Praise for A. C. Grayling

'A. C. Grayling's eloquent book . . . The question is not rhetorical, and Grayling's answers are illuminating. His subject is as much about the search for the best way to live as the best way to live itself . . . Grayling effectively demystifies a subject that is all to often discussed as though its secrets are accessible only to long-bearded gurus. He writes like a dream and with impressive but not overbearing erudition'

Times Educational Supplement

'Grayling's style is straightforward and comprehensible, and his overarching fondness for what is rational over what is sensational or emotional is highly appealing: Grayling wants to see the rational life triumph, as that is precisely where he locates the good life . . . but he loves the poetic too . . . he shows the importance of the sensual as well as the intellectual'

Lesley McDowell, *Sunday Herald*

'This elegant and controversial critique of religiously based ethics . . . As a demolisher of . . . pretensions Grayling deserves to be heard' John Habgood, *Church Times*

'Perhaps not since Julian Huxley's *Towards a New Humanism* (1957), or his *Essays of a Humanist* (1964), has a British humanist of such stature provided his generation with so sweeping a panorama of the fortunes of humanism. This ought not to deter those of a religious persuasion from reading this book, for Grayling is careful to put forth their best arguments in the debate . . . One of the joys of the book is Grayling's profiling of the movers and shakers in the struggle. His sketches of Erasmus, Hume, Mill and Nietzsche, for example, are the most enjoyable that I have ever read. Nor does he talk down to us non-philosophers . . . I plan to return to this book often'

Hazhir Teimourian, *Literary Review*

A. C. Grayling is Professor of Philosophy at Birkbeck College, University of London, and a Supernumerary Fellow of St Anne's College, Oxford. He is the author of numerous books, and is also a distinguished literary journalist and broadcaster. He has been a columnist for the *Guardian* and *The Times*, is a Contributing Editor of *Prospect* magazine, and Editor of Online Review London. He is a Fellow of both the Royal Society of Literature and the Royal Society of Arts. His website can be visited at www.acgrayling.com.

By A. C. Grayling

The Refutation of Scepticism
Berkeley: the Central Arguments
The Long March to the Fourth of June (*as Li Xiao Jun*)
Wittgenstein
China: A Literary Companion (*with S. Whitfield*)
Moral Values
An Introduction to Philosophical Logic
Russell
The Quarrel of the Age: The Life and Times of William Hazlitt
The Meaning of Things
The Reason of Things
What is Good?: The Search for the Best Way to Live
The Mystery of Things
The Heart of Things
Descartes
The Form of Things
In Freedom's Name
Among the Dead Cities
On Religion (*with Mick Gordon*)
Against All Gods
Truth, Meaning and Realism
Towards the Light
The Choice of Hercules
Ideas that Matter

AS EDITOR

Robert Herrick: Lyrics of Love and Desire
Philosophy: A Guide Through the Subject
Philosophy: Further Through the Subject
The Continuum Encyclopaedia of British Philosophy
Schopenhauer's 'Art of Always Being Right'

WHAT IS GOOD?

The Search for the Best Way to Live

A. C. GRAYLING

PHOENIX

A PHOENIX PAPERBACK

First published in Great Britain in 2003
by Weidenfeld & Nicolson
This paperback edition published in 2004
by Phoenix,
an imprint of Orion Books Ltd,
Orion House, 5 Upper St Martin's Lane,
London WC2H 9EA

An Hachette Livre UK company

Reissued 2007

12 14 16 18 20 19 17 15 13 11

A CIP catalogue record for this book
is available from the British Library.

ISBN 978-0-7538-1755-1

Printed and bound in Great Britain
by Clays Ltd, St Ives plc

The Orion Publishing Group's policy is to use papers that
are natural, renewable and recyclable products and
made from wood grown in sustainable forests. The logging
and manufacturing processes are expected to conform to
the environmental regulations of the country of origin.

www.orionbooks.co.uk

For Katie:
tremulae sinuantur flamine vestes

CONTENTS

The good is, like nature, an immense landscape in which man advances through centuries of exploration.

Jose Ortega Y Gasset

The conflict of faith and scepticism remains the proper, the only, the deepest theme of the history of the world and mankind, to which all others are subordinated.

Goethe

Reason can wrestle terror, and overthrow it at last.

Euripides

PREFACE

This is a book for the general reader. Its aim is to introduce some of the best of what has been thought and said about the most important question facing mankind: what values should we live by in order to live the genuinely good life? Its method is historical, using some of the standard nodes in the development of Western civilisation to trace the story of thought and discussion about this question. This in part involves looking at aspects of the development of ethical debate, and in part looking at the moral presuppositions of climates of thought. The distinction between 'ethics' and 'moral presuppositions' can for present purposes be explained like this: 'ethics' means thinking and theorising about what is good and bad, and how people should live; 'moral presuppositions' are what, either consciously or unconsciously, govern what people do, or aspire to do, in the practice of life. Although it weaves together the story of ethical reflection and moral presuppositions, this book does not aim to be a scholarly treatise. It is an informal survey, a conversation rather than a lecture, an aerial view rather than an exploration on foot; and because it covers such a vast terrain, it represents a personal route and not, by far, an encyclopaedic one.

Much more detailed and deep-going explorations of these themes are to be found both in the original literature of such debates, from Plato to Nietzsche, and – in scholarly and ambitiously circumstantial guise – in the vast industrial output of academic literature generated by the professionalisation of philosophy in the last century or so. The bibliography provides a starting guide to this wealth of resource. I vigorously recommend the classics of ethics themselves, some of which are to be found even among the professional output of recent times. But it has to be acknowledged that much recent philosophical writing is for specialist readers only, a fact that is in one way a great pity, but that in another is an inevitable result of the endeavour to gain increments of understanding of ourselves, our world and our thought by work of uncompromising analytical care – which has the inevitable tendency of multiplying fine distinctions, complicated theories, and an impenetrable (from the outside) jargon in which to discuss them. No doubt a lot of academic work is of very minor value to the world, motivated more by the pressure to publish than by the discovery of priceless truths; but some of the rest of it really does add to the stock of human insight, and puts in place another riser in the staircase that, by dint of hard work, takes us towards the stars: *per ardua ad astra*.

So: this is a non-academic survey of debates about the good life for humankind. But it is not just a survey. I have a point to argue, which is that mankind's quest for the good has been a struggle between humanism, on the one hand, and religious conceptions of the world, on the other hand. The latter have proved resistant in the face of efforts by the former to free not just the imagination but the very life of man from the authority of religious world views, whether in the classical epoch, the Renaissance, or the eighteenth century and since. The durability of religious views might be variously explained, but one main historical reason is that most people are naturally superstitious and insufficiently reflective, and that religious hierarchies have been successful in getting political power or at least influence, as demonstrated by Christianity through most of its history – and as with Islam likewise, and contemporary fundamentalisms of various kinds in India, Israel and the United States.

As these remarks more than hint, the point I make is a partisan one. My claim is that most human progress has occurred in the face of religious reaction, and that most human suffering other than that caused by disease or other natural evils has been the result of religion-inspired conflict and religion-based oppression. This is an unhappy fact, but one that is overwhelmingly attested by the evidence of history. My hope is that this sketch of the search for the good will help some, perhaps even many, to see afresh what is at stake in the broad opposition of perspectives between humanistic enlightenment and traditional religion in their debates about the best life for humankind.

There is an allied point. This book appears at a remarkable juncture in human history, namely, the point at which the secrets of human genetic endowment have been unlocked and laid open not just to our view but our intervention. Increasingly, the human beings who people our planet in the decades and centuries to come will be different from us now and from our ancestors. Utopian expectations have it that they will be more beautiful and intelligent than we are; they will have teeth that do not decay, eyes that give perfect vision, genetic profiles that exempt them from cancer and cardiovascular disease – and so on for all the things that people with bad teeth, spectacles and high blood pressure now wish could be immediately cured with a turn of the genetic screwdriver. No doubt once these trifles (cancer and the rest) have been dealt with, attributes and characteristics currently unimaginable will come under the geneticists' expensive care, producing people more and more remote from us, their primitive, natural, accidental and imperfect ancestors. Many now find this picture disturbing, but mainly out of a nervous sense of prospective inferiority. Whatever does indeed happen, my hope is that the intelligence and access of knowledge enjoyed by future people will allow the enlightenment project to triumph at last. Then this book and others like it will be records of a struggle that will seem remote and absurd, but which has been one of the two or three chief determinants of human history so far, and which remains so even as these words are written in the morning of the twenty-first century.

Yet even future paragons, if such there be, will still have to ask themselves the questions whose history of answers is sketched here: What is the best life? What is the good? Another prediction is that whatever form future answers take, they will have something in common with the best of past answers, and will find inspiration in them.

The informality of this book, and the fact that it expressly addresses a general, non-specialist readership, means that it does not seek to be exhaustive in canvassing ethical ideas and moral hopes; but in one sense of the term 'comprehensive' it does aim at being comprehensive, in that it seeks to sample the best and most important contributions in Western civilisation to its subject, I hope leaving none of the most important aspects of this story untouched, however lightly.

The text has been kept deliberately free of footnotes. The works used and cited in each chapter are listed in the chapter bibliographies at the end; those readers who wish to track a quotation to its source will have the pleasure of seeking it in the appropriate places on their own account, indulging thereby in one of the greatest pleasures of the good life: reading.

The plan of this book follows the main contour of its argument. For six or seven centuries from the height of classical Athens to the last flourishing of the Antonine dynasty in Imperial Rome, thinking about the good life was premised on principles which, as the following pages show, were fundamentally those of enlightenment and humanism, so nameable not just because they are the source of intellectual attitudes which bear those labels in later times (the Renaissance and the eighteenth-century Enlightenment), but because that is exactly what they were in themselves.

Then, for a period more than twice as long, the Western world – for most of that time restricted to Europe – lay under the ideological hegemony of Christianity, which, although it adopted and adapted much from the ethical thought of classical antiquity, also flatly rejected most of its bases in favour of a quite different view, namely that the source of value lies outside the world, embodied in the commands and requirements of a personal deity.

Since about AD 1400 – which is to say, in the six centuries up to the present – the project of enlightened humanism has been fighting back against this theistic transcendentalism, which, imposed on European civilisation from the Orient (it is important to note that the 'Religions of the Book' – Judaism, Christianity and Islam – are Oriental faiths), has had a very mixed influence on its development and welfare.

The chapters to come observe the line of this history of six centuries of ancient thought, twelve of Christian hegemony, and then a following six centuries of struggle between the revival of the former against the latter. Chapters 1–3 canvass ancient ethical thought. Chapter 4 describes and discusses religious ethics through the example of Christianity. The remaining chapters discuss the revival and development of ethical thinking from the Renaissance period – here called 'the second enlightenment' – onwards, together with the tension and frequent conflict between the two broadly different bases for ethical perspectives at issue. The book, therefore, has a design that is at the same time chronological and conceptual.

1

INTRODUCTION:
SHADOWS AND SHAPINGS

Many important and difficult questions arise in the course of a human life, but few can compare with the most significant question any individual can ask, namely, 'How shall I live, in order to live a good life?' The purpose of this book is to survey the chief answers proposed from classical antiquity to the recent present. The focus is largely though not exclusively Western (not exclusively because, beneath the surface, there are many conformities of view between Eastern and Western traditions of thought), and it is historical because it aims to reveal a persistent fact: that when one looks at the best that has been thought and said about the good life for human beings, it transpires that there are two large but very different conceptions of what that should be, which have remained consistent in essentials through time. One is a broadly secular attitude rooted in views about human nature and the human condition. The other is a broadly transcendental one that locates the source of moral value outside the human realm, a transcendent source that places on the human realm a demand to realise aims and attain ends likewise located beyond the boundaries of this world and its circumstances – standardly, in a life after death.

These two fundamentally different ways of understanding the nature and sources of value have often competed and sometimes overlapped during the course of history; but since the rise of science in the seventeenth century they have come increasingly into competition, and the resulting accumulation of tension between them is one of the greatest problems faced by the modern world. Understanding the divide is necessary to managing and perhaps bridging it.

As an illustration of the divide between these fundamentally different ways of thinking about the good life, consider the following two sketches.

In his delightful essay on Japanese aesthetics, *In Praise of Shadows*, Junichiro Tanizaki writes of taking his soup from a lacquerware dish:

Whenever I sit with a bowl of soup before me, listening to the murmur that penetrates like the distant song of an insect, lost in contemplation of the flavours to come, I feel as if I were being drawn into a trance. The experience must be something like that of the tea master who, at the sound of the kettle, is taken from himself as if upon the sigh of the wind in the legendary pines of Onoe. It has been said of Japanese food that it is a cuisine to be looked at rather than eaten. I would go further and say that it is to be meditated upon, a kind of silent music evoked by the combination of lacquerware and the light of a candle flickering in the dark.

Throughout his essay Tanizaki selects for praise things delicate and nuanced, softened by shadows and the patina of age, and he celebrates everything understated and natural – the patterns of grain in wood emerging after many years, the sound of rain dripping from eaves and trees, or washing over the footing of a stone lantern in a garden and refreshing the moss that grows about it – and by doing so he is suggesting an attitude of appreciation and mindfulness, especially mindfulness of beauty, as central to life lived well. It is a striking thought, on its first appearance, that aesthetic considerations are fundamental to ethics, in ways to be explored in later chapters; but as reflection shows, it is in the end a deeply natural one. It reaches from the grandest things, as suggested by contemplation of the stars, to the simplest things, as Tanizaki shows in praising the colour of a common sweetmeat called 'yokan':

> The cloudy translucence, like that of jade; the faint, dreamlike glow that suffuses it, as if it had drunk into its very depths the light of the sun; the complexity and profundity of the colour – nothing of the sort is to be found in Western candies. When yokan is served in a lacquer dish within whose dark recesses its colour is scarcely distinguishable, then it is most certainly an object of meditation. You take its cool, smooth substance into your mouth, and it is as if the very darkness of the room were melting on your tongue.

The outlook suggested by Tanizaki's remarks is one in which the world and our experience of it are good things in themselves, and in which, when life is lived with attentiveness and sensitivity – an intellectual as well as sensory attentiveness that can be educated by practice – it is rich and good. It is not a long step from such an attitude to one in which attentiveness and sensitivity to others make the life of community good too; and it is hard to imagine such an attitude of mind being anything but tolerant and full of fellow feeling.

An educative contrast to the conception of life suggested by Tanizaki's evocative praise of shadows is given by Augustus Hare's account of his Victorian childhood. Hare was the author of a series of superior nineteenth-century guidebooks to various English counties, European countries, and notable cities, and he otherwise occupied his time by being a minor socialite, drifting from one country house party to another, and during each year's London season making up the numbers as a dinner guest. He was brought up by an aunt, Maria Hare, who was descended from an ancient Norman family that had stocked the Church of England with rectors and bishops for centuries. She was a pious woman, and because Augustus was intended for a clerical life in the family tradition, she was determined that he should be suitably prepared for his future. She accordingly gave him a careful Christian upbringing, which proceeded as follows.

Hare's training began the minute he arrived in Aunt Maria's care. When he was eighteen months old she told her journal, 'Augustus has grown much more obedient, and is ready to give his food and playthings to others.' He could read by the age of three, which is when his German lessons began; and when he reached the age of four his playthings were stored away in the attic so that he could understand, in accordance with St Paul's injunction about putting aside childish things, that life is too serious for toys. He was forbidden to play with other children – mainly because the only ones available were servants' offspring, and therefore unsuitable – and his uncle Julius, near whom they lived, was summoned whenever Aunt Maria thought corporal punishment was required. Julius used a riding whip for the task. Once, during a rare encounter with other children, Augustus was given a peppermint sweet by their nanny. Aunt Maria smelled it on his breath when he returned home so, to teach him to avoid fleshly pleasures, she used a forcing spoon to cleanse his digestion with rhubarb and soda.

Aunt Maria's methods are well illustrated by a lesson she taught Augustus when he was five. First, he was repeatedly told that a delicious pudding was to be served at dinner, so that by the time dinner arrived he was agog with expectation. Just as he raised his spoon to take a first mouthful of this treat, the plate was whisked from under his nose and he was told to take it to one of the poor in the nearby village. 'The necessity of obedience without reasoning is especially necessary in such a disposition as his,' Maria told her journal.

Augustus's lot was not improved when his uncle Julius at last married. Julius did so to Maria's distress, for although Maria was Julius's deceased brother's wife, which meant that there could be no thought of marriage between them, they had lived as close neighbours for many years, in great intimacy, and Julius had dined at the home of Maria and little Augustus every night – occasionally, as noted, plying his horsewhip to the benefit of Augustus's soul. Now that he was married the dinner arrangements were reversed, Maria and little Augustus going to dine at his rectory every night. The woman Julius married was not as high-born as Maria (a fact that gave Maria much unhappiness), but she had almost as many clergymen in her lineage, and what she lacked in breeding she made up in piety. Her name was Esther. When Maria and Augustus had to remain overnight at the rectory after dinner because of bad weather – which happened often, especially in winter – Esther made Augustus sleep on a straw palliasse laid on a trestle table, and although he suffered severely from chilblains, which caused open sores on his hands and feet, he was made to wash in the mornings in a pitcher of cold water, first breaking its covering of ice with a brass candlestick. These amenities were intended to educate him in the virtues of endurance. For Sabbatarian reasons Maria and Augustus did not dine at the rectory on Sundays, but lest Augustus should do anything improper to that holy day, he was locked in the church vestry between services, with a sandwich for his lunch.

Esther's notions of how to raise a child in the true Christian spirit were, if anything, stricter than Maria's. When she learned that Augustus loved his cat, she told him to give it to her so that he could learn to yield up to others what mattered to him. Sobbing, he took the cat to Aunt Esther at the rectory, and Esther had it hanged.

Augustus Hare grew to be a self-indulgent snob as an adult, whose one act of rebellion was to refuse to take holy orders, but who more than compensated by writing a sentimental biography of his Aunt Maria which became a best-seller. Even the terrifying Thomas Carlyle was moved by it; he told Hare, 'I do not often cry and am not much given to weeping, but your book is most profoundly touching.' Throughout Hare's life he observed the customs of a Victorian Christian household, at breakfast every day obliging guests and all his domestic staff to listen to the appointed lessons and psalms, and to say the collect and the Our Father. One visitor noticed that the prayers sounded odd, so he inspected Hare's copy of the Book of Common Prayer, and there found certain lines inked out. 'I've crossed out all the passages in glorification of God,' Hare told him. 'God is certainly a gentleman, and no gentleman cares to be praised to his face. It is tactless, impertinent and vulgar. I think all that fulsome adulation must be highly offensive to him.'

There is a great moral to be drawn from the contrast between what is implied by these sketches of Tanizaki's attitude to soup and sweetmeats, and Hare's upbringing. Hare's tale, ordinary enough in the Victorian context, might seem distasteful and even shocking now, but in comparison with the lives of scores of millions of children and women living today in countries where religion is a major social force – living as their cultures have expected women and children to live throughout much of their religions' history – it is neither unusual nor extreme. For just one of many possible examples, girls who suffer female circumcision in Islamic regions of Africa suffer far more than Augustus did, and not just in that respect. The point, however, is general: variants of Hare's childhood experience – some of them far severer – can be seen to this day among Christian fundamentalists in the southern United States, in ultra-orthodox Jewish families, in Saudi Arabia, and anywhere that religion remains the dominant influence in the life of human beings.

What a contrast is offered by Tanizaki's relish of the world and its ordinary pleasures. Although he approaches the question of how to live from a cultural perspective different from Western varieties, there is nevertheless something essentially humanistic and therefore familiar about it. It addresses the felt quality of experience in the course of life, not just as an end in itself but because each moment of experience belongs to a life-long series (in the ideal) in which thought and an emphasis on value are important components of the well-lived life. It does not take much to show that this idea has many expressions in the Western tradition; for one famous example, a close analogy is to be found in Walter Pater's concluding remarks in his *Renaissance*, where he says, in a passage worth quoting in full,

The service of philosophy, of speculative culture, towards the human spirit, is to rouse, to startle it to a life of constant and eager observation. Every moment some form grows perfect in hand or face; some tone on the hills or the sea is choicer than the rest; some mood of passion or insight or intellectual excitement is irresistibly real and attractive to us – for that moment only. Not the fruit of experience, but experience itself, is the end. A counted number of pulses only is given to us of a variegated, dramatic life. How may we see in them all that is to be seen in them by the finest senses? How shall we pass most swiftly from point to point, and be present always at the focus where the greatest number of vital forces unite in their purest energy? To burn always with this hard, gem-like flame, to maintain this ecstasy, is success in life. In a sense it might even be said that our failure is to form habits: for, after all, habit is relative to a stereotyped world, and meantime it is only the roughness of the eye that makes two persons, things, situations, seem alike. While all melts under our feet, we may well grasp at any exquisite passion, or any contribution to knowledge that seems by a lifted horizon to set the spirit free for a moment, or any stirring of the sense, strange dyes, strange colours, and curious odours, or work of the artist's hands, or the face of one's friend. Not to discriminate every moment some passionate attitude in those about us, and in the very brilliancy of their gifts some tragic dividing on their ways, is, on this short day of frost and sun, to sleep before evening.

This in its turn is simply an encapsulation of one aspect of what, in many different ways, has been a powerful theme throughout Western thought – a point that becomes clearer when one notes that Pater's view, like Tanizaki's, does not restrict itself only to the sensual (although both emphasise it), but demands an intellectual awareness, a mindfulness lit by reason, which with different emphases has been central to ideas about the good life from Aristotle to the eighteenth-century Enlightenment.

In what follows I explore the various ways in which human-ist perspectives on the good life have been articulated, and I contrast it with views that locate the source of value outside the realm of human experience – centrally, in 'divine command', an external source of obligation upon us as moral agents to live and work for a reward, or an avoidance of retribution, in a world other than and posterior to the human world. My claim is that the great ethical debate that has always confronted mankind, and does so still, is between a fundamentally humanistic view and the religious moralities it opposes.

An account of the chief moments in the quest for the good life needs to look beyond the history of philosophy, narrowly conceived, to the more diffuse social and literary manifestations of ethical ideas – which is to say, to culture, especially high culture – and to the evidence of how these latter expressed themselves in concrete historical terms. A scholarly account of such matters would fill many volumes. Here I undertake some-thing more modest: a sketch of how ethical sentiment was expressed and debated in several important epochs in the intel-lectual history of Western mankind. My aim is to remind the interested general reader of the rich inheritance of ideas that constitute some of the best that has been thought about these matters, not only for its intrinsic interest, which is great, but so that this inheritance can help us now towards good, or at least better, lives and societies.

I start where Western civilisation starts, with classical Greek thought, the first fully recorded enlightenment in the history of humanity. The discussion of the good life it contains is not only the source of all ethical enquiry in Western history since, but is a marker for the best such thinking which that tradition has produced.

2

THE CLASSICAL CONCEPTION
OF THE GOOD LIFE

The Greek view of life

To say that Western civilisation owes its existence and much of its character to classical Greece is to make a very familiar claim. Now that few people study the classical languages and the culture and thought associated with them, however, the truth of this claim is much under-appreciated. But true it is; and in such pervasive and profound ways that it is impossible properly to discuss ideas of the good life without beginning in ancient Athens.

As if by magic, when contrasted with the Dark Ages and even the archaic period that preceded it, the Greek world of the classical epoch – the fifth and fourth centuries BC, and in that period especially Athens, home of Pericles and Socrates – produced literature, art and ideas of seminal importance to the subsequent history of the Western world. It bequeathed a vocabulary of civilisation, education, science, politics and poetics – not just the words ('democracy', 'politics', 'tyranny', 'philosophy', 'history', 'anarchy', 'geography' and countless others) but thereby the concepts themselves, which constitute the Western intellectual resource. Rome took its culture from Greece, and spread it through Europe; when an Orient religion called Christianity irrupted into the European world, it borrowed Greek language and philosophy to clothe itself as a means of penetrating the more mature polity it invaded.

It is important not to romanticise the classical Greek world. There was much in it that was disagreeable then or which now seems so: it was racked by war and civil war, the economies of its city states were based on slavery, and women were excluded from full citizenship. Since in fundamentals human nature varies little across time or cultures, it is salutary to remember that Plato castigated his fellow Athenians for their greedy love of money and their perjuries in law suits. Still, a number of outstanding individuals among enfranchised Greeks thought and felt in ways which were strikingly original and made a permanent difference to the world, not least on questions about the good life and the good society. There was no settled consensus among them – different thinkers and different schools of thought offered competing views – but the atmosphere of enquiry into these vital matters breathed a distinctive and remarkable spirit, which has, in all subsequent centuries, inspired admiration in those who have studied what the finest of the Greeks achieved.

When viewed in general terms as an ethos, the Greek view of life appears at its best in its appreciation of beauty, the respect it paid to reason and the life of reason, its freedom of thought and feeling, its absence of mysticism and false sentimentality, and its humanism, pluralism and sanity of outlook – which, taken all together, specifies living nobly and richly in spirit as the aim of life. In Plato one aspect of this ideal is encapsulated as *sophrosyne*, a word for which no single English expression gives an adequate rendering, although standardly translated as 'temperance', 'self-restraint' or 'wisdom'. In his most famous dialogue, *The Republic*, Plato defines *sophrosyne* as 'the agreement of the passions that Reason should rule'. If to this were added the thought – reflecting the better part of what other Greeks besides Plato thought – that the passions and the senses are important too, something like their ideal conception of human flourishing results.

According to some students of classical civilisation, notably those who view it from a set of assumptions explicitly or implicitly Christian in perspective, it is a mistake to see the

Greeks as placing moral striving at the focus of their endeavours. Such critics think that Greek ethics is tepid and insignificant in comparison to the hot moral enthusiasms of St Paul, who in excited language denounced homosexuality ('let it not be named among you'), accumulation of wealth ('the covetous man has no inheritance in the Kingdom of God') and much besides that the Greeks regarded as unexceptionable. The difference between the Pauline and Greek views in these respects is, of course, that the Greeks had no sense of sin. They called moral failings *amartiai*, 'bad shots', the sort of things that can happen to anyone and are best put behind one, except as reminders to take better aim next time. To this phlegmatic view the vehement attitudes of St Paul are completely opposed. Sin is very terrible to him; it stands for all eternity as an offence to God, unless God legislates otherwise in the individual case; and it can result in the destruction or endless torment of the sinner. Such a view would have seemed at best hysterical and at worst barbaric to Greeks of the classical age.

The supposed contrast being drawn here between Greek moral tepidity and Christian moral enthusiasm is, however, a false one, for the true contrast lies elsewhere. The Greeks were indeed eager to identify and live good lives – very much so. But their conception of a good life was much broader and more inclusive than the Christian one. St Paul preached a circumscribing code of restraint – with the honourable exception of his promotion of 'charity', his morality is mainly a war against natural human impulses and interests – because he believed that a Second Coming was imminent, and thought he was legislating for years, or at most decades, rather than millennia. This point is standardly made by apologists when his embarrassing views about (for example) women and marriage are mentioned, but they are forgotten in other respects.

The classical Greeks would have thought Paul very one-sided, and limited even in that one side. They would have deprecated his indifference or even hostility to the arts, to the acquisition of knowledge, to the enjoyment of pleasures of the senses and especially of beauty – for an important example, to the beauty of the naked human form. It is impossible to imagine St Paul even beginning to appreciate the Greek view in this regard. The healthy, fit, trained body seemed the summit of perfection to the Greeks, and its beauty was a matter of moral significance as well as visual delight, for its proportion, harmony and poise expressed humankind's role as the measure of things. The idea of the free movement of limbs in running and wrestling, of fleetness and suppleness, of grace in acts of throwing the discus or riding a horse, brought intellectual as well as sensual pleasure. The word 'gymnasium' comes from *gymnos*, meaning naked, and denotes the place where the virtues of physical beauty were cultivated. Nudity, in the orthodox Judaeo-Christian view, is by chilling contrast a state of shame: witness what Adam and Eve did upon first understanding that they were unclothed.

An admirer of ancient Greek culture who at the same time was unpersuaded by the claims of Christianity would be inclined to say that, in comparison to the generous celebration of life expressed by the Greek ideal, Pauline morality is therefore not merely pinched and dry but misdirected in its aims. For the Greeks, to live well is to live now, for the lifetime of man, aiming to flourish, achieve, learn, appreciate and enjoy. For St Paul, to live morally is to be prepared for the Kingdom of God; and when the centuries wore away, and Christians came to accept that the Kingdom was not coming particularly soon, the preparation metamorphosed instead into one for the 'next world', demoting this world and making everything in it unimportant by comparison, as merely instrumental at best, or at worst – and this was the majority category – a huge set of snares set by the devil to impede the individual's chances of getting into heaven at last.

As to the specific question of the Greek interest in matters of ethics, the criticism that they were not much concerned with them is handsomely refuted by the single most important fact about the life and teaching of Socrates – namely, that with a tireless sense of urgency he directed Greek philosophical attention away from 'physics' – enquiry into the nature, origins and laws of the physical universe – to questions about how people should live. This was his aim and his passion, and in the end it got him into fatal trouble; but his legacy was that the philosophical genius of Greece always thereafter gave a central place to discussing that vital matter, and that debate has shaped the thinking of the Western mind ever since.

The first enlightenment and the first humanism

The intellectual spirit that produced Socrates and his successors is well and simply illustrated by the example of Thales, an Ionian who flourished about 585 BC and is standardly considered the 'father of philosophy'. He wished to know what the 'principle' of the universe is – that is, what it is made of and where it comes from. On the basis of observation and reason he concluded that the answer is – water. That now seems a quaint conclusion, but a little reflection reveals something interesting about how Thales arrived at it. First, he did not resort to invoking supernatural agencies to explain the world. Secondly, he made a tremendously important assumption: that human reason is competent to answer ultimate questions about the world's nature and origins. Thirdly, he looked at the world itself and noticed a significant fact: that liquid is everywhere – in the sea, rivers and rainfall, in the sap of trees and the veins of men; that it is essential to life; and that alone of all substances known to him it can take all three material forms as solid, liquid and gas, the first when it freezes into ice and the third when it boils away as steam. Its ubiquity, necessity and metamorphic capacities therefore suggested to him that it is the basic stuff out of which all things are made.

What is significant about Thales is the manner rather than

the conclusions of his thought. The independence of mind, the clear-eyed attitude of looking at things and thinking about them without superstition or reliance on traditional beliefs, is an essential feature of the Greek mentality. To see things as they are and to understand them – this is the aim of the Greek classical mind that characterises its literature and philosophy, and that makes it the first true Enlightenment. Thales is thus the first known Enlightenment thinker.

Moreover, the reference point was, in this attitude, man himself. For this reason the Greek outlook is well described as a form of humanism. The most famous expression of it is the dictum of Protagoras, *anthropos metron panton* ('Man is the measure of all things'). One application of this idea is that a good life is one which is fulfilling and appropriate for an inhabitant of the human condition, living in the material world among other people, and aiming to do so with moral success. If Greeks used such phrases as 'doing things that are pleasing to the gods', they did not thereby mean that the chief point of life was spiritual or other-worldly, and certainly not as this would be understood in various mainstream forms of Christianity. Life was unquestionably for living in the here and now, with human interests at the fore.

There are a number of informative characterisations of what thoughtful Greeks meant by a good life in their humanist sense. One is given by Xenophon, like Plato a pupil and memoirist of Socrates, and most famously the author of the *Anabasis*, the story of the Ten Thousand in their retreat after the failed Greek expedition to help Cyrus in the Persian civil war. Xenophon's sketch of life lived well, according to the outlook of educated Greeks of his day, occurs in what he says of various friends who, like himself, were associates of Socrates. They listened to Socrates not in order to become popular orators or wealthy lawyers, said Xenophon, but so that they could 'grow into good and noble men, and learn how to conduct themselves aright to their households and servants, their relations and friends, their country and countrymen'. He praised them for their temperate outlook, their cheerfulness and gentle manners, and their desire to live nobly. This was the ambition likewise of Ischomachus, a leading figure in Xenophon's dialogue *The Economist*, who in addition to these other goods sought 'health and physical well-being, the respect of my fellow Athenians, the affection of my friends, an honourable increase in wealth, and honourable safety in war'. These recognisable ethical sentiments had their greatest spokesman in Aristotle, as we shall later see; but what is noteworthy about them is the fact that they were then, in that period of history, something striking and new, for they expressed civic virtues, and in doing so represented a very different outlook from the one that had prevailed beforehand: celebration of the warrior or heroic virtues, as in Homer.

Heroic virtues

The Homeric poems tell of a splendid era of mighty men, who walked and talked with the gods and performed feats of incomparable valour. They fought great wars, went on perilous adventures full of supernatural intervention and encounter, slew monsters, descended into and returned from the underworld, faced appalling horrors, temptations and sufferings, and enjoyed triumphs beyond the dreams of mortals of the more prosaic (as it must by comparison have seemed) classical times. Most of the legends were drawn from the Mycenaean age, six and more centuries before the classical epoch; their Homeric subset had become an organised set of poems by the eighth century BC, collected and committed to writing in the time, and perhaps at the injunction, of Peisistratus, ruler of Athens in the sixth century BC. The poems had long been a central part of the education of Greek youths, and continued to be so right into the classical period – although by then with somewhat changed emphasis. As part of the school curriculum the ancient tales inculcated an ideal of manhood in which the individual pursues honour. In the original heroic conception, honour was sought in a life of action, each man using his physical and mental endowments to the utmost to earn the applause of his comrades. Since honour was the central pillar of this ideal, aspiring heroes were expected to be active in seeking opportunities to display courage and prowess – best of all in the teeth of danger. Fame was the recompense for honour, and it was a great recompense indeed, because it meant a multiplied existence in the admiration of following generations of men and in the plaudits of poets.

Everything that conduced to the realisation of the heroic life was therefore counted a virtue. Fitness and strength of body, a quick, alert mind, endurance, fortitude, courage and boldness – these were what made a warrior, a hunter, a sailor on the treacherous seas. So powerful was the idea of heroic qualities as distinctive of true manhood that the very word 'virtue', although etymologically drawn from the later source of Latin, still carries the original conception in it: for its first syllable 'vir' connotes 'man', not in the generic sense of 'mankind', which includes women, but specifically in the sense of 'male of the species' (*virtus* means 'manliness', 'strength').

The philosophers of Greece's classical period did not share the Homeric idealisation of these manly characteristics. They respected them, but did not place them as high as the virtues required for their own preferred best life, which was the life of contemplation and the pursuit of knowledge. In Socrates' thought, the expressly civic values of justice and friendship became paramount. This is precisely the change one would expect to result from the increased importance given to notions of community, where old-fashioned heroic ideals were more of a threat than a boon except in time of war. But that did not mean they were altogether dismissed. Among Socrates' predecessors they were given their due; Pythagoras said that men can be classified in the same way as those who attend the Games: the spectators, the competitors, and those who come to buy and sell under the stands. Generalised to life, the first group typifies those who seek knowledge, the second those who seek honour, and the third those who seek gain. Pythagoras rated them in that order, which means that although he did not think the desire for honour as worthy as the desire for knowledge – a great change from the Homeric view – still it was above the mere quest for gain. That ordering remained the standard for the classical outlook.

An honour code is one in which the greatest punishment is shame, and in which revenge is a duty. A remarkable comment on the shift from heroic to civic values that characterises the rise of classical civilisation in Athens is given in Aeschylus's *Eumenides*, third in his great trilogy the *Oresteia*. In it he tells how the old rule of revenge and blood feud was replaced by a due process of law before a civil jury. Orestes, pursued by the Furies for killing his mother in revenge for her murder of his father Agamemnon, throws himself on the mercy of the goddess Athene. She convenes a court on the Hill of Mars in Athens, the Areopagus, with a jury of Athenian citizens – the first ever assembled – to try his case. They acquit him, with the help of her casting vote. This innovation maddens the Furies, who accuse Athene and the other 'young gods' of usurping the rights of the 'old gods' whom they represent. She placates them by giving them an honourable home in her city, and thereafter the concept of a due process of law replaces might as the arbiter of right.

This brilliantly dramatises the change of outlook as between the Homeric and classical conceptions of the good. Of course, it would be a mistake to think that theory accords fully with reality. The classical and Hellenistic ages were as riven by war and strife – the natural element of the warrior virtues, and their field of exercise – as any period in the history of the Greeks. But although Homer often speaks of the dreadful character of war (he describes it as 'hateful', 'baleful', 'tearful'), he also relishes the glory it offers and the joy of ultimate and dangerous physical commitment as experienced in combat. In the classical era, by contrast, an unblinking acceptance of the evil nature of war was the norm. Euripides' *Trojan War* is a stark account of what military defeat really means, and during the fateful Peloponnesian War (431–405 BC), which closed Athens's brightest period, Aristophanes spoke out for peace and satirised the warmongers who profited from the conflict.

It is significant that, even in its most self-confident vein, the heroic conception of virtue was not confined to the strength, courage and endurance that made a man, despite being chiefly focused upon them. As the Homeric poems in their quieter moments show, it also extolled beauty, eloquence, open-handedness and sound judgement. Although the warrior excellences as such were most manifest in battle, they increasingly came to be enjoyed and celebrated on the field of athletics, to the extent indeed that winners at the Games became national heroes, the greatest of them being immortalised in the odes of Pindar. As this suggests, the Homeric view of virtue contained fertile seeds from which many aspects of thought about the civic virtues could grow.

Still, heroism was open to relatively few, and ordinary folk were apt to be on (at best) the serving end or (if less lucky) the receiving end of its exercise. The shift to civic values meant that, by contrast, every citizen could be included – and indeed, not only could be but *should* be, for a civil polity needs good citizens in order to flourish. This transfer from the singular man to the plurality of men is subtly embodied in one of the orations of Pericles, where, contrary to the ancient vein of singing the exploits of a great named hero, he speaks of the many unnamed Athenians who died fighting for their city, speaking of all of them as men of honour. This is a description Homer would never have applied in such general terms to those whose slain bodies lay on the plain before Troy; for the majority among these were the likes of Dolon and Thersites, lower-born men of whom Homer speaks with contempt because, not being higher-born, they were not capable of aspiring to honour's heights.

As the example of Pericles' oration implies, in the warrior ideal the hero aims at his own glory, while in the civic ideal the new demotic hero aims at service to his community. It is interesting that Homer's principal heroes were Achilles and Odysseus, while Virgil – so much later a writer, in thought as in time, profiting from centuries of reflection on ethics in the Hellenistic and Roman periods, and writing with perhaps eight or more centuries of philosophical development after the Homeric epics were circulating in oral versions – draws his inspiration rather from the example of Hector, who fought for Troy rather than himself, and had the safety of his wife and family in mind when he went to his fatal confrontation with the grief-enraged Achilles. Virgil's hero is a Hector-type hero; he is, of course, Aeneas, who escaped the flames of Troy carrying his father on his back and leading his small son by the hand – a highly significant pair of details – and his escape was the legendary beginning of the adventure of another and indeed greater city, namely, Rome.

If there is one writer in the age of Pericles who more than any other signalises the epic civilisation-changing shift from warrior to civic morality, it is Pericles' friend Sophocles, through the medium of two of his plays in particular, each dealing with a mighty hero: the *Ajax* about the eponymous warrior and the *Trachiniae*, telling of the death of Heracles. The respective downfalls of Ajax and Heracles flow from the same fact: their remoteness from ordinary men, not just in their courage and strength but in their implacability, insensitivity and pride. Ajax angers the gods with his contumacy; Heracles turns his back on his wife Deianira, whose fault was to love him too much. Both die terrible deaths. Sophocles brings the ancient heroes to earth – to the grave – because of the opposition they represent to the values which are the new values of Periclean Athens. The lesson cannot have been lost on the enthralled audiences who saw the plays on first performance.

Civic virtues and Socrates

Such was the turn from the old world to the new. It happened in practice first, but the Greeks were always quick to seek the theory in things, in order to understand them and to bring clarity into them – not for merely speculative reasons, although they were great speculators, but so that they could bring the best to bear in life, in the interests of yet greater attainment.

In the new dispensation, discussion and debate mattered because they brought office, fame, civic honours and financial gain to any citizen who sought them ably enough. For that reason teachers of rhetoric flourished, and many of them became famous for their skill not just in teaching the forensic arts of oratory and advocacy but in showing how to argue about the great political and moral issues of the day. These were the Sophists, some of the more popular among whom impressed their audiences with their skill at marshalling extremely persuasive arguments both for and against any given proposition, and by showing how to make weak arguments appear stronger. They were, accordingly, able to charge high fees for teaching their craft. Their indifference to truth was a special provocation to Socrates and his pupil Plato, as was the fact that they asked for money. For Socrates, all enquiry was free; and it was all the more important that it should be free given that the questions it addressed were the most important any man could ask himself.

The source of Socrates' passionate view to this effect is easily explained. He saw the shift from the old to the new way of thinking about values as exactly right, and as raising tremendously important concerns; and he introduced his own shift of perspective accordingly, by turning philosophy – which had hitherto, among his predecessors, been almost exclusively concerned with questions about the nature and origins of the universe, as exemplified by Thales – to the dedicated task of enquiring into the good life and the good society.

From our longer perspective it seems that Socrates' rejection of his predecessors' thought was too hasty. It is obvious that the work they did was important in its own right. It initiated the tradition of science, which at last, especially from the beginning of modern times in the seventeenth century AD, transformed the world vastly for the better (though creating some desperate problems too). Their endeavour was rational, secular, objective and disciplined. Some of the ideas they developed proved of lasting value in philosophical thought. Why, then, did Socrates turn his back on them?

Both Xenophon and Plato give the reason. They report that as a young man Socrates listened to debates about the views of his predecessors, and became disillusioned on two grounds. The first was that their enquiries seemed futile, arriving at no settled conclusions and degenerating into a Babel of differing opinions. Secondly and more importantly, it seemed to him astonishing that these thinkers could devote themselves to unresolvable questions about the nature of the world while ignoring far more immediate and significant questions – namely, those about the human good. To arrive at answers to these latter was to be noble and free; to be ignorant or confused about them was to be a slave. He asked, 'How can study of the stars or the weather be expected to bring a man self-knowledge, and to teach him how to live?' As Xenophon puts it, Socrates thought that scientific knowledge is of no practical use to mankind – a view that, in the infancy of science, at least seemed temporarily cogent – and that therefore all one's energies should be focused instead on the infinitely more important question of the good life and how to live it.

That question was not as rarely asked by ordinary men in the Athens of Socrates' day as it is now. But in all times and places the great majority of people have accepted conventional views about what life is for, and by entering into a particular line of work, as most must, they thereby accept the goals native to those endeavours. That remains as true today as ever. Teachers and administrators, doctors and lawyers, in a local sense know what they do and why, and any larger or more diffuse goals they might have tend to be the usual (and perfectly worthy) ones of raising their families, succeeding in their careers, and enjoying leisure pursuits such as reading, gardening, music and sport. Their overall aim is that, at the end of their working lives, they will be able to retire to some pleasant spot to enjoy a measure of repose at last, reasonably satisfied in the knowledge that they have done their best in what is conventionally asked of people of their kind and time.

But whereas it is usual for people to become teachers, administrators, doctors and lawyers, it is highly unusual for them to ask: 'What is the value of education, organisation, health and law?' They simply and unreflectively assume that such things have value, and give the matter little further thought. Very occasionally a related philosophical question prods them; most people at some time find themselves dis-cussing – for example – the place of wealth in life, and iterating platitudes (which they widely ignore in practice) about money as such not bringing happiness or fulfilment. But deep-going questions about what really matters either remain unasked, or are addressed only in the skimpiest fashion.

Socrates, however, felt compelled to devote his energies to asking questions about what constitutes the good life, and he put his question in a distinctive way. Is there a goal, a purpose, a value in life which is worthwhile as an end in itself and not merely as a means to other things? If one presses people on the question of what overall good they wish to have, most would undoubtedly say 'happiness'. Further pressed on what this vague term means, they might well offer (as many of Socrates' near-contemporaries did) one or other of wealth, pleasure or wisdom as the chief ingredient of happiness. This echoes Pythagoras's description of the three classes of men who attend the Games. And naturally enough, the debate about the three candidates for happiness took then, as it takes now, the form of trying to determine which is the most important, and whether or not two or perhaps all three are required for happiness in its fullest sense.

For Socrates, however, happiness consists in what he described as 'the perfection of the soul'. In the *Apology* – Plato's dramatised version of Socrates' defence at his trial for 'impiety and corrupting the youth of Athens' – he tells his fellow Athenians that his primary concern is to seek wisdom, and to urge the view that it is not wealth and success that make goodness, but goodness that gives value to wealth and success. Moreover, he argues, goodness consists in having a particular kind of knowledge, namely, a knowledge of the intrinsic value of the things that men do and desire. This is part of what Socrates meant when he said, in a famous phrase, 'virtue is knowledge', and by arguing that once a person knows what the good is, he cannot do otherwise.

On the face of it, the statement 'Knowledge is virtue' looks empty. It seems to say that virtue consists in knowing what virtue is, which is unhelpful. But it can be understood in the light of Socrates' method, which was the largely critical and negative one of getting people to see that they did not really know what they thought they knew. A classic example is given in Plato's dialogue *Meno*, in which a rich young man (called Meno) visits Socrates while on a business trip to Athens, to ask the great philosopher what he thinks should be the answer to a question much pressing the Greek mind at the time, namely: Is virtue teachable? The problem was that the offspring of upstanding citizens were quite as likely to behave badly as they were to be as virtuous as their parents. How could this be? To Meno's astonishment Socrates answers that he does not know; and – to Meno's even greater astonishment – he does not know because he does not know an even more important thing, namely, what virtue is. Pretending to be struck by Meno's surprise at this, Socrates asks him if *he* knows what virtue is, to which Meno confidently replies that of course he does. 'Tell me!' cries Socrates in feigned delight. 'I've longed to meet someone who knows!' It does not take long for him to demolish Meno's attempts at a definition, and when Meno finally collapses and admits his ignorance, Socrates says, 'Now that you know that you do not know, we can begin to make progress.' They thereafter begin to make progress indeed; but still do not arrive at the definitive statement Socrates seeks.

Most of the Socratic dialogues by Plato have this inconclusive air, and in the *Apology* he has Socrates admit that, although he has sought knowledge all his life – mainly by asking everyone to tell him what they know – he has not found it. The Delphic oracle had called him the wisest of men; but that, says Socrates, was because he knew that he knew nothing, whereas other men did not understand their own ignorance.

This suggests that what principally mattered to Socrates was the quest itself – the quest for ethical understanding, the living of the examined life – rather than the conclusions he or anyone else came to. Or perhaps his point was that even though the ideals suggested by such a quest are in practice unattainable, the life of striving towards them is itself the good life.

Socrates' avowed aim was to try to find definitions for such notions as justice, courage, temperance and beauty. He assumed throughout that these notions indeed have definitions, despite the great difficulty he and everyone else experienced in specifying them. It is therefore plain enough, in an initial way, what he took goodness and the good life to be; and even the failed attempt to define the essential nature of these values goes a considerable way to clarifying them. The business of getting people to shed their confusions about these matters, especially when they mistake their confusions for knowledge, is more than half the task of getting things right, which is a large gain. So perhaps Socrates' apparently inconclusive and negative methods were neither so inconclusive nor so negative after all: for we at least know that he wished to know the essence of justice, courage, temperance and beauty.

Plato

One thing immediately apparent to any enquirer into Socrates' views is that, since he never wrote anything, and we have accounts of his life and teachings always at second hand in Xenophon, Aristophanes, Aristotle, and – chiefly – Plato, one has to be cautious about what to attribute to him. Plato used Socrates as his mouthpiece in most of his dialogues, but went far beyond him in setting out his own theories, which consisted in a set of interlinked views resting on metaphysical and epistemological premises.

Two dialogues of Plato contain important moments in the development of his ethical views. One, the *Gorgias*, is a relatively early dialogue. The other, a great classic written in Plato's 'middle' period, is *The Republic*. In the first he had not yet developed the metaphysics that came to underlie his mature views, and for that reason its focus is more exclusively ethical. In the second his concerns are wide-ranging, but focus principally on a notion he thought fundamental: the notion of justice.

Gorgias was a Sophist, a teacher of rhetoric, who claimed that since the highest good is freedom to do as one wishes, and since rhetoric – the art of persuading and influencing others – is the instrument that will get one that freedom, it follows that to live the good life one should study rhetoric. In a beautiful argument Socrates demolishes Gorgias's view. There are, he says, two kinds of persuasion: one gives rise to knowledge, because it involves giving reasons for accepting a belief, whereas the other does not give rise to knowledge, but simply consists in using rhetorical tricks to sway the minds of hearers to accept a proposition, whether or not it is true. Socrates asks Gorgias: Does the rhetorician need a knowledge of the difference between right and wrong? Gorgias is vague in his reply, but he insists that rhetoric itself is morally neutral: a bad person will use it for bad ends, a good person for good ends. To show what is wrong with this view Socrates engages two of Gorgias's pupils in a discussion that raises, among other things, two points of great importance to Plato. One is the thought that an unjust person will be denied the friendship of the gods and other people if he is not capable of sharing. The second is the even more significant thought that to live well is to have an ordered soul, one which is in harmony with itself. These ideas anticipate *The Republic*, where they feature centrally.

Despite its name and most of its content, *The Republic* is offered by Plato as being only incidentally a work of political philosophy, for he ostensibly intends its discussion of political justice and the ideal state to be an illustration of justice as the moral ideal for individuals. In the central portions of the dialogue Plato argues that an ideal city state is one in which each of the community's three orders of citizens – the governors, the 'guardians' or military men, and the general population – do what is appropriate for their position in society, and thereby preserve a balance (which is to say, social harmony) between them. Then Plato draws his analogy between the state and the individual. Just as the city state has three components, so an individual soul has three parts: reason, the emotions, and the appetites. When these are in harmony the individual is happy. In the later part of *The Republic* Plato accordingly likens disharmony in the soul to disorder in the state, as happens when tyranny and democracy (both of which he regards as unjust political dispensations) are in force.

Plato has Socrates say, at the conclusion to Book 9 of *The Republic*, that even if the ideal city discussed in the main body of the dialogue cannot exist in fact, it nevertheless provides the right model for individual moral excellence. Achieving internal harmony is, he says, 'the object of the intelligent man's life'; and he makes Socrates continue as follows:

> The only studies [such a man] values will be those that form his mind and character accordingly. As for his physical condition; he will not live merely with brutish and

irrational pleasures in view, indeed he will not even make his bodily health his principal concern, for strength, health and beauty will mean nothing to him unless self-control accompanies them, and we shall always find him keeping his physical values in tune with his moral and intellectual values. He will observe the same principle of harmony in acquiring wealth, and will be careful not to become too rich, thereby accumulating problems; and he will think the same way about honours.

The idea of justice performs two tasks in Plato's account of the moral life. In addition to the internal justice-as-harmony conception just described, he also advances the idea of a justly lived life, which he wishes to show is happier than an unjustly lived life. By this Plato does not mean a life in which the individual deals justly with others. Rather, he means a life lived according to a balanced arrangement of reason and the passions in their practical, outward-directed activity. It is a life distinguished, in other words, by a sense of proportion. One of his arguments for the preferability of the just over the unjust life is that a man without a sense of justice (that is, without a sense of proportion) will not be able to set a limit to his desires, and will always therefore be discontented. Another argument is that an individual who lives justly will know, as a result of reflecting on his life in order to make it balanced and harmonious, which pleasures are true pleasures, and in particular he will know that the pleasures of the mind far outweigh those of the body.

This reveals a characteristic feature of Plato's outlook: his sharp division between reason and the appetites, between things intellectual and things of the senses – and that in particular means between rational temperance and sensuality. Famously, he argued in his dialogue *The Symposium* that the best kind of love should not express itself physically, but intellectually only – a conception familiarly known as 'Platonic love'. To force the analogy between justice and continence,

Plato has to make the unjust man one who pursues pleasures with a gross and ungovernable appetite. This suggests that the analogy between justice in the state and justice in the individual is too strained, and in the case of personal morality looks like a rationalisation for, rather than an argument in support of, Plato's somewhat puritan attitude.

Of course, *The Republic* is in truth principally a work of political philosophy, to which the moral teaching is actually – despite Plato's avowals – somewhat incidental, so this sketch ignores Plato's detailed conception of the ideal state, which is, in most respects, a very questionable one, for it is a state both paternalistic and totalitarian in character. But as an account of the nature of the person who attains the good life, in the express sense of a life of inner balance and moderation, it is a very classical Greek view – even if Plato harnesses the ideas of harmony and restraint to a much more intellectual and puritan conception than many of his contemporaries favoured.

Aristotle

Plato's great pupil and successor Aristotle was a far more down-to-earth thinker, and expressly distanced himself from the refined abstraction of Plato's views. A principle adopted by Aristotle in his wide-ranging and remarkable enquiries was that of 'respecting ordinary opinions and beliefs', not because they are necessarily right, but because they might contain clues to what is right, or at least will make the salutary demand on us to explain why people believed them, and to justify such corrections to their views as enquiry shows are necessary. A theory that offered no map of the route from ordinary beliefs, however mistaken, to better views would thereby lack an important connection with common sense and perhaps even truth. This principle, usually referred to as 'saving the *endoxa*' where *endoxa* means 'common beliefs', served Aristotle especially well in the development of his ethics, in which he sought to provide a commonsense account of human nature and the best life for man.

The classic statement of Aristotle's outlook occurs in the *Nichomachean Ethics* (so called because it is believed to have been edited by his son Nichomachus after his death). Two other works attributed to him, the *Eudemian Ethics* and the *Magna Moralia*, are characteristically Aristotelian in content, whether or not they were actually written by him; but they neither differ from nor add to the main source. In the *Nichomachean Ethics* is found the first ever systematic attempt to explore the basis of ethics, and to set out an ethical theory in due form. Yet for all that it is a treatise stating a doctrine, it is strikingly open-minded and mature – not the preachings of a zealot nor the dreams of a mystic, but the reflections of a careful, clear-minded, sensible intelligence. A clue to its character lies in Aristotle's belief that discussions about the good life are not for the inexperienced, who will not be able to appreciate their point; rather, they are for people who have seen something of the world, felt its sharp corners, tasted success and defeat in the concerns of humankind, and who will therefore be able to recognise what conduces to moral success in life's manifold business.

Indeed the *Nichomachean Ethics* has an exploratory, tentative air in some respects, suggesting that it is the work of someone feeling his way and trying to get clear about what is right. It works on the material that Aristotle saw as the true lode from which ethical insight is mined, namely, human psychology. As with Plato and all the Greeks, Aristotle did not see ethics as something different from politics, on the grounds that politics is the science of how to create a good society with the express intention of providing the best opportunities for its citizens to live the good life.

If we start from the *endoxa*, Aristotle says, we can see what the good is most commonly held to be. Following the familiar Pythagorean classification of types of men, Aristotle says that 'persons of low tastes (always the majority)' hold that the greatest good is pleasure, while the businessman thinks it is wealth and 'the gentleman' holds that it is honour. But these common conceptions are not wholly satisfactory, for in each case the supposed goods are merely instrumental to an end beyond themselves, which they are supposed to bring within a man's reach. By common consent, says Aristotle, that highest good is happiness. So the task is to specify what happiness truly is, and how to attain it.

Aristotle begins with a statement of what he takes to be a plain fact, namely, that the good for man is what man's nature makes him desire, as shown by the correlative fact that the good is what is desired and sought by all men. In identifying the good with happiness Aristotle had a particular concept of happiness in mind, to which he gave the name *eudaimonia*. By this he meant an active kind of well-being and well-doing – a much richer notion than is now generally meant by 'happiness'. More precisely, *eudaimonia* means a flourishing state of the soul. The English word 'happiness' (especially in contemporary usage) embodies a very pallid conception in comparison; one could make everyone happy by putting suitable medications in the public water supply, but that would scarcely convey what Aristotle had in mind.

The reason why happiness (in the sense of *eudaimonia*) is the aim that human nature selects for itself, says Aristotle, is that human beings are rational creatures, who reflect and make choices, and in particular are capable of thinking about what is in their ultimate interest. Happiness is in everyone's ultimate interest because it is desirable for its own sake; all other goods are merely instrumental in helping to bring happiness about, whereas happiness is complete and self-sufficient.

The appeal to man's rationality is an important feature of Aristotle's view. Man is part of the natural world in that, like the plants, he ingests nutriments and reproduces himself, and like animals he moves about, perceives, and has desires. But in addition, and alone among all things, man is rational, and this is his defining mark or essence. To be human is to reason – more particularly, to employ practical reason in thinking how to live. Since the good life for man is the life lived in accordance with his essence, it follows that the good life for man is a life of 'practical wisdom' (in Greek, *phronesis*). Aristotle describes such a life as one lived 'in accordance with virtue'.

By 'virtue' Aristotle means what reason will choose as the middle path or 'mean' between opposing vices. Thus the virtue of courage is the mean between cowardice and rashness, and generosity is the mean between miserliness and profligacy. Like Plato, Aristotle recognised people as having both rational and non-rational desires, and saw virtue as being the condition in which reason governs the latter. So rationality is what guides a person between, on the one hand, the overindulgence of non-rational desires and, on the other hand, the suppression of them. This is not quite the same thing as 'moderation' in the sense of the commonplace advice to 'take all things in moderation', although sometimes it might mean this; for Aristotle's virtuous individual is not simply a continent one, but one who lives according to the dictates of practical wisdom. Such wisdom will allow an appropriate expression of needs and appetites, for it is indeed sometimes appropriate to feel angry, or to desire the approbation of others, or to feel a sense of shame or pride.

Consider the example of anger. Aristotle saw it as an emotion capable of great power and good effect if wisely directed. 'It is easy to fly into a passion,' he remarked, 'anyone can do that; but to be angry with the right person, to the right extent, at the right time, in the right way, with the right aim; that is not easy.' He thought that knowing how to be appropriately angry is an essential part of the moral life – providing that it does not overthrow reason and become merely destructive in consequence.

An attractive feature of Aristotle's view is that it requires the moral agent to determine, from the actual facts of an individual case, what is the right course of action in that case. There is no code or list of rules, no 'thou shalt' and 'thou shalt not', but a requirement to do the sensible thing, based on practical wisdom or prudence. If one cannot oneself be practically wise, says Aristotle, one should imitate those who are. Eventually this has a good chance of helping one learn how to be prudent, for in any case identifying the mean and acting in accordance with it in given situations is a matter of developing habits of practical wisdom, and becoming skilled in ethical judgement. Living the good life is a whole-life project, and accordingly is something in which one can perfect oneself.

It is a counter-intuitive result of the views Plato put into Socrates' mouth that if a person does wrong, he does so only out of ignorance. Surely people can sometimes know what is right, and yet do the wrong thing for any of a variety of reasons, not least among them an inability to exercise sufficient strength of will to do the right thing? A trivial example of 'weakness of will', or *akrasia*, is a dieter's accepting and eating a piece of chocolate cake when he knows he should refuse it. Aristotle's account of the moral life makes room for weakness of will by diagnosing it as a contest between rational choice and non-rational desire in which the latter wins, making it happen that the incontinent person 'sees the better but does the worse'.

The person who lives according to practical wisdom attains *eudaimonia*, and is accounted virtuous, where the virtues are such traits of character as courage, temperance, liberality, justice and honesty. A person in whom these virtues are cultivated is said by Aristotle to therefore have the special virtue of magnanimity, the possession of a 'great soul', for which the Greek is *megalopsychos* (the English word derives from Latin *magna anima*). Aristotle's great-souled man is the original model of what might be called a 'gentleman' if this term had not acquired connotations of social class resulting from birth and inheritance, which mostly obscure its moral sense of a person who acts in a distinctive way – the way that is meant when someone is described, in the vernacular phrase, as 'a real gent'.

Aristotle's own portrait of the *megalopsychos* is not – or at any rate is no longer – an especially attractive one: he has a deep voice, a steady gait, and a self-important air, as befits one who lives according to the mean in all situations, prudently considering what to do, never overrating the value or importance of anything, but certainly not underrating his own value and importance. This alas is not a mere caricature of what Aristotle had in mind, and it exposes the vulnerability of his view to the criticism that his doctrine, in focusing upon the middle way, is therefore too middle-aged, middlebrow and middle-class, suggesting a rather limited individual prone to pomposity, who, in shunning the extremes of passion, love, anguish and like states, cannot know the value of them as sources of insight and creativity. For all that Aristotle did not mean the middle way to be the same thing as moderation or restraint just as such, this criticism has a certain bite, as is admitted in advance by his remark that his kind of reflection on ethical matters is for people whose experience of life has already revealed to them the value of choosing its quieter and more even terrain as the home of the good.

An important feature of the good life, in Aristotle's view as in almost everyone else's, is that it should involve a concern for others. To show why this is so, he examines the idea of friendship, in a justly famous and much-quoted passage of the *Nichomachean Ethics*. He there distinguishes genuine friendship from two superficially similar kinds of acquaintanceship, one in which the basis of the relationship is pleasure, the other in which it is mutual usefulness. These shallow forms of friendship last only as long as the pleasure or utility they afford, says Aristotle, whereas true friendship lasts because it is 'grounded in good', in the sense that one wishes for one's friend what is best for him. Aristotle calls this friendship 'perfected' or 'completed' because its goal lies wholly within the relationship itself, and does not treat it as merely instrumental for some other or further end.

Aristotle says that a friend is 'another self', meaning that the kind of concern one properly has for one's own good is extended to one's friend too. Proper self-concern is appropriate for an ethical individual, who will be motivated thereby to act nobly, and to make intelligent decisions about how to choose and act – and who will therefore always see, as a social being, that what is best for himself is at one with what is best for his friends and (ultimately) community. Thus, to treat a friend as another self is always to wish the best for him for his own sake, and to act accordingly.

The Aristotelian ideal of friendship is personal and mutual, and involves sharing activities, discussing decisions and actions, co-operating, and supporting one another. Because a friend is another self, everything that benefits him in these activities will benefit oneself, and the capacities and possibilities of each as rational agents will be enhanced thereby. The fullest development of each individual therefore requires friendship and all that it brings in the way of growth and realisation of moral character for all parties to it.

The very highest ideal of the good life is, however, reserved by Aristotle for contemplation, in the sense of thought and study for its own sake. His motive is not hard to see: if reason is the highest feature of man, and its possession his distinguishing mark, it follows that the pure disinterested exercise of reason will express man's essence in the most fitting way possible for it. The life of contemplation is thus the best life, because contemplation is, as the essential activity of humankind, the one attended by the greatest possible happiness. In this connection Aristotle allows himself a flight of poetry, having walked the landscape of ethics with prosaic tread so far. He writes,

We ought not to listen to those who counsel us to think as mere mortal men should think, and to remember our mortality. Rather we ought to strive towards attaining something great, and leave nothing unattempted in the effort to live conformably with the highest thing in us. Our rationality might be modest in quantity, but in power and value it outstrips everything else about us. We may indeed believe this is a man's true self, being the sovereign and best part of him.

This leads Aristotle to his conclusion:

The rule is that what is best and pleasantest for each creature is what intimately belongs to it. In applying that rule to man we see that the life of the intellect is best and pleasantest for him, because the intellect more than anything else *is* the man. So the life of the intellect will be the happiest life for man. (*Nichomachean Ethics*, Book 10, chapter 7)

What, though, should the intellect be exercised upon? Aristotle's answer is characteristic. The chief object and aim of contemplation is, he says, *theoria*, which means 'speculative enquiry into eternal truths'. This is the avocation of the philosopher – though Aristotle concedes that it is not to everyone's taste, nor within everyone's grasp. This means that the very highest kind of life is restricted to a small group of people who have the required intellectual capacity, and a sufficiency of wealth to give them enough leisure to devote themselves to thinking for its own sake.

Some critics have denounced this as elitism, and claimed therefore that Aristotle's ethics is not for ordinary people despite its apparent ambition at the outset to describe, in general terms, the good life in the good society. The criticism is not, however, quite fair. Aristotle concedes that good fortune plays its part in helping some to live the best kind of life by providing the necessary opportunities; but much else of what he says is applicable more generally, not least his views on justice. In line with his theory of the mean, he defines the doing of injustice as getting more than one ought, and suffering injustice as getting less than one ought; and therefore justice is equity – to deal justly is to do what is fair. This applies irrespectively of social status or moral luck.

Still, it remains true that Aristotle lived in a society whose economy was based on slavery, and he not only saw nothing wrong with slavery but even held that some people are naturally born to be slaves. Moreover, there is a good deal of the complacent, comfortably-off citizen about Aristotle's ideal man; and the idea of a deep-voiced, steady-gaited burgher is somewhat at odds with the ideal of the philosophic contemplater of eternal truths – or it would be, if the burgh in question were not Athens in the classical age.

3

THE PHILOSOPHIC IDEAL

The Hellenistic condition

From the time of Aristotle until Christianity's conquest of the Roman world there were many competing conceptions of the good, shared among a number of different philosophical schools and – far less consciously and clearly – many different popular religions. The most notable of them in this long period was the outlook that came to be known as Stoicism. It began as a philosophical school that contributed original ideas of a technical nature in logic and metaphysics as well as in ethics, but it was the influence of its ethics that especially flowed into the wider culture of the Hellenic and Roman worlds. Stoicism became the chief outlook of educated people for over half a millennium before Christianity put an effective end to 'pagan philosophy' by imposing a deliberate hegemony over thought, signalised finally by its closing of the schools of Athens – those founded by Plato and Aristotle among others – in AD 529.

Stoicism is best understood in its historical context, as framing itself in answer to needs and interests that, although universal among mankind, took a particular form in the periods between the empire of Alexander and the later Roman Empire. It also profits from being understood alongside two other important schools of thought in the same period, Cynicism and Epicureanism. All three schools took their rise in the Hellenistic period (for rough purposes the years 350–30 BC), an age marked by two distinctive traits. First, the city states of the pre-classical and classical periods lost their independence and became part of a large empire. Individuals no longer played a role in governing themselves and their local community, and one result was that thought and literature ceased to have immediate connection to public affairs, instead becoming focused much more upon personal matters. Where Socrates, Plato and Aristotle had simply assumed that ethical and political considerations are seamlessly connected, and therefore moved without question between them in the statement of their views, their Hellenistic successors concentrated instead upon the private and interpersonal spheres only, making no assumption that what weighed in them applied by direct analogy to the far larger spheres of public, and still less imperial, concerns – or vice versa.

Secondly, whereas the classical period had been one of entirely fresh thought, new challenges, and concentration upon the present and future in the affairs of individuals and states, the Hellenistic period was conscious of the fact that it was a successor epoch, following upon a more glorious past. It was accordingly a reflective, historically minded period. It would be natural, but too simple, to see the Hellenistic world as the tired residue of the brilliant burst of creative energy that characterised the classical age. Of course, a measure of truth attaches to this thought, for it is impossible to deny the extent of the classical achievement. But even so, the more introverted and troubled Hellenistic thinkers had much of value to offer, and they profited from standing on their predecessors' shoulders.

The classical period had not been a time of peace; on the contrary, just as Athens reached its peak as the crucible of Western civilisation, so it suffered the debacle of the Peloponnesian War, failing in its military expedition against Sicily and in the end, after a quarter of a century of hot and cold conflict, being decisively beaten in 405 BC by Sparta in the naval battle of Aegospotami. The military and political failure of Athens was what disaffected Socrates and Plato against the democracy – they belonged to the aristocratic party, which explains the character of Plato's political views. Yet neither of them reacted to the turmoil of their times by seeking to disengage from practical affairs. Rather, they argued for remedies, alternatives, improvements; they took it that Athens' glory could be restored.

Alexander's imperial successes, and the world that followed them, caused, or were otherwise somehow involved with, the change in philosophical ambition described. The old ambition and confidence were gone. Thinkers did not ask, 'How is the state to be organised so that its citizens can have the best life possible?' Rather they asked, 'What should the individual do to live with as much fortitude and tranquillity as he can, in this uncertain and insecure world?' As this change of focus implies, the chief aim of ethics after the end of the classical epoch was to teach people how to find *ataraxia*, which means 'peace of mind', or at very least as much inner psychological stability as possible in the face of the changes, chances and pains of life in a troubled world. Each of the three schools (though it should be acknowledged that 'school' is not an accurate description for the Cynics) prominent in the Hellenistic and Roman periods offered distinctive responses to this challenge.

The way of the dog

The Cynics were, in essence, hippies, drop-outs, anti-establishment figures who rejected ordinary life and its aims and goals, and asserted instead a life of self-sufficiency according to nature. It was more a movement than a school, started by Diogenes of Sinope in the fourth century BC and his disciples, chief among them Crates. Although Diogenes and a number of his followers – then and later – wrote treatises and letters stating their views, nothing beyond quotations in other people's works survive, and our knowledge of Cynicism is the result of painstaking analysis of legends, anecdotes and attributed doings and sayings. Not infrequently such records of the Cynics as remain occur in the writings of people hostile to them, for which, therefore, a large adjustment has to be made. But it is obvious that so distinctive an outlook, and such an unignorable group of people, could not have failed to make a clear impression on history, and that is indeed how it seems on looking at the traces they have left.

Diogenes was not a tramp by birth. His father was a banker in Sinope on the Euxine Sea, and if the titles of Diogenes' lost works are an indication – they are listed by Diogenes Laertius – he was a highly educated man. Perhaps as a result of a scandal involving his father, or perhaps even himself, in connection with counterfeit money, Diogenes left Sinope for Athens, and there might have associated with one of Socrates' most famous pupils, Antisthenes. Some commentators suggest that the latter was the true founder of Cynicism, for he was a blunt-speaking, plain-living man in very much the Cynic style as it was soon to become. The writers who nominate Antisthenes as Cynicism's founder lived mainly in later antiquity, which raises a suspicion that they chose him in order to give the school a dignified lineage from Socrates, while allowing them also to play on the fact that 'Cynic' is thought to come from the Greek word for dog – thus illustrating the simple, free, convention-spurning attitude of the Cynics – and, conveniently, Antisthenes was nicknamed 'Plain Dog' because of his mannerisms and simple apparel.

Whatever the truth about Cynicism's origins, it remains that its primary focus was repudiation of a world in which poverty, slavery, exile, death or injury in war, capture by pirates, and other insecurities and horrors, were common facts of life, making it seem that the only divinity still at work in the world was Fortune, who was more likely to dispense ill luck than good luck. In response, Diogenes taught that the best life is one of simplicity and naturalness. The traditional desiderata of life, he said, are worthless, and with them the conventional restrictions on behaviour, all of which go against natural human impulses. People devote themselves to worthless aims, wasting themselves in the futile and shallow endeavour of pursuing them, and fretting themselves when failure ensues. Man's suffering is the result of his passions, his anxiety and ambition, his attraction to vacuous pleasures, and his enslavement to the desire for wealth and fame. In such a life people are dependent on others, trapped in obligations and stress, doomed to disappointments, vulnerable to external accidents of fate over which they have no control. The remedy, said Diogenes, is to turn one's back on the whole rat race. There are three essential conditions for peace of mind: autarchy, apathy and freedom. By 'autarchy' is meant self-government and self-sufficiency; by 'apathy' is meant indifference to what the world outside oneself can do to one; and by the last is meant freedom from dependence on other people and on material possessions. Animals provide a model of such a life: they support themselves from what the world offers, and are otherwise free. 'It is the gods' privilege to need nothing,' Diogenes said, 'and of the godlike man to need little.'

In line with this last sentiment Diogenes went about clad only in a dirty cloak – which served him in all seasons as both apparel and a blanket to sleep under – and a staff and little bag. He did not wash, and he let his hair and beard grow matted and long. He performed all his natural functions, including masturbation when he felt the need, in public. He hurled abuse at passers-by, or at the least spoke with excoriating bluntness, disdaining everything conventionally admired and urging people to drop convention and taboo, to ignore the law and to give up their money, homes, ambitions – and with them, therefore, their misery. He described himself as a citizen not of a city or a state, but of the universe – a 'cosmopolitan'. Naturally he was regarded as scandalous, and so were his followers, not least Crates and his consort Hipparchia, who enjoyed each other sexually in public, to general amusement or embarrassment.

So far did Diogenes go, indeed, that his encouragement of complete personal freedom and the abolition of taboos against anthropophagy and incest, together with his call to destroy all weapons and money, seemed too extreme even for his own later followers. But they agreed with his attack on religion, which he said was an obstacle to apathy (in his sense of this term) because it promoted fear of death and the vengeance of the gods, and it enslaved people to superstition, rituals, interpretations of auguries, priestcraft, and unnatural life-denying limitations. An entirely natural life, lived in nature and in accordance with nature – with no regard to alleged supernatural entities or truths – was, said Diogenes, the only route to freedom and therefore happiness.

An advantage offered by Cynicism was that it was open to anyone who could grasp its simple teachings. Understanding it required neither education nor sophistication, and in its wholesale rejection of the apparatus of ordinary life and ordinary ambitions it was an attractive alternative – as hippiedom has always been – to those who seek a very short short cut to happiness. Study and enquiry were unnecessary; this was a rejection altogether of the intellectual path to enlightenment. Enlightenment came from living a life as much like an animal as possible, simple and in direct touch with instincts and impulses, close to life's most basic needs and their satisfactions.

Diogenes and Crates were famous, or perhaps infamous, in their own day in the fourth century BC. Unlike the sadhu of India, those ascetic pilgrims who live on alms as they wander from one holy place to another in the subcontinent, most of the Cynics did not inspire the admiration, still less the veneration, of their contemporaries. Diogenes himself, 'the Heavenly Dog', prompted a shocked affection among some, and Crates (in any case a more humane and accessible individual) was liked; people called him 'the dear hunchback'. But the Cynic way was regarded as eccentric at best and excessive at worst, and did not survive in its early extreme form. Yet aspects of the radical alternative life it proposed continued to have an attraction for some right until the fifth century AD, typically in the form of bluntness of speech, simplicity and austerity of dress and lifestyle, and a close adherence to nature. In the usual way of these things, it was during the luxurious period of Rome's empire, especially in the first century AD, that a form of Cynicism became popular, in large part as a nostalgia for Republican austerities that some in Rome mourned when they observed the effeteness and loss of moral fibre – as they saw it – among their contemporaries, who took to the opposite extreme the teachings of another Hellenistic school of thought: Epicureanism.

The pursuit of pleasure

Nothing could seem further from the Cynic view than the ethical teaching of Epicurus, when first encountered in summary form as the injunction to 'pursue pleasure and avoid pain'. That is what an 'Epicurean' in the modern sense is committed to doing, where 'pleasure' is understood as eating and drinking and 'pain' as having to get up in the morning to go to work. But Epicurus held that the highest pleasure was sitting in the shade of a tree discussing philosophy with friends; and he thought that gourmandising and carousing, promiscuity, idleness and other conventional pleasures carried in them the seeds of pain and were therefore to be avoided.

Epicurus was born in Samos about 342 BC, and moved to Athens in 306 BC, where he bought a small garden and in it established his philosophical school. He and his disciples liked to say that they 'philosophised together', rather than following the method of a master instructing pupils. By good fortune a number of Epicurus's writings have survived, and in one, the *Letter to Menoeceus*, he makes his famous remark, 'Let no one when young delay to study philosophy, nor when he is old grow weary of the task; for nobody can come too early or too late to secure the health of his soul.'

To make ourselves strong and secure from harm, said

Epicurus, we need to get a clear understanding of four matters: god, death, pleasure and suffering. All our fears and desires are comprehended in these four subjects, so to grasp the truth about them will free us and give us peace of mind. And Epicurus proceeded to elucidate them as follows.

If there is a deity it is a blessed and tranquil being, not concerned with the burden of administering the world – for the world governs itself according to the laws of nature, consisting as it does of nothing more than physical objects and the void – and therefore a deity is not actuated by anger or favour, nor possessed of any interest in imposing requirements of any kind on us. From such a being we have nothing to fear. We can instead treat the idea of such a deity as a model for us to emulate; its peacefulness, detachment and unending pleasure are exactly what we should seek to achieve in our own lives.

By the same token, death is nothing to us. It is simply the dissolution of the physical elements we are made of, which return into the cosmos they came from. To fear the non-existence that ensues is as irrational as to regret that we did not exist before we were conceived and born. Those who fear death perform an impossible feat: they imagine themselves witnessing their own non-existence, and lamenting it. Superstitions and religious beliefs that tell of punishment in a post-mortem state make people afraid of dying, but as soon as we see that death is simply an end, all such fear evaporates, and once again we are free.

From ordinary observation of the world, said Epicurus, not least from observation of babies and animals, which act from their innate promptings only, it is clear that pleasure is the chief value, and goes naturally with a desire to avoid pain. Since the absence of pain is itself a pleasure, it follows that pleasure and pain mutually exhaust the options, and therefore provide the entire framework of ethics. Human unhappiness results from ignorance of how to understand and measure pleasures properly. Hedonists, who believe that pleasure is attained by self-indulgence, and especially indulgence of the appetites for luxuries including excessive food, drink and sex, make two mistakes in Epicurus's view. First, self-indulgence does not increase the amount of pleasure, but at best only iterates or varies it. But secondly, it anyway has the harmful effect of increasing desires and appetites, thus increasing one's vulnerability to pain by exposure to the vagaries of fortune.

Epicurus was of course fully aware that others nominated non-hedonistic values as the aim of ethics, chief among them virtue. His response was to say that such values are not truly ends in themselves, but instrumental to the great goal of pleasure.

Given this view and his strictures on conventional pleasures, it seems that Epicurus's idea of pleasure must at least be unusual; and so it is. To explain it he gives an account of how intellectual and physical pleasures are to be measured relatively to one another, and how we are to rate 'static' and 'kinetic' pleasures. In the light of the intellectualism of philosophers and the powerful examples of Plato's and Aristotle's celebration of the mental over the physical life, one might expect later philosophers to follow suit. But Epicurus does not dismiss physical pleasure, arguing that it is an important component of pleasure overall, on the grounds that mental pain and pleasure in the end express themselves in satisfaction or dissatisfaction with one's degree of bodily well-being. In this way, bodily well-being is the ultimate reference of pleasure. But this is not to underrate the mental component of pleasure; on the contrary, mental pleasures are such a powerful aspect of overall pleasure that they actually determine bodily pleasure – as when an ill person can, by thinking about happier times in the past or to come, ameliorate his bodily pains. The power of the mind is equally displayed in the fact that fear – of imaginary ills, possible disasters, and death – can ruin one's present pleasure and reduce one to living in anguish. It is the mind's connection with time that makes the difference between physical and mental pleasures: the former are always of the moment, occupying exclusively the present, whereas the latter inhabit the past and future as well, thereby multiplying their intensity and value.

By a 'static' pleasure Epicurus meant the absence of pain. Absence of physical pain he called *aponia*, and absence of mental pain he called *ataraxia*, which as noted means peace of mind. The latter is attained by understanding the nature of the universe, thereby seeing that it is not a frightening or threatening place. This is where Epicurus's accounts of god and death figure prominently, for these are topics that cause so much unease among men.

'Kinetic' pleasures also have physical and mental versions and, as the word suggests, they involve activity of some kind. In the physical case kinetic pleasure is the process of attaining a static pleasure (putting an end to hunger by eating, say) or varying a static pleasure (eating not to quell hunger but to enjoy the taste of food). In the mental case kinetic pleasures are such activities as discussion with friends and the solving of problems. Both the physical and mental varieties have to be carefully supervised, however, because they easily include desires and appetites that either are not good in themselves, or quickly lead to pain; most of the conventional aims of life, such as the eagerness for wealth or fame, are of this latter kind. To be secure from the harm that fortune can bring, only natural and necessary desires should be indulged, said Epicurus, and then mostly in moderation. But he taught that we should be moderate even in our moderation, and the simple-living Epicurean communities therefore occasionally held banquets.

There are a number of features of Epicurus's theory that place it in a class above the Cynic outlook. Two are especially worth mentioning. First, the view is an egoistic one, in that the aim and measure of the good is one's own pleasure, even if it is the modest and restrained pleasure extolled by Epicurus. What, then, of the two important social values of justice and friendship – is there room for them in this view? The answer is yes.

Justice is one of the instrumental values mentioned earlier, which serves the best interests of everyone's pleasure, as a form of contract between members of a community to ensure that they do not harm or disadvantage one another. Each individual stands to gain from such an arrangement, and therefore it contributes to the pleasure of each.

Friendship is a quite different matter in Epicurus's view. Unlike justice it is not merely an instrumental good, but has intrinsic value, being in itself one of the supreme pleasures. Its pleasures derive not only from what friends can do for each other and give to each other, but in disinterested and altruistic actions. Unquestionably, though, there is a tension between the egoism that lies at the basis of Epicurus's view and the great importance he attached to friendship and the pleasure of altruism. Later Epicureans debated the matter extensively, trying various ways of finessing the problem. To their credit, none attempted to resolve it by jettisoning the idea that friendship is among the highest of goods.

The second point is Epicurus's innovatory recognition that the question of the will's freedom is central to ethics. The point arises for him because of the naturalism of his metaphysics: he held that the universe is a material realm consisting of bodies (e.g. the planets, ourselves) and the void (the empty space in which bodies exist), entirely governed by natural laws. Since these laws are causal, it is a problem to explain how human beings can truly be moral agents – that is, beings who act from free will according to choices and decisions of their own, not causally determined by previous states of the universe. The problem of free will and determinism has since remained one of the most intractable of metaphysical difficulties – and one of great importance, for freedom is required for the very possibility of ethics. This can be seen by considering that if everything we do is necessitated by natural laws acting on and through us according to fixed principles, we are not free and therefore do not truly choose, and so cannot be praised or blamed for what we do. In such a setting the idea of morality is empty. Only if we are genuinely the authors of our choices and actions can we be regarded as moral beings. Epicurus saw this, and dealt with the problem by asserting that humans have free will. It might even have been part of his view that the mind is governed by its own causality, involving laws separate from those operative in the natural world; but whether he indeed held such a view remains a matter of scholarly interpretation.

Epicureanism remained influential in the Hellenistic and Roman periods, commanding some distinguished adherents, including Cassius, one of Julius Caesar's assassins (Cassius evidently did not obey the Epicurean injunction to keep out of politics). The poets Horace and Virgil were influenced by Epicurean teachings, and later, when the mainly Stoic emperor Marcus Aurelius established four professorships of philosophy in Rome, one of them was for Epicureanism. Later, the attacks on the largely atheistic and naturalistic outlook of Epicureanism by Christians kept the doctrine alive in the Western mind, and it again became of interest to intelligent speculation in the Renaissance. Naturally enough, it was the somewhat degenerate popular forms of it which settled that the very name of the school should become associated with attitudes and practices far from Epicurus's original teachings, by caricaturing it as a crude form of hedonism. But that is a fate that greets many names and what they first denoted.

Even at its most influential, however, Epicureanism did not compare with the dominant school of thought before Christianity, at least among educated people. This was Stoicism, whose two best remembered figures are a slave and a Roman emperor.

Stoicism

Such was Stoicism's impact on the Hellenistic and Roman worlds that it has left its mark on the language we use today when we describe as 'stoical' or 'philosophical' an attitude of self-disciplined, uncomplaining and courageous acceptance of all that life brings. This is only part of Stoic ethics, but a distinctive one, and it was one reason why it recommended itself to some of the best and most intelligent minds of the ancient world.

Stoicism had a long continuous history as a movement, with many contributing thinkers who debated and occasionally disagreed among themselves on points of detail and emphasis, as in any school of thought, but who shared much in the way of assumptions and basic principles. Unfortunately, all the writings of early Stoicism are lost, only their titles and a scattering of quotations remaining. As with Cynicism, our knowledge of early Stoic teaching is drawn from summaries, discussions and refutations in other writers. Later Stoicism is, by contrast, well represented in extant literature, especially in the writings of Seneca and Marcus Aurelius, and in the careful record kept by Arrian of the teachings of Epictetus. By this time Stoicism had become almost entirely focused on its ethical doctrines, either because the detailed work of the early Stoics in logic, epistemology and science had come to be generally accepted by their successors, or because the importance of identifying the good life and living it absorbed the interest of the school's later members to the exclusion of all else. Both points are likely to be true in part, not least because the later leaders of Stoic thought were, with the exception of Epictetus, not teachers and intellectuals only, but busy men of affairs: Seneca was a minister in the government of the emperor Nero, and Marcus Aurelius was himself an emperor – the last of the great Antonines in Rome's Indian summer of the second century AD. The early Stoics were, by contrast, all teachers and thinkers. They considered the connection between the technical and the ethical aspects of their doctrines as especially important, because a founding principle of their view was that man ought to live as far as possible in accordance with nature – and that meant understanding what nature itself is (the task of science) and getting clear about how we come by that understanding reliably (the task of epistemology).

The founder of Stoicism was Zeno of Citium (334–262 BC). He taught in Athens in a porch embellished by the paintings of Polygnotus and therefore known as the Porch of Paintings, the *Stoa poikile*, which is how the school acquired its name. His immediate successors, also major contributors to early Stoic doctrine, were Cleanthes of Assos (331–230 BC) and Chrysippus of Soli (280–208). Cleanthes was the poet of early Stoicism, Chrysippus its scholar and systematiser; but along with Zeno himself they were all inheritors of ideas developed in the classical period that preceded them, for example, the logic of the Megarians and the metaphysics of Heraclitus, who taught that reason is a creative principle and that the universe is in a perpetual state of flux, changing back and forth according to principles of natural justice that never allow (as Heraclitus put it) the hot to go too far in driving out the cold, nor the cold to go too far in driving out the hot in return. From Socrates himself the early Stoics had the example of rationality, self-mastery, and the tireless search for truth. That model had also inspired the Cynics, who were another and important source of influence on Stoicism; the Cynics' advocacy of cosmopolitanism, life in accordance with nature, and the supreme value of 'autarchy' (individual self-government) was a major factor in the development of Stoic ethics. But there was an immensely important difference between the Cynic and Stoic outlooks: whereas the Cynics recommended turning one's back on one's community and the world, the Stoics believed in civic engagement and social relationships, and their ethical views reflect this commitment.

The ethics of the early Stoics was a direct expression of their view of the universe. For them the universe is a single orderly system, existing in ever-returning cycles as a rational organisation of the four elements (earth, air, fire and water) by *logos*, or reason. The activity of reason brings the elements into 'tension' with one another, that is, combining, shaping and holding them together through the cycles of change that constitute one of the cycles or 'great years' of the universe's ever-returning, ever-recurring history. The *logos* – by which they meant (and which they variously called) 'creative power', 'fire', 'ether', 'soul of the world', 'order of the world', 'order', 'providence', 'reason' – was also called by the early Stoics 'god' or 'Zeus'. By this they did not mean anything remotely similar to what theism traditionally involves, for they did not think of deity as a separate being, but rather as a principle of organisation of things. Just as the soul or mind is the principle of individual life, so 'god' is the soul of the universe; and just as the soul of a man is interested in the man it inhabits and his welfare, so the soul of the universe is benevolent and cares for its well-being. Indeed the soul of an individual man is a part, a spark, of the world soul.

Such was the metaphysics on which the teachings of the early Stoics rested, and from which their ethics readily flowed. To attain peace of mind and inner security, they said, one need only live in accordance with benevolent nature. One does this by schooling oneself to live intelligently, courageously, justly, and with self-control. Each of the virtues thus implied – intelligence, courage, justice and self-mastery (this is Plato's list of the cardinal virtues, which the Stoics adopted) – involves a species of knowledge. Intelligence enables one to know the difference between what is good and bad. Courage tells one what to fear and what not to fear. Justice tells one how to give others their proper due. And self-mastery (or temperance, Plato's *sophrosyne*) tells one how to adjust one's emotions and passions, and how to judge what really matters in one's experience.

At the outset the Stoics were austere in teaching indifference to such conventionally recognised goods as health, wealth and honour. But they soon came to accept that the possession of these things has advantages, and their lack disadvantages. The advantages are that they help their possessors to live with intelligence, courage, justice and self-mastery more adequately; but they are not, said the Stoics, necessities, and their lack should not be regarded as a barrier to living well.

As noted, Stoicism differs markedly from Cynicism in its attitude to others and society. In line with their belief that the mind of each individual is part of the universal organising reason in things – the 'world soul', or divine fire – the Stoics taught that all rational beings, slaves included, are brothers, and merit each other's respect and concern. They believed therefore that everyone has a duty of service to their fellow human beings, irrespective of nation, class, race or creed. The aim of fulfilling this duty was to create among all men a rational cosmopolis reflecting the universal order and beneficence of the universe.

This admirable humanitarian cosmopolitanism had part of its source in an interesting view of human psychology. Epicurus had invited his fellows to observe animals and newborn infants in order to see that the natural impulse of unsophisticated nature is towards pleasure. The Stoics drew a different conclusion from the same data. They argued that the primary impulse one observes in the young as in animals is towards self-preservation and, as an aspect of this, self-enhancement – which involves accepting pain and discomfiture in order to achieve goals seen as worthwhile, such as learning to walk and speak. As an individual develops, he extends this concern and striving towards others – first to his family, whose interests he wishes to further because they are intimately connected with his own; and then more generally to his fellow men, although of course in attenuated form, since the same degree of affection and affinity does not apply. This is simply a fact about the propensity of humans to feel concern for others as a natural extension of their innate self-concern, the Stoics argued, and does not yet amount to goodness; for goodness requires in addition a conscious desire to conform one's life to the rational order of the universe. Recognising that this natural humanitarian impulse is indeed in accordance with the rational order turns it from a psychological into an *ethical* impulse.

In saying that the good life is life lived in harmony with the rational order of things by means of the four cardinal virtues, the Stoics were restricting the meaning of 'good' in a specific way. This is illustrated by further consideration of their argument that such conventional goods as health and wealth are strictly speaking 'indifferent' in moral worth, in the sense of being neither good nor bad. The inspiration for this idea came from Socrates, who typically insisted that most traditionally conceived goods are only good if wisely employed, and could be bad otherwise. Whereas the Cynics derived from this a general contempt for conventional goods, the Stoics, as noted, tempered the view, and treated the 'indifferents' as dispensable adjuncts to the good life, giving as their justification the argument that we have natural instincts in favour of the comfort or happiness that health and a measure of material comfort bring, and that we naturally like the recognition our community gives in return for services rendered. Acceptance of these under government of a sound understanding of their true indifference in value is an aid, although a dispensable one, to living in accordance with the rational order of things. By this subtle and perceptive move the Stoics made their view of the good life a widely acceptable one, unlike the far less compromising teaching of the Cynics.

They also took account of the fact that desires and appetites are not necessarily bad. According to one view, passions are, in effect, rebellions against reason, forcing people to act contrary to what reason dictates. But the Stoics regarded the passions as natural, and said that the way to deal with them properly is to master them by understanding them. Consider the example of fear: reason commands that we be courageous in the face of danger, but fear disobeys, and makes one run away. By understanding the true nature of fear, and bringing it under the control of self-mastery, one turns it into something positive:

carefulness or appropriate caution, say. In this way the passions can be converted into what the Stoics call 'good feelings', among them kindness, generosity and amity. In this they again followed Socrates' claim that virtue is knowledge, and that vice is nothing other than ignorance.

It was a concern of the Stoics that their teaching should not be merely an abstruse idealisation that people might find hard to put into practice. They therefore developed a full theory of 'preferred' actions and attitudes among the indifferents, which could be encapsulated in guidelines or rules – such as honouring parents, developing friendships, furthering one's education, looking after one's diet and general health, and the like. And they suggested that a self-education in Stoic living is to be effected by emulating an ideal wise man who has fully mastered the Stoic way – even if such a sage exists only in imagination, and even if one cannot oneself attain to that state of moral perfection. The endeavour is the thing; and the goal – to repeat – is to live in agreement with nature, in the sense of living in conformity with the rational order of things, thereby achieving peace and strength of mind.

The Roman Stoics

As already mentioned, the only Stoic works still extant are those of Seneca and the emperor Marcus Aurelius, together with full notes of the lectures of Epictetus. And as also mentioned, all date from the first two centuries AD and therefore embody late Stoicism, when it was almost exclusively ethical in aim and doctrine. Seneca's writings, which contain treatises on anger, mercy, tranquillity, steadfastness and the brevity of life, and which also – yet more importantly – include a series of *Letters to Lucilius*, which are his most influential work, are the earliest complete Stoic writings remaining to us, and for that reason have great importance to historians of thought even though they do not attempt to give a record of the earlier phases of Stoic philosophy. The *Letters* were especially influential in the Renaissance, not least as models for Montaigne's essays; afterwards they were much quoted by Rousseau, and long beforehand they had served as one of the chief routes by which Stoic thought entered the Christianity of the Church Fathers.

Seneca had a busy and, in the end, troubled public life, serving as a senator and as an adviser to the emperor Nero, who in AD 65 compelled him to commit suicide for alleged participation in the conspiracy led by Piso. He was born in Spain in AD 1, one of three sons of a wealthy dignitary, and was carefully educated there by Stoic teachers. Both his brothers achieved distinction, one as a provincial governor most famous for being the official who arraigned St Paul for trial in Rome, the other as a private intellectual and father of the epic poet Lucan. All these men met their deaths simultaneously as a result of the Pisonian conspiracy. (This fact alone is sufficient to illustrate one reason why Stoicism recommended itself as a bulwark against the violent changes of fortune that were a commonplace of life in those arbitrary times.)

Seneca's contribution to Stoicism was to further its adaptation to the life of men of affairs. He followed Stoic tradition in regarding himself not as a sage but as one merely attempting to make progress towards moral worth. His importance in the history of thought is that he in effect revived philosophy in Latin literature, and gave Stoicism a further impetus in humanistic directions. He was also the most distinguished writer of his day, giving Latin prose a new style marked by a pithy, declamatory rhetorical technique – which was, however, a subject of much controversy, being criticised by some contemporaries for its affectation and for being (in the words of Aulus Gellius) 'sand without lime', yet commanding the admiration of many others, who were therefore influenced by his style into adopting the Stoic outlook.

In extending the Stoic doctrine of the universal brotherhood of man Seneca was far ahead of his times, most particularly in applying this doctrine to an adamant hostility towards slavery, gladiatorial contests and any form of cruelty by man to man. It is interesting to speculate whether, if he had retained his position as a minister in the Imperial government, or if he had served a better emperor, he might have done something towards ameliorating the condition of those many who suffered the careless inhumanities of the time.

Seneca's picture of the true Stoic is given in his letter *De Constantia Sapientis*, 'On the Firmness or Constancy of the Wise Man' (abbreviated in English as 'On Firmness'). Its theme is that the wise man can suffer neither injury nor insult.

> Fortune can only snatch away what she has given [he wrote]; but she does not give virtue, and therefore she cannot take it away. Virtue is free, inviolable, unmoved, unshaken, so steeled against the blows of chance that she cannot be bent, much less broken. Facing the instruments of torture she holds her gaze unflinching, her expression changes not at all, whether a hard or a happy lot is shown to her. Therefore the wise man will lose nothing that he will regard as loss; for the only possession he has is virtue, and of this he can never be robbed. Of everything else he has the use only on sufferance.

As a practical philosophy of life Stoicism received its fullest expression in the teachings of Epictetus (AD 50–120), by far the most considerable figure of the three chief late Stoics. Epictetus was a Greek who had been brought as a slave to Rome to serve as a tutor in a patrician household. His pupil, Arrian, made careful notes of Epictetus's lectures and subsequently published them; these are the *Discourses*, which are one of the principal sources of our knowledge of his thought, the other being the *Enchiridion*, a 'handbook' to his philosophy also compiled by Arrian.

Of the three late Stoics, Epictetus was the least eclectic and the closest to the tradition of early Stoicism, especially to the teachings of Chrysippus, whom Epictetus greatly admired; describing him as 'our great benefactor', he said: 'Chrysippus discovered the truth, and brought it to light, and communicated it to us all – not merely about living, but of living well.'

The outline of the Stoic teaching given above concerning the four cardinal virtues, life according to nature, the doctrine of 'indifferents' and 'preferred' indifferents as a non-necessary adjunct of the good life, characterises Epictetus's view. His central tenet is that we must distinguish between what lies within our power and what lies outside our power, learning how to master the former and to accept the latter with fortitude. Only our own emotions, thoughts and appetites – our inner mental life – are in our own power, so we must govern these while cultivating stoic indifference to factors beyond our control. These latter include not only what the world and other people do to us, but some of the ungovernable facts of our own nature, mainly those associated with pleasure and pain. As Arrian in the *Enchiridion* reports him saying, 'Some things are up to us and some things are not up to us. Our opinions are up to us, and our impulses, desires, aversions – in short, whatever is our own doing. Our bodies are not up to us, nor are our possessions, our reputations, or our public offices; that is, whatever is not our own doing.' This is the key item of knowledge that liberates us from the false beliefs and hopes that make us unhappy slaves of fortune; for once we grasp it, and live and think accordingly, we are free and possess *eudaimonia*.

As a way of managing life according to this distinction, Epictetus enjoined rational anticipation of what our actions and choices might result in, and firm self-government and orderliness. Together these help towards the well-lived life. 'The proper goal of our activity is to practise how to remove from one's life sorrows and laments, and cries of "alas" and "poor me", and misfortune and disappointment,' he said; and added, 'No one is master of another's moral character, and in this alone lies good and evil. No one, therefore, can secure the good for me, or involve me in evil, but I alone have authority over myself in these matters.' And he asked his pupils, when he had explained to them that their own happiness thus lay in their own hands, and that they could therefore immediately begin to be happy, 'How long will you delay to be wise?'

The most notable individual to be influenced by Epictetus's teachings was Marcus Aurelius Antoninus (AD 121–80). Aurelius was both a Roman emperor and a philosopher, a rare combination, and in its way a happy one; for he was one of a succession of emperors, the Antonines, who made the second century AD a Golden Age for Imperial Rome. It was the century that saw Galen in medicine, Ptolemy in astronomy, and Lucian in literature – and not least, Marcus Aurelius himself in philosophy. 'Golden Age' is Gibbon's description of the period; it might better be characterised as the Indian summer of the Roman Empire, for after Marcus Aurelius's reign its decline and fall began in earnest. The first signs of the fall were already present during Aurelius's reign, in the form of repeated barbarian attacks along the borders of the Empire, which the naturally peaceful and reflective emperor had to spend many difficult years defending. Some commentators blame Aurelius himself for his problems, but the fact is that the second century was an era of mass migration pushing relentlessly against Rome's margins, straining the Empire's military and economic resources. Aurelius was faced with an unturnable tide of history.

Although Aurelius's philosophy was Stoic in content and inspiration, it was also to a certain degree eclectic, for he read widely and helped himself to worthwhile insights wherever he found them. While campaigning on the Empire's northern border Aurelius kept a notebook, in which he entered his choicest thoughts, written in Greek, together with admonitions to himself and comments on how to live with fortitude and probity. He gave this notebook the title *To Myself*. When it was published after his death it was recognised as a classic of *lebens-philosophie*, and it has retained its reputation ever since as a graceful and noble homily on life. In English translation it is standardly known as *The Meditations*.

In *The Meditations* Aurelius iterates the basic Stoic view of the universe as a living organic unity, in which everything is mutually related, and in which human individuals are 'limbs' of the whole. It follows that the well-being of individuals is dependent upon the well-being of everything else. Similarly, each individual is inseparably an organic part of his society, so that individual flourishing cannot be detached from the flourishing of the community. People are essentially social creatures – using 'essential' here in its primary philosophical sense to mean that they cannot on pain of impossibility be otherwise – and this means that the attainment of good by an individual cannot take place other than in a social setting. Reciprocally, the well-being of society depends on that of its members. The community's interests neither outweigh nor negate individual interests: the two coexist inseparably, and must be fostered together.

One of the principles of Stoicism from the outset was, as noted, that whatever happens 'in accordance with nature' is for that reason good, and that therefore the only bad things that can happen to people are the outcome of their own failings. When what might ordinarily seem a bad thing happens to a good person, it is not, from that person's perspective, really bad; indeed, nothing bad can happen to the good. Consider the example of disease: to the good person disease is simply a natural occurrence, and as such something to be calmly accepted. People who behave badly should not be punished but taught, for as soon as they understand what is good they will do it. In adopting this optimistic and debatable view, Aurelius follows the teaching of Socrates as Plato presents it; for Socrates, everyone is seeking his own good, and if he does wrong it is because he is ignorant of the right way to attain it.

The most Socratic of Aurelius's views is that the good life is one based on reflection. By this means we attain the self-government enjoined by the Stoic tradition, and thereby happiness. One of the themes that exemplifies Aurelius's commitment to this thesis is his view about death. Human life is a small matter in cosmic terms, he says, and its cycles of life, change and death are natural and inevitable. We should therefore see our own deaths as natural and inevitable likewise, good because natural, nothing to be afraid of, and indeed not even very important as measured against the great scheme of things. If we rationally base our beliefs on what we know to be inevitable, we will suffer neither fear nor anguish.

The Stoic view is a courageous one, and Aurelius's version of it is true to its quiet but profound dignity. Of course there is much to question in it, not least what some might see as the Stoic's too cool attitude to what more energetic souls will see as the ecstasies of love, vivid experience of the arts, the welcoming even of terror and despair as creatively fruitful experiences in their own right. No Stoic could accept the idea that excess and psychological risk can be or can lead to good, yet one can imagine strong arguments to the conclusion that they are wrong. Nevertheless, for many aspects of life, and for many phases of life, the courage and tranquillity enjoined in Stoicism's noble outlook, not least in Aurelius's rendering of it, have not just their attractions but considerable power.

Not least among its virtues is that it is a philosophy which, while enjoining self-mastery and the courage to treat both good and ill fortune as irrelevant to true inner stability of mind, also encourages engagement in the world of men, giving the demands of social responsibility their full due, and basing social morality on the same view of the connectedness and naturalness of things as underwrites the personal aspect of the outlook.

Stoicism was eclipsed by Christianity, for reasons now to be discussed; but when, after many centuries, the hold of that powerful religion over people's minds began to weaken in the face of learning and the desire for liberty – liberty, first, of thought and conscience, later of the whole person – many distinctive elements of Stoicism returned to the attention and the approval of thinking people. As the best of the pagan ethical humanisms it was bound to recommend itself in this way to the later chapters of enlightenment in Western history. And that is how it proved.

4

THE ORDINANCES OF GOD

The Religions of the Book

One thing a reader of Marcus Aurelius, Epictetus and Seneca will note, perhaps with some surprise if they do so after reading the humanistic account of their tradition of thought as given in the previous chapter, is the frequency with which they invoke the notion of a god. But it is important to understand that their notion of deity is profoundly different from any that figures in the major historical forms of religion which make expressly moral demands of their adherents. In what follows, Christianity – for all the variety of its manifestations – is taken as a paradigm of such, sharing with the other 'Religions of the Book' (Judaism and Islam) a central commitment to a morality of divine command, in a sense to be explained and examined shortly. Not all religions are expressly ethical, even when they have systems of taboos about (for example) when to eat and what not to eat, and elaborate rituals designed to make the spirits, the ancestors, or the gods, perform their functions as required by humans – for example, to provide needed amounts of rainfall, or safe childbirth, or any of the other practical concerns for which religion is, mostly, the technology of man's impotence, originated in earliest times, in the face of an indifferent and often cruel nature.

The Stoic conception of deity is of a universal rational principle that governs the functioning of the cosmos in accordance with inherent laws. They called it the *logos*, reason, the ether, the eternal fire, the unifying principle, and other such things, to denote its function as something unifying, cohesive, and order-imposing. This principle of order and unity is called 'reason' because its action makes the universe a rational place, that is, something comprehensible, organised and systematic. It is because of its rationality and orderliness that nature is for the Stoics the model to follow for the achievement of goodness.

In view of the Stoics' commitment to the view that the history of the universe eternally recurs, repeating itself endlessly in cycles of 'great years', the 'god' or 'word' that is the organising principle of the universe is not anything like the supposedly conscious, aware, interested, creative and interventive deity of the Religions of the Book. This latter deity is a person, a king writ very large, who issues instructions and who punishes or rewards their observance or otherwise. The Stoic deity is a principle, in essence a logical principle. Logical principles do not issue commands, or mete out rewards and punishments, or take a personal interest in individuals. The Stoics' *logos* is a concept, a theoretical idea employed to systematise an account of the natural order.

The way of thinking made possible by Stoic metaphysics and ethics was important to educated people in the ancient world because religion was then a matter neither of metaphysics nor of morality, and accordingly offered no satisfaction to intelligent minds. The variety of cults in the Roman world was great, a Babel of different local superstitions, indifferently mixing gods of the hearth, rustic or 'pagan' vegetation spirits, the tribal deities of conquered peoples, and much besides. Judaism was different; its monotheism, its written tradition, and its peculiar sense of its votaries' being especially elected by their god, made it distinctive, and were among the principle determinants of the forms that Christianity and Islam later took. But the Roman (and, beyond the borders of the Empire, barbarian) kaleidoscope of cults and superstitions was distasteful to educated minds, who therefore accepted with pleasure the rational metaphysics of Stoicism, or the effective atheism of Epicureanism.

As regards the cults, educated Romans shared the view of Polybius that indulging popular religions was a way of managing the mass of the population, who were kept in some sort of order by their superstitious beliefs and the rituals and ceremonies that came with them. 'This would not be necessary if it were possible to have a state peopled by the wise only,' Polybius remarked; 'but as every multitude is fickle, appetitive, unreasoning, passionate, and given to violent anger, it must be held in check by the thought of invisible terrors and a lot of pageantry.'

Yet this very fact explains the weakness of the philosophies. They were too difficult, too dry, too austere, too rational for the vast majority of the populace. Both Epicureanism and Stoicism taught indifference to fortune in order to gain peace of mind; but for ordinary people faced by harsh and difficult lives, the counsel to cultivate a fortitudinous self-mastery in the face of hunger and illness, poverty and perennial confrontation with pain, was useless. These things were their common lot, and they wished to escape it. Their popular religions gave them hope of a change in their luck: charms and amulets, bribery of the gods, petitions – all were sources of hope, just as with someone praying that a lottery win will save him from his money problems. In teaching patience and acceptance with no further relief, not even reward at the end of life beyond the satisfaction of having lived courageously and independently, the philosophies had little to offer the ignorant. One powerful source of comfort and hope among the welter of cults was the mystery religions, such as Orphism. But soon after the age of the late Stoics another religion was to capitalise on these same popular needs in a way that led to spectacular secular and political success on the back of its spiritual appeal: Christianity.

A full scrutiny of religion would require starting at a logical point a long way prior to consideration of relatively so developed a matter as the ethics offered by Christianity. There are three separate questions in the offing: one is a metaphysical question about the intelligibility of the idea that there are supernatural forces or entities in the universe; the second is the interesting psychological question of why people believe that there are; and the third is the question of what value attaches to an ethics based on beliefs thus held. The metaphysical question is a complex one, but it can in part be illustrated by noting that if there were any reason to think that there existed realms, entities or forces other than those known or hypothesised in the natural universe, that fact would not, without supplementary premises, be a reason for thinking that such supernatural forces or entities are intelligent, that they are persons, that they have intentions, purposes and memories, or that, even if they were or had any of these things, they are interested in any aspect of the universe, still less in human beings on this particular planet. The fact that the ancient religions were premised on the idea that this planet (with its starry skies) constitutes the whole universe, and that nothing could be more interesting to the gods who made it than the human beings who rule the sublunary realm, is the explanation for the amazing self-importance that religious beliefs reveal in mankind. The highly anthropomorphic character of most deities variously believed in during the course of history reveals the extent to which they are man's own creations. The reason why man had to create them, and the result of his submitting to his own creations, involve the two other questions – the psychological and evaluatory ones – mentioned. I turn to them later.

Despite the fact that an inspection of the metaphysics of religious belief makes it hard to take seriously anything based on it, the historical fact is that religions exist, and that some of them seek to direct and control the lives of individuals according to a given set of imperatives. These are the concern of this chapter.

Divine command

The Religions of the Book are distinctive, and perhaps unique, in postulating a personal deity who in each case makes a set of moral demands on its worshippers. The ethics of these religions is accordingly based on 'divine command'. Before looking at the way Christianity expresses such a view, the concept and implications of an ethics of divine command bear scrutiny.

In all three Religions of the Book the fundamental presupposition is that a god commands and we must obey. Sin is disobedience to the commands of god; virtue is obedience to them or, in the more graphic conception of Islam, submission (which is what 'Islam' means). In what Christians call 'the Old Testament' two minatory morality tales are told to underpin the premise that it is for god to command and man to obey. One is the story of the expulsion from Eden, and the punishment that accompanied it (for their disobedience Adam and Eve, *and* the entire human race that flowed from their loins, were condemned to 'eat their bread in the sweat of their brow, to bring forth children in agony, and to suffer death'. If a deity were passing this judgement now, it would be in violation of the article in most human rights conventions forbidding excessive, cruel and inhuman punishment – a point mentioned not out of levity, but because the conflict between divine morality and contemporary humanism is a very sharp one, a point that becomes important later). The other is the story of the fall of Satan, once an archangel high in the ranks of heaven, but whose pride – he desired autonomy, independence, self-determination – was the cause of his being cast from heaven, just as Hephaestus was thrown to earth from the summit of Olympus by an angry Zeus. (Hephaestus thereafter occupied an underground estate of fire – to make armour for gods and heroes, not as a punishment, which shows how the old tales become mixed and adapted in different mythologies.)

Suppose there is a personal deity interested in mankind, whom it commands to do such and such and to live in such and such a way. Why should it be obeyed? There are several standard answers. One is that the deity will punish you if you do not obey. This is the chief response of Christianity in its earlier or more basic versions – some still extant. More fully, it says that if you disobey you will be thrown into hell, a place of eternal punishment. Early church murals graphically represent the torments inflicted by fire and devils with instruments of torture. In modifications of this teaching, for example the Catholic doctrine of purgatory, this state is limited to a certain number of thousands or millions of years, depending on the severity of the sins that require purging.

Since this answer consists in a threat, as a reason for obeying god it can only be a prudential one ('If you do not wish to be punished, do as you are told'), for it is otherwise not a logical reason for obedience, since it commits the fallacy of *argumentum ad baculum*, the appeal to force. A threat of force is not a logical ground for accepting a conclusion, even if self-preservation dictates otherwise; but self-preservation or, more generally, self-interest is a corrupting reason to accept a moral injunction. It is also self-defeating – for one of the things that most moralities enjoin, including religious ones, is a degree (and usually a considerable degree) of altruism, the opposite of self-interest.

Another answer standardly offered is that one should obey god because god is good. The problem with this answer is that if what is good is what god says is good, and if what it says is good *is* good *because* it is itself good, then we have moved in a circle. The goodness of god, if god is good, is something that attaches to god in virtue of some fact other than that of its being god. It is good, in other words, because it satisfies a criterion of goodness, or passes a test of goodness, which is independent of itself. As Bertrand Russell put it, 'The proposition "god is good" is not a tautology.' But then if there is an independent criterion of goodness, I can judge what is good and bad on my own account, and do not need to be instructed in the matter by anyone else, even by a god.

The move that theists make in response is to appeal not merely to the goodness but to the omniscience of the deity. This latter guarantees that it will know infinitely more about the consequences of our actions and choices than we ever can, and therefore, since it is good also, its guidance is sure to be right, and far better than anyone else's. This answer requires us to take on trust that a deity really does intend our long-term benefit, and knows what will produce it. Now, a cynic (in the modern sense) might be forgiven for thinking that the evidence warranting such trust is highly equivocal. Using what we must suppose is our god-given reason, which (with Descartes) we will further suppose is generally trustworthy since a good god would not have equipped us with a faulty instrument for use in so crucial a matter, we can look at the evidence of history to see whether it would be rational to trust in providence. The result is dismaying. The 'Old Testament' is full of examples of a deity changing its mind, repenting of earlier decisions, committing genocide in some cases and mere mass murder in others, in fury as a result of mankind's exercise of the free will it gave them and which they have used in ways it seems not to have foreseen.

Moreover, so-called 'godly' lives appear in some cases to be amply rewarded on earth, whereas others have to wait for presumed rewards in heaven later, while not infrequently appearing to suffer harsh and sometimes terrible pains here despite their devotion. The inscrutability of god's purposes, and its propensity to 'move in a mysterious way', are invoked to explain, or more accurately to explain away, such things; but to be asked to accept such non-rational or irrational defences of such apparently non-rational or irrational phenomena is to be asked to take an even greater risk in placing our trust in the providence which thus unpredictably operates. That, as it happens, is indeed the line taken by those, for a chief example Søren Kierkegaard, who take it that the essence of religion is *faith*, and faith is a commitment made in direct opposition to reason, in the very teeth of the evidence. Such irrationalism has a purely emotional basis, which no doubt might prompt some to say that it therefore requires not argument but therapy.

Still, if the question 'Why should I obey a god if there is one?' has received not an answer but an appeal to the fundamental non-rationality of faith – in short, to the answer that there are no answers, just blind acceptance – then the honest enquirer has not been helped. Perhaps therefore he should turn to look at the substance of the ethical teachings of one of the great moralising religions, to see whether they are intrinsically of such a character as to command respect and assent, independently of whatever metaphysical justification they are said to receive from the supposed existence of a deity. One reason why this might be helpful is that it adds specific content to the general idea of what a god commands. For example, in Christian guise, another justification that can be invoked for obedience to god's will is the idea that god loves the world, and that therefore we should love one another – or, more circumstantially put, god loves us (and made us, etc.), and we should therefore love it in return, and further therefore we should obey its moral injunctions (for example, that we should love one another). Unfortunately, none of this quite stands up without the supplement of the supposed special character of the deity and its relationship, as creator and governor, to the world and us; for if one tried to use the same reasoning to explain why someone we love should do everything, or even just anything, that we wish them to, we would quickly see that loving them, or the house they live in, and so on, is no reason why they should do what we require, still less love us in return.

This equally applies to a closer analogy to the supposed love of god for mankind: parental love. My loving my children is not a reason for my children to live as I wish they would, still less as I order them to – even if my greater wisdom and experience mean that my choice of life for them would be in their interests. They might, if they love me in return, and trust me because of our mutual affection, be guided by me; but that is a different matter. The argument offered by Christian apologists does not rest on any such voluntary mutuality of trust, since it would be unthinkable on their terms that a creature of god can choose to favour or oblige god with his affection and obedience, or not, as he wishes; god's laws are non-negotiable. So in this version of the argument putatively showing why we must obey a god if there is one, we are being asked to accept as sound the following reasoning: 'A loves B and therefore B must do as A requires.' This is an obvious non sequitur.

In short, the answers to the question 'If there is a god, why should I obey it?' are unsatisfactory, and this is unsurprising, because for most of the history of the Religions of the Book, god's edicts have been seen to rest either on the promise of punishment and reward, or, in Christianity as it reinvented itself in softer terms when it lost its institutional and political grip, on the vaguer sentimental appeal of the paternity and love of the deity as somehow making a demand that its creatures respond in kind. Or both.

Christian ethics

At this juncture it pays to look more closely at specifically Christian morality, chiefly in its early manifestation. It involves leaving aside the kinds of interpretation offered by Christian philosophers who supplement the teachings to be found in the gospels and the letters of St Paul by insisting on such metaphysical underpinnings as the claim that 'good is what god wills in accordance with his nature' and that 'the end or purpose of all things is the glorification of God', because to the enquirer who, without prior commitment to its theology, wishes to know whether Christian ethics recommends itself by its intrinsic appeal, such assertions are unmeaning. It might, however, turn out that without them the ethics is itself ultimately unmeaning – which would not in the end be a surprise, given that its ultimate ground, as noted, has to have something to do with the will or nature of a suitably understood deity.

In the gospel account of the teaching of Jesus, direct models of right moral action are offered, and with them, although indirectly, a model of the moral man. The first is given in various parables, for a striking example the parable of the good Samaritan. The second is given by implication in the Beatitudes delivered in the Sermon on the Mount, for in describing who will inherit the kingdom of heaven Jesus is thereby painting the portrait of the good person. Such a person is poor in spirit, mournful, meek, hungry for righteousness, merciful, pure in heart, a peacemaker, generous (going two miles when asked to go one), unjudgemental, not concerned with material preparations for the future, and happy to be persecuted for Jesus's sake. A third model is given by the example of Jesus himself, and this time the model is not quite of the virtuously meek and peaceable person portrayed in the Beatitudes, but of the warrior for god, who overturns the money-lenders' tables in the Temple, and who is also unquestioningly obedient to god's will, as witness the conclusion to the agony in the Garden of Gethsemane, 'Not my will but thy will be done' – a sentiment incorporated in the Lord's Prayer.

These basic features of the Christian ethic are supplemented by more particular directives and suggestions, as when the rich young man asks Jesus what he should do to inherit eternal life, and as when the adulterous woman is brought before him. To the rich young man Jesus says that he should obey the ten commandments; whereupon, when the rich young man says he does so, Jesus tells him to give away everything he has to the poor, and to follow him. This injunction to holy improvidence is in accordance with the instruction to consider the lilies of the field, which neither toil nor spin; in these teachings Jesus seems to be offering a Judaised version of Cynicism, a turning away from the world and an adoption of an eremitic life of poverty and denial. The hard saying about the rich finding it impossible to enter the kingdom of heaven adds to this picture.

Jesus was kind to the adulterous woman, saving her from being stoned to death by inviting anyone who was sinless to throw the first stone. In line with his injunction that we should forgive one another as we hope to be forgiven our own sins, and that we should do unto others as we would have them do to us (the 'Golden Rule'), he let her go with the injunction to sin no more. He certainly held adultery to be a sin; he reinterpreted Jewish morality by saying that if you look with lust on another's spouse, you have committed adultery in your heart, where you have also committed murder if you are so much as angry with your fellow. These intensifications and internalisations of moral prescriptions denote a shift from externally observable virtue to an inner authenticity or integrity of goodness.

In St Paul we find an almost unrecognisable Jesus, transformed by metaphysics and high theology into a being of abstractions and conceptual subtleties. For St Paul the chief virtue is faith in Jesus interpreted as Christ the divine redeemer, the Messiah, the new covenant between god and man, who by his death and resurrection has provided an atonement for man with god, so that anyone who believes that Jesus was sent by god and is one with god and the holy ghost (constituting the 'trinity', a three-in-one person) – here meaning vanishes in the murk cast by a thousand tomes of theology; but essentially the alleged monotheism of Christianity is bought at the cost of a miracle of arithmetic – will be saved to everlasting life. Everything else in Pauline ethics follows from this theological construction – which is not to the point here, for whereas having faith in, say, a fairy story might be a virtue in the eyes of fellow fairy-tale believers, it scarcely counts as recognisably a contribution to debate about the good. So although for St Paul the chief virtue is 'faith in the metaphysical Jesus-as-one-with-god', he recognises other virtues besides, and these amount to an ethical view we can evaluate.

For Paul a cardinal virtue is charity – *caritas*; in Greek, *agape* – meaning 'love for one's fellow men'. This notion, which is wholly inclusive – 'There is neither Jew nor Greek, slave nor free, male nor female' – he takes from Jesus's own summary of the moral law, which is to love god with all your heart, and your neighbour as yourself. Paul's more particular recommendations were based on the belief that the *Parousia*, the Second Coming, was imminent; and so he instructed everyone to stay as they were – if single, single; if married, married; unless they were the former and could not be continent, they should become the latter, for 'it is better to marry than to burn'.

Most of these teachings – the urge to love one's fellows, to forgive them their trespasses, to make peace, to avoid judging, to quell anger – appear attractive, as does the idea of the sort of person (the good Samaritan, or the person who will go two miles with you when you need his company for one) pictured in the scriptures as exemplary of the charitable individual. These sentiments retain their attraction even when shrived of the theology that gives them their point and motive. As prescriptions to be applied universally they need qualification; there is, after all, appropriate anger, as Aristotle showed; and there are acts, such as the Nazi attempt to exterminate European Jewry, that are unforgivable in any circumstances; and there are people and situations that require us to judge their worth, not least when they are good and deserve admiration. But the drift of the ethic is clear, and on the whole worthy.

It is not, however, unique; it is scanty, in comparison with the great ethical philosophies of the classical world which were its predecessors and contemporaries; and it does not fare well in comparisons with the much richer and more universally compassionate teachings of Buddhism, or the doctrine of universal brotherly love in the philosophy of China's Mo Ti (470–390 BC), or the Taoist search for the inner 'Way' that will bring the individual and all things into harmony. Read beside these other traditions, which say and enjoin more with less theological undercarriage, Christian ethics is not outstanding. Take just two examples: the respect for animals in Buddhism, and the defence of the poor in Mohism. The first powerfully extends the idea of moral sensitivity and concern by making the whole world a target of respect. The second brings moral piety down to earth with a demand to relieve the suffering of the poor by practical means – in Mo Ti's view, by diverting funds from the wasteful expense of state rituals to direct help for those starving and in need: an early version of the welfare state. Jesus's impracticable adjurations to individuals to 'give your all to the poor' in the gospels seem like a gesture by comparison, especially since the chief moral beneficiary of the act is not the poor but the giver.

This, indeed, is one aspect of the more direct criticism that can be levelled at Christian morality. In some views, Jesus was not aiming to state an ethical view as such, but rather to challenge a prevailing set of moral practices, namely, those of the Pharisees. The Pharisees were strictly observant conservative Jews who at the time of Jesus had become immensely influential as a result of the moral authority they wielded. Jesus attacked them for being hypocrites who made a great outward show of piety in their observance of rules and duties, but who had little real inner goodness. In advocating a rejection of such social norms as providing for the morrow (which means providing for your family, their future, your own old age, and the like) Jesus was rejecting the conventional morality they represented, saying that you lose your soul by trying to gain the world. But your soul is the crucial thing; and Jesus is quite explicit and unabashed in making this self-regarding principle central to his view. That is what is implied even in the overtly altruistic injunction to 'love your neighbour as you love yourself'.

The narrowness of the gospel ethics, and the temporary nature of the Pauline additions, are what led later Church thinkers to borrow heavily from the Greek schools – and most notably from Stoicism – to flesh out an ethical theory (as well as an appropriate metaphysics for their theology). Plato was an early resource for the Church Fathers, and Aristotle a later one for Aquinas and the theologians of the medieval schools. Plato had divided the universe into two, a Realm of Being where the eternal and unchanging Forms of all things exist, and a Realm of Becoming, the world of our ordinary experience, in which everything is impermanent and imperfect. He likened the soul to a two-horse chariot in which the charioteer, Reason, tries to drive up to the Realm of Being; one of the steeds, the soul, aspires to reach that realm, but the other, the physical appetites, keeps trying to plunge back to earth.

The demotion of the body and promotion of the mind or soul, as exemplified in Plato's views about non-physical love being the highest form of that sentiment, was adopted by the Church for its teachings on sexuality, resulting in an emphasis on chastity and celibacy, and – in one tradition of thought about sex – in the belief that people should expressly avoid feeling pleasure in sexual congress, which they were to undertake solely as a duty to reproduce. If women were wicked enough to feel sensual pleasure when conceiving, so this view went, they risked producing a deformed or otherwise blighted child as a result.

Another perspective on Christian morality is offered by Nietzsche, whose principal objection to it was that it represents the slave morality derived from the experience of the Jewish tribe in exile – impotent, trapped and suffering. That experience, he argued, is figuratively speaking the source of the Beatitudes, which turn the wretched conditions of weakness and misery into virtues, and promise them a reward. For Nietzsche, whose moral ideal was Homeric in character, which therefore meant extolling the individual who faces life heroically and creatively, striving to attain heights of self-realisation and mastery of his fate – a figure he called the 'Superman' – such a morality seemed profoundly negative and unhealthy. As a classical philologist with an intimate knowledge of the ancient world and its outlook, who especially admired the heroic aspects of the Greeks' ethics and liberality of thought, Nietzsche was hostile to the corruption of such values by the success of Christianity, whose promotion of what he saw as weak and inverted principles had the effect of subverting the qualities of the ancient world and depriving subsequent history of them.

A thought suggested by Nietzsche's critique, although not expressly part of it, is that, properly understood, Christianity – and by extension any religion sharing its assumptions about the perilous and unhappy state of the embodied soul in this life, yearning for its true home in a posthumous dispensation – amounts to a profoundly pessimistic and negative world view. It explicitly teaches that solace, hope and meaning are not to be found in this world, except in such constrained states as manage, with great effort, to reproduce something of what the posthumous state will be like. It therefore demands resignation, blind faith, submission, negation of this-worldly things, mortification of bodily nature, and in related versions (such as Islam) passivity and fatalism. Apologists say that the optimism of their faiths lies in the various forms of salvation they proffer; but it is remarkable how much the life of man in this world has to be denigrated to make the promise of happiness after death – but only if you do as you are told – appealing.

The irrelevance of religion to morality

Independently of these strictures, it is pertinent to ask what Christian morality has to offer the contemporary world. There is a widespread supposition that a religious ethics, Christian or otherwise, or some vague version of it that involves the deity as in effect an invisible and ubiquitous policeman, has to be good for individuals and society because it is inherently more likely to make them seek the good. This view is troubling because it is false: religion is precisely the wrong resource for thinking about moral issues in the contemporary world, and indeed subverts moral debate. The reasons, polemically stated, are as follows.

In the contemporary Western world human persons are characterised chiefly by their rationality, self-awareness, and desire for a degree of autonomy consistent with reasonable and (in the best dispensations) democratically adjusted requirements of responsible social living. Human beings are natural entities, intelligent animals, part of the order of nature although strikingly significant in it by virtue of their individual and collective intelligence and its effect on their relationship with everything else. Recognition of these facts has given rise to the view that the kinds of problem faced both by individuals and societies are for this reason best handled naturalistically, and by reference to the actual experience and needs of mankind – which means history, and the principles produced by agreement as a result of debate well and responsibly conducted. One such principle, which has emerged in the last several centuries as fundamental to the complex circumstances of modern societies, is tolerance. Although as honoured in the breach as in the observance, this principle – even as an intermittently realised ideal – is pivotal to the very possibility of the existence of populous, multi-ethnic, multi-cultural societies of the kind now standard in the West. Often the implicit settlement wrought by tolerance seems fragile and parlous, but it is practically the only hope for the survival of those societies. One way of enshrining tolerance in a firmer and more explicit set of principles has been the institution of national and international frameworks of human rights. These aim to protect individuals in all the ways most fundamental to their chance of forging good lives for themselves, and their effect is permissive: a wide variety of lifestyles and beliefs is protected by a blanket right to choose in these respects, and obligations are laid on states to ensure that this is the case for all their citizens equally.

Against this background it is easy to see that religion – and, in the present case, particularly Christianity – is the wrong resource for morality because it is irrelevant to the practical questions of contemporary life thus organised. Modern societies value personal autonomy, achievement in earning a living, providing for a family, saving against a rainy day, and being rewarded for success. Christian morality, as noted, values exactly the opposite. It tells people to take no thought for the morrow, to give their possessions to the poor, and to beware the fact that a well-off person will find heaven unwelcoming. In one hyperbolic moment Jesus even repudiates his family affiliations, saying that his family are only those who submit to the will of god. Moreover, Christian ethics, in common with the other Religions of the Book, explicitly disvalues the concept of personal autonomy, preaching instead heteronomy in the form of obedience and subjection to a deity.

Religious – and especially Christian – morality is not only irrelevant but inimical to modern interpersonal relations and sexual attitudes, and thus attempts to perpetuate its distorting influence on human nature in this fundamental respect. Almost all religions confine sex to marriage, and their more orthodox members oppose homosexuality, contraception and abortion, and restrict women to the domestic sphere. Most people ignore the contrast between such views and today's ethos, and the Churches accordingly either temporise or contradict their own earlier teachings. But they still stand in the way of enlightened attitudes to domestic arrangements, reproduction, abortion, sex and love, and in many parts of the world the endeavour to liberate people's private lives from the moralising interference of state and religion is far from complete.

Religious morality is not just irrelevant in these ways to contemporary attitudes about what is acceptable and appropriate: it is anti-moral. This is because the great moral questions are those identified by the discourse of human rights: oppression, war, poverty, and the vast disparities between rich and poor. In the Third World a child dies every two and a half seconds because of starvation or curable disease, while in the First World churchgoers decry pre-marital sex and debate the theology of divorce and contraception. As arms are manufactured for export to warring countries in the Third World, Church leaders complain about teenage pregnancies. By distracting attention from what really counts and focusing instead on trivia, they do much harm to the cause of good in the world.

Religion is not only anti-moral, it is often immoral. Elsewhere in the world religious fundamentalists and fanatics incarcerate women, mutilate genitals, amputate hands, murder, bomb and terrorise in the name of their faith. It is a mistake to think that Christian clerics in Western countries would never behave likewise, for it is not long in historical terms since their predecessors were burning heretics at the stake or mounting crusades against them, whipping people or slitting their noses and ears for adultery, or preaching that masturbation is worse than rape because at least the latter can result in pregnancy. To this day adulterers are stoned to death in certain Muslim countries; if the priests still had their once-held powers in the Western world, how different would things be? If one looked to religions to provide historical examples of the moral life in practice, one would have to forget a great deal of immorality to find it.

The perfumed smokescreen

Apologists for religion and religious morality are apt to respond to the foregoing blunt criticisms by drawing what might appropriately be called a perfumed smokescreen over the evidence of religion's own signal failures to be moral. Inquisitions, burnings at the stake, witch-hunts, crusades against heretics and 'infidels', missionary impact on colonised cultures, and much besides, might be summoned to the witness stand against Christianity as an organised force in history; but one response is to say that these are failings of men in the Church, not the god who inspired it. This argument founders, however, on one of Christianity's own teachings: 'By their fruits ye shall know them'. And of course it marks a retreat behind a smokescreen of metaphysics, for if one treats religion as a human phenomenon produced by the needs and fears of mankind, then the practice of a Church just is the religion itself in action; and the evidence of history emphatically condemns its record.

The real perfume in the smokescreen lies in the claim that the contemporary Churches, with their charities and their aid for the suffering in the Third World, are models of goodness in action. They accordingly present themselves as institutions devoted to peace, kindness, brotherly love and charitable works. But this soft face is turned to the world only when the Church is on the back foot, increasingly a minority interest and still losing members, and therefore wishing to recruit (not untypically among the lonely, the desperate, the uncertain, the directionless, the timid, the anxious). For whenever a religion is in the ascendant, with hands on the levers of secular power too, it shows a very different face – the face presented by the Inquisition, the Taliban, and the religious police in Saudi Arabia. The instinct of a religion, when it has power, is to coerce compliance with its orthodoxy, and to pursue or punish those who will not conform.

In modern secular ethics great weight is given to concern for the welfare and rights of people, animals and the environment. This concern is motivated not by divine threats and promises but by a sense of the intrinsic worth of these things, and their importance to us. To a secular view, the notion of the intrinsic worth of others and of nature is the only true source of morality. By contrast, as noted earlier, religious ethics is ultimately based on a sanction of posthumous rewards and punishments, with goodness consisting in the diktat of a supernatural agency of some kind. A person does good, by the lights of his religion, in order to achieve eternal bliss. If there are indeed supernatural powers in the universe, it might well be prudent to do what they require, whether for good or ill, in the interests of saving oneself from the harm they might do us; but, as noted, even when what the supernatural agency requires is that we should do what we independently recognise as good, that motivation is not a moral but a self-regarding and self-interested one. The contrast can best be put this way: if I see two men doing good, one because he wishes to escape punishment by a supposed supernatural agency and the other because he respects his fellow man, I honour the latter infinitely more.

Why belief happens

In line with the 'perfumed smokescreen' policy of contemporary established Churches, the ethical motivation for believing in supernatural agencies has come to be a prominent inducement offered by the leaders of those Churches. This is a very recent development. For most religions in most of history it has not been the ethics but the metaphysics of the religion that has bound people into belief in it. The power, 'sacredness', terror, mystery and kingship of the gods, and their control over health, wealth, life and destiny, compelled ignorant and superstitious minds into awe of them, and therefore into obedience to the priests who served those gods and 'knew' what they required.

In the case of Christianity there were added inducements. Whereas the ethical outlook of educated people, for example Stoicism, offered little to ordinary people, the appeal of Christianity was considerable. It made everyone a hero; where once only the likes of Hercules could expect to get to heaven (in Greek mythology by becoming a god himself), the Christian believer became a hero of the faith, and was guaranteed to get to heaven in consequence. The faith thus provided grand rewards, including especially succour for the poor and the lowly, no matter who or where they were. This gave the religion universal appeal. It had always made perfect sense that a brave man might die for his fatherland, city or tribe for the sheer glory of it; now people were prepared to die for their faith because of those guaranteed rewards. An even purer and simpler form of this outlook, if that is possible, is found in Islam.

Early Christianity succeeded not only because of these attractions, nor only because it was persecuted (persecution is a good way to ensure the survival of what is persecuted), but because as a Church it imposed an iron discipline, crushing heterodoxy and demanding absolute loyalty by the faithful. As in all successful organisations, the demand made and the reward offered had to be simple and direct: obey god, and you will become, as it were, a god yourself in heaven. Once one recognises these facts, the idea that religion is a peculiarly authoritative source of moral value in the world evaporates.

Four reasons are standardly given to explain why religion exists. One is that it provides answers to fundamental questions about the origin of the universe, the way it works, the currently mysterious or inexplicable things that happen in it – and why it includes evil and suffering. Another is that religion provides comfort and solace, giving hope of life after death, providing reassurance in a hostile world, and a means (by prayer, sacrifice and conformity to one or another form of prescribed behaviour, either ritualistic or moral) to live more securely and successfully. A third is that it makes for social order, in promoting morality and social cohesion. And a fourth is that it rests on the natural ignorance, stupidity, superstitiousness and gullibility of mankind.

Among those who disagree that these are the right explanations are, of course, religious people, who think that religion exists because there are gods (or a god, and perhaps spirits and ancestors too) and that therefore religious belief is the natural and obvious response to this alleged fact. But there are others who, without being in the slightest religious, also do not think that the standard answers are right.

These are those who, for a contemporary example, think that religion is the result of the way the brain works. Brains are complicated mechanisms evolved to process information and draw inferences. These tasks are carried out by a large number of specialist systems that operate at deep levels of brain structure. Most of the brain's work is done in this way, out of sight of the conscious mind. Using a small number of 'ontological categories' that classify things in the world into five orders – animals, plants, tools, natural objects and persons – the subroutines of the brain form expectations and hypotheses, and then draw inferences from them, thus allowing the brain to represent the world to itself, and to interpret it.

The structure of the mind is by itself sufficient to produce all the typical manifestations of religious belief, nothing special or additional being required. The chief way is as follows. Because minds can detach concepts from their normal settings and yet retain most of the standard inferential connections that accompany those concepts, they can easily generate notions of the supernatural. For example, a spirit is a being that cannot be seen, and can pass through walls – and thus is different from ordinary animals and persons – but it can hear and see what we do, and interact with us in other ways – thus retaining the normal characteristics of animals and persons.

Using this explanatory paradigm, psychologists and anthropologists, who study religion as a human phenomenon from the point of view of their disciplines, observe that religion is a practical matter for most people, who in most cultures do not regard it as something odd or different from their other beliefs about the world. They note that most people are vague about what they believe, and do not have a polished theology to account for their commitments and practices. Just as they accept at face value natural phenomena such as rain, thunder and wind, so they accept that there could be beings very like themselves who nevertheless are stronger, cannot be seen, can walk through a wall without materially interacting with it, and then – by materially interacting with them – affect them in some way, for example, by causing them to speak foreign languages they never knew, or making them ill, or even killing them.

This idea, that the occurrence of supernaturalistic beliefs is best explained by the way brains work, is very likely true; for the mental operations in question are well understood and wholly adequate for the explanatory task. It is a thesis well supported by empirical research. As an explanation of how concepts are formed, including religious ones, it is especially illuminating. But it does not by itself provide a complete explanation of religion, for the standard explanations described above are consistent with this account, and are not displaced by it.

The reasons are many, but one merits special mention. Culture is not merely an epiphenomenal outcome of lower-level computational systems in human brains, but in part at least is the result of feedback upon those systems by the high-level concepts and practices that earlier mental activity produced. Culture assumes an existence of its own outside the individuals who make it or subscribe to it, and it affects them as much as they affect it. The majority of people may be passive consumers or spectators of culture, but significant minorities have a crucial influence on cultural development and content – chief among such people are religious leaders, demagogues, writers, and thinkers – and the ordinarily vague grasp of the majority is a set of diluted versions of what they think and say. The theory just described offers a mechanism for the formulation of the types of concepts that figure in religious culture, but the 'how' of their formation does not explain why they, rather than close competitors, acquire the special grip they do in concrete historical and social circumstances.

Much of the theory just described is premised on the reflex, untheoretical character of religious belief displayed in the sort of societies that anthropologists typically study – the Fang of Cameroon and the Kwaio of the Solomon Islands, for example – but it might be seriously misleading to think that such peoples get us closer to unadulterated evidence than do, say, Western Christians and Jews. These latter have highly articulated religious literatures and traditions, which provide a rich vein of material other than the subroutines of the brain for thinking about why religions exist – not least in explicitly offering themselves as elaborate theories about origins, morality and the rest, exactly as the standard accounts of religion say. Nevertheless, the subroutines of the brain have their place in the overall story; in the light of them and the facts of cultural history, the religious devotee's appeal to metaphysics is no more than a hopeful distraction.

The return of the ghosts

A result of the long process of growth that for historical convenience is successively named the Renaissance, the Reformation, the scientific revolution, and the Enlightenment – this sequence of labels denoting some of the most important events and changes in, very roughly put, the fourteenth and fifteenth centuries (the Renaissance in Italy), the sixteenth century (the Reformation), the seventeenth century (the scientific revolution) and the eighteenth century (the Enlightenment) respectively – was the eventual major clash of science and religion in the nineteenth century, triggered by the publication of Darwin's *Origin of Species*. There had, of course, been constant skirmishing and some outright war ever since the sixteenth century: in the early seventeenth century the Vatican made Galileo retract his claim that the Earth moves, and he was put under house arrest for having seen through his telescope things that contradicted the official teachings of the Church. But the tinder was fully lit in the mid-nineteenth century, and the ensuing debacle seemed to be the beginning of religion's demise. Religious observance became increasingly a private matter; church attendances dwindled; a career in the Church lost its interest and its social cachet. As tends to happen in such cases, the shrinking residue was captured and carried forward by enthusiasts – chiefly evangelicals and missionaries, these latter proselytising captive audiences of colonised peoples, who have since blended what the missionaries taught with their own local faiths to produce (the figure is literal) tens of thousands of fundamentalist sects, often wildly superstitious and wholly emotional or ecstatic in observance.

The intellectual defeat of religion that culminated in the nineteenth century is accordingly responsible for the revival, usually in more fundamentalist terms, of religions in the century that followed. A number of remarkable features mark this process. One is the difference between the attack on Darwinian evolutionary theory in the famous Scopes trial of 1925, and the way that 'creationists' or 'intelligent design theorists' now marshal their arguments and personnel against biological science, especially in the United States. Another is the rapid increase in the influence wielded, and not infrequently the danger posed, in the form of terrorism and 'holy war', by fundamentalist religious movements from the second half of the twentieth century onwards.

The Scopes case involved a young biology teacher, John Scopes, who defied the laws of Tennessee prohibiting the teaching of evolutionary theory in schools. (Florida, Mississippi, Louisiana and Arkansas also banned Darwin.) The American Civil Liberties Union sent Clarence Darrow to defend Scopes' First Amendment rights, while one William Jennings Bryan defended Tennessee – and with it, religion. It was an epic confrontation, but not much of a battle, for Darrow was a brilliant advocate with a strong case, and Bryan's best argument was that the people of Tennessee had a right to defend themselves against the 'untested hypothesis' of evolutionary theory, given (as he and the people of Tennessee claimed) its danger to morality. Both legs of this argument were easily cut away by Darrow, who went on to force Bryan on to the witness stand, where he was cross-examined and, in short, humiliated. He died a few days after the trial, having confessed that he 'did not think about things he didn't think about' and 'only sometimes thought about the things he *did* think about' – and had neither studied other religions nor made a critical evaluation of the Christian religion, nor (despite having written a Christian refutation of Darwin) was his understanding of evolutionary theory good.

Despite the demolition of Bryan's case, no Tennessee jury was likely to find in Scopes's favour, so he was duly convicted. But though Scopes lost, science had won: the rest of the nation poured scorn on the Tennessee hicks, whom H. L. Mencken called 'the gaping primates of the upland valleys', and the cause of religious fundamentalism seemed doomed.

But the religious lobby in the United States is a powerful entity, and although it took a long time to recover from its defeat in Tennessee, by the end of the century it was able to publish a volume in which no fewer than fifty holders of PhD degrees in various sciences asserted their allegiance to creationism, and their correlative rejection of evolutionary theory. The book, edited by John F. Ashton and called *In Six Days: Why 50 Scientists Choose to Believe in Creation*, more specifically explains why these scientists believe in the literal truth of the story told in the Book of Genesis. That story (which in fact is there told twice, in somewhat different versions) comes down to the assertion that in six days a god created heaven and earth and all they contain, and then rested for a day. Because the fifty have science PhDs they felt obliged to do more than merely assert their faith in the correctness of the Genesis account – rather than, say, in one of the dozens of very different alternative creation myths found round the world – and they therefore had to offer arguments and evidence, instead of relying on the non-rational 'leap' that Kierkegaard pointed out is the true believer's only proper resource.

Their task was two-fold. They had to show why scientific cosmogony – theories about the origins of the universe – and evolutionary biology are wrong; and they had to demonstrate the truth of Genesis. Either by itself is a tall order. First, they fastened on the fact that science is self-confessedly provisional and undogmatic, neither claiming that its theories are conclusively proven, nor that the data supporting them are complete. Creationists carefully avoid pointing out that the evidence for these theories is nevertheless stunningly and overwhelmingly good, with immense explanatory and predictive power, and that the detailed science accompanying them has given us electric light, computers, aeroplanes, antibiotics and much besides. They focus on the caution of the scientists, and say, 'See? Even they are not sure they are right.' And then – unconscious of the irony attaching to their own dogmatic faith in the accuracy of an ancient text – they assert instead that a particular religious document is not only preferable to science as an account of the universe and the origin of life, but is definitively and unimpeachably true.

Creationists explain the apparent antiquity of the Earth and its fossil record by appeal to the Flood, which they say laid down the Earth's geological sediments, in an instant crushing and burying in them all antediluvian life. But their principal argument is that the world exemplifies design, and could only be as intricate, various, beautiful and wonderfully organised as it is if made by a god. This argument – called the 'argument from design' or 'teleological argument' – is one that first-year philosophy students at university learn to dispose of rapidly. They do so as follows.

First, the appearance of order in any given complex phenomenon can be explained by one of two things: either as the result of the human propensity to impose an appearance of order on complexes, or as a function of some objective order in the complex itself. It is a feature of the human mind naturally to interpret complexes as manifesting patterns or designs even when they are not intrinsically there, as exemplified by our reaction to Rorschach blots. We are likewise over-apt to interpret symmetries and coincidences as evidence of purpose – for obviously advantageous evolutionary reasons. This is merely a cautionary point; but physics teaches that the universe is entropic – that is, is constantly moving in the direction of disorder – and that local reversals of entropy (as in biological phenomena) take a great deal of energy to start and maintain them. So order, as something static and inertial, is not a physical norm. Despite that, it is something we humans almost invariably manage to project onto things, because our minds naturally dislike unstructured or incoherent appearances.

Secondly, evolutionary theory explains the emergence of pattern and structure very well without any supplementary premises. If life forms give the appearance of design, it is because they have evolved that way under selective pressures, survival of the species ensuring that anything unfitted to survive will die out of the record. So the butterfly wing's pattern of eyes, making it look like a larger and fiercer creature to frighten away predators, is economically explained by hypothesising that those of its ancestors which survived to pass on their genes had an adaptation which conferred survival value in this way, an adaptation preserved and perhaps improved over the course of the species' genetic history. On classical Darwinian views this would happen by random mutations proving reproductively advantageous. According to other versions of evolutionary theory, adaptation in response to environmental pressures might happen more swiftly and directly, with evolutionary change taking place in spasms punctuated by periods of equilibrium ('punctuated equilibrium' is the name given by Stephen Jay Gould and his colleagues to just such a process).

Thirdly, if there is indeed conscious design in the universe, the most that its presence entails is a designer or designers; it tells us nothing about how many, who or what they were, and certainly not that it or they fit the notions of a particular religious tradition. Moreover, since suffering and death, the preying of animal upon animal, natural disasters, diseases and plagues, deformities, pain and anguish seem to be part of the design, it is not as good as it might be, so if there were indeed a designer, it's clear it could have done with more practice – unless the natural and moral evils built into the design are there on purpose, which by parity of reasoning (if beauty implies a good designer) implies malice or evil on the designer's part.

In short, the argument is a bad one, and it is very surprising to find educated people still invoking it.

Among the many puzzling things about literal believers in the contents of the Bible is the fact that they do not appear to ask the simple questions that make the collection of writings – its poetry, history, sex and humour aside – so implausible as an alleged account of the activities of a deity. Why, if the god it portrays is omnipotent, did it take it six days to create heaven and earth, and why did it need a rest afterwards? Why is a 'day' for this god and the universe twenty-four hours long, when that merely happens to be the period of rotation on its axis of our planet? Why do hours and days apply to the god anyway, since it is supposed to be eternal, which means 'outside time'? If the god knows everything and is wholly good, why did it repent of having created humans, and proceed to murder all but a very few of them in a flood? Obviously this deity is not as advertised; it makes bad mistakes and gets into genocidal rages. Why, therefore, do those who believe in the literal truth of the Old Testament not blench in horror at the portrait it gives of a despotic, jealous, violent, temperamental, petty and murderous deity? And as to the New Testament's supposedly more avuncular deity, how can they tolerate a god who makes an unmarried teenage girl pregnant and then arranges for the resulting offspring to be tortured to death? None of the fifty PhDs sought to offer a satisfactory account of these matters. A different set of PhDs, this time in theology, would doubtless respond that it is a mistake to read the Bible literally, and that some or all of these things are to be understood metaphorically, symbolically, mystically, or all three. A different set of questions therefore arises. Which bits are to be taken literally, and which figuratively? Whose interpretations of the latter are the authoritative ones – and why are they so? How does one know which of competing interpretations to accept?

The book of the fifty PhDs would be amusing if it were not saddening. It would be the former because in it one finds remarks, wonderfully lacking in self-perception and irony, such as this: 'It is nothing but *blind faith* to assume the linearity of isotopic decay over time' (my italics) – meaning thereby to impugn the validity of scientific techniques for dating rocks and fossils, so that the theory of the Flood can be asserted instead. And it contains such claims as that Neanderthals lived for up to three hundred years, and are therefore suitable candidates for Methuselah and the patriarchs.

But the book of the fifty PhDs is in the end not amusing because it makes one despair. If people can still base their lives on belief in ancient superstitions despite an education in open-minded use of reason, experiment, observation and careful evaluation of data, the world has an uphill task in trying to reach sanity and peace. For books such as this show that the tenure of religious belief has nothing to do with reason – and that is an unpromising fact.

This raises the question of how it is that religion has experienced a resurgence in fundamentalist form since the second half of the twentieth century. This has happened not only in the Religions of the Book but also in Hinduism. Islam is by nature fundamentalist, and its recent history has seen an unleashing of the destructive forces fundamentalism too often contains. Fundamentalism's manifestations have taken sometimes horrifying forms, from the murder of medical staff working in abortion clinics to the massacre of worshippers in mosques; from small and large acts of terrorism involving mass murder, such as the events of 11 September 2001 in the United States, to open warfare between people of different religious persuasions. In every case fundamentalists, whether or not they use the gun and the bomb in defence or furtherance of their views, are opposed to democracy, liberal pluralism, multiculturalism, religious toleration, secularism, free speech and equal rights for women. They reject the discoveries of modern science in the fields of physics and biology, and assert the literal and unrevisable truth of their ancient holy writings. All the major fundamentalisms are determined to take control of the states in which they exist, and to impose their view of the world upon them.

No doubt the main sources of fundamentalism lie in the increasing secularisation of society started by the eighteenth-century Enlightenment, itself fuelled by the advance of science. In the light of both enlightenment and science, religion appeared to be retreating into the domain of private eccentricity, and in most advanced countries had adopted a social and symbolic guise as a way of coping with its loss of literal credibility and public authority. There have, of course, always been religious enthusiasts who have resisted what they see as attacks on their cherished beliefs; in the earlier centuries of the second millennium they were the critics who attacked the Church for its lack of zeal, its corruption and its loss of true spirituality. In the twentieth century the enthusiasts had a different target: the unbelievers and their liberal, tolerant, secular society whose education and science saw religion as at best marginal and quaint, but mainly as an absurdity, a hangover from the infancy of mankind, the withered fig leaf that hid mankind's ignorance and fear in ancient times. Along with secularism came a relaxation of morality – at least, from the enthusiast's viewpoint. All this doubtless felt like an insult and a threat. To the passionate soldier of god, the sight of an advertisement in which a scantily dressed attractive girl leans nonchalantly on an expensive motor car of phallic design must seem an intolerable incitement and blasphemy. In the case of Islam, the backwardness of Islamic states relative to the advanced West, and the frustration caused by their own Islamic governments, must seem an added offence to many, for whom militant forms of Islam provide everything needed in the way of excuse to engage in a violent struggle against the hated enemy.

Some have felt sympathy for those embattled in their beliefs in this way. Others feel sympathy for them for the different reason that they are victims of a false and distorting perception of the world, a view into which they are trapped typically because of their upbringing and circumstances. For the continued existence of religions is largely the product of religious education in early childhood – itself a scandal, since it amounts to brainwashing and abuse, for small children are not in a position to evaluate what they are taught as fact by their elders. (The vast majority of religious educational institutions are for very young children.)

The main point of interest for present purposes is to ponder for a moment what kind of ethics would be imposed by, say, a fundamentalist Christian government in the United States, if such came to pass. The world has seen Taliban rule in Afghanistan, where music was banned and women had to walk about covered completely from head to foot – two facts quite staggering in their meaning when one contemplates them. And of course the whole of history is an object lesson in this regard. From it one knows that a religious morality imposed by enthusiasts for their faith would controvert almost every tenet of liberal views about tolerance, openness, personal autonomy and choice, and would impose instead a harsh and limiting uniformity on behaviour and opinion, and doubtless even on dress and recreation. It would be done in the name of a god, in the alleged interests of our souls; and it would not reflect or accommodate much in the way of facts about human nature and human occupancy of a natural physical world.

Transcendentalism in ethics

The point of the foregoing excursus is to show two things in connection with the belief held by many that religion provides a basis for ethics (many of those many claim, even more strongly, that it provides the only *genuine* basis for ethics). The first is the questionable character of religion's proposal that the source of our values lies outside the human world, in the commands of a supernatural agency. Both this claim itself, and the character of the resulting ethics, are unsatisfactory for the reasons given. The second is that, in any case, the ethical dimension of religion – even in the expressly moralising Religions of the Book – is marginal to the metaphysics of the religion, that is, the claims about the existence of a supernatural being or beings of some sort, whose existence – or more usually whose power, 'sacredness' and the rest – automatically means that we must worship and obey them, obedience being the key virtue. When Abraham set about killing his only and long-awaited son Isaac as a sacrifice because god had commanded it, he exemplified the obedience required by god, and which Adam and Eve had so signally failed to give. Neither Abraham's obedience, nor Jesus's, if they were truly acts reconciling mankind and god after the Fall, have yet relieved mankind from the terrible punishment inflicted on it as a result of that first sin of disobedience – which is not, of course, taken as a refutation of the claims made in the Bible, for to people emotionally committed to their beliefs nothing can so count. (As Karl Popper pointed out, a theory that admits of no refutation is no theory; it explains everything, even the apparent counter-evidence that ought to refute it; and therefore it explains nothing.)

In the most direct statement of it possible, then, and ignoring perfumed smokescreens of sophisticated apologetics and interpretations, religious ethics comes down to this: the good is obedience to a deity; the good life is a life of submission and obedience (which in practice means obedience to the instructions found in ancient writings and/or issued by a priesthood). The motive for obedience, no matter what the command, is gaining the reward for compliance, and avoiding the punishment for disobedience. The punishments were once graphically represented as torment and agony; the perfumed smokescreen now has far more subtle and complicated stories to offer about 'being excluded from relationship with god', and so forth. The rewards were once graphically represented as eternal bliss in heaven, singing with the cherubim and seraphim – a prospect, cynics might say, so unattractive as to be almost as bad as eternal hellfire, unless the 'eternal bliss' is like being on an unending heroin trip – so of course the soft-voiced latter-day interpreters have a different story to offer. But the fact remains that divine ethics rests on a demand and a threat, not on reasons, and certainly not on reasons prompted by reflection on the facts of human nature and human experience.

It is against this conception that the projects of enlightenment and humanism have striven. In the second enlightenment – the Renaissance – the effort was made to work from within the religious tradition. In the Third Enlightenment – the Enlightenment of the eighteenth century and thereafter – the effort to accommodate religion was in effect abandoned. The next two chapters tell these two tales respectively.

5

THE SECOND ENLIGHTENMENT

Renaissance humanism

No discussion of the Renaissance begins without much foot-shuffling by scholars about what it was, when it happened, or even whether there was truly such a thing. The brightest minds of the period itself were in no doubt; the man who inaugurated, if not the Renaissance itself, then at least the humanism distinctive of it, Francesco Petrarch, himself coined the term 'Middle Ages' to denote the long period which separated his own time from the world of classical antiquity whose art, architecture, thought, outlook and values were in the process of being increasingly rediscovered. More to the point, they were being increasingly appreciated and adopted – or, more accurately still, adapted. As his coining of the label 'Middle Ages' (*aequem aeve*) implies, Petrarch took himself to occupy a new world and a new epoch; and he was right, for across many fields of endeavour the Renaissance was truly not just a rebirth but a fresh birth. It brought with it a conception of the good for man which was, in contrast to the medieval outlook, radical in its invocation of values that sprang wholly from the secular humanism of the first great enlightenment in classical antiquity, despite being expressed in terms conformable with the religious hegemony of its time.

The Renaissance as a distinctive historical epoch is conveniently described as the period stretching for two centuries before, and a century and a half after, the year 1500. It began with a brilliant and sustained flourish in Italy, and spread north into Europe, this northward diffusion mainly happening from about 1490 onwards. One reason for choosing this more precise date as pivotal is that the superpower of the day, France, invaded Italy in 1492, and was conquered by its culture. (This was a watershed year in other ways also. In it the last of the Moors were driven from Spain, and shortly thereafter the Jews likewise. Lorenzo de Medici died, ending one spectacular period in Florence's history. And – with much longer-term effects – Columbus reached the West Indies.) Of course the art and learning of Renaissance Italy had long been filtering outward into the rest of Europe. But thereafter Renaissance ideas and ideals spread into and fertilised the regions of Europe still struggling out of their Gothic past. The spread was most rapid in the thirty years preceding 1520; in that fateful year, in which Luther nailed his theses to the church door in Wittenberg, thereby inaugurating the Reformation, other and more difficult currents began to flow in addition.

Because what most people associate with the Renaissance is its art, the emblem of its origins might well be the work of Giotto, with its striking new three-dimensional realism replacing the two-dimensional formulaicism of Byzantine art. Giotto was born in 1267 and died in 1337, and therefore was a contemporary of Petrarch and Dante – indeed, he was a friend of the latter, who according to legend served as his assistant on a painting commission in Naples. Giotto's naturalistic style was not simply a matter of improved technique. It was inspired by an interest in how things are in the real world, as a subject not merely instrumental and secondary to the transcendent realm that the Gothic imagination made central to all its works, as expressed by its soaring cathedrals and almost exclusively religious art and scholarship. In Giotto's paintings there are real people solidly occupying space, true individuals with human sentiments registering on their faces, in contrast to the repetitive pattern of expressionless Byzantine figures. In this is implied an interest in all things human as a subject of keen importance in its own right, and not simply as representing a temporary and tragic phase in the history of embodied souls whose true home lies elsewhere.

Giotto's outlook is accordingly a humanist one, in the general sense of this term, inspired by the set of intellectual interests involved in the rediscovery and appreciation of the literature of classical antiquity. These interests rapidly became organised into a new curriculum of studies quite different from traditional studies in the universities, which retained their medieval curricula for several centuries longer. The new interests were collectively called 'humanities', *studia humanitatis*, and a votary of them was called a 'humanist'. The model for Petrarch, as the first self-conscious humanist of the Renaissance, and for the many who followed his example, was the liberal intellectual education described by Cicero, Aulus Gellius, and especially Quintilian when his works were soon afterwards rediscovered. In the course of the century following Petrarch's death (he died at the age of seventy in 1374), the humanities became a regular course of education, comprising grammar, rhetoric, poetry, history and moral philosophy. The striking thing about this list is that it does not include theology, law or medicine, which were the three great subjects of the universities, for which the preparation was the *quadrivium* of arithmetic, geometry, astronomy and music, supplemented by logic. All through the Renaissance, while this traditional curriculum continued to be the staple of their instruction, the universities suffered serious decline and marginalisation. The Masters of Arts in many of them ceased to teach, living in idleness on their endowments, while their students, protected by their clerical privileges, devoted themselves to dissipation and riot. Secular authorities found the universities hard to control and almost impossible to reform because of their charter privileges and the protection they enjoyed from the Church. Where serious study survived, it continued and elaborated the tradition of Scholastic thought, in which philosophy and theology became immensely complexified, jargon-laden, accessible only to scholars, and often embroiled in ferocious technical disputes over minutiae of doctrine and dogma quite impenetrable by the ordinary man, and almost invariably irrelevant to him.

The humanists mainly stood outside this introverted and miasmic world, and quite deliberately so. Most of the great humanists of the Renaissance were non-academics, and if some were clerics they were usually so only in the notional sense that any educated man might be in minor orders. The situation is rather similar to the disjunction between the academic and intellectual worlds of today. Not all, and perhaps surprisingly few, university academics in the contemporary English-speaking world are intellectuals in the sense of having wide interests of the mind and deep commitments in moral or political terms, often together with a vocation for deploying these in debate about matters of public concern. A university academic today is a specialist in a narrow field, under pressure to publish technical work in journals of interest only to other specialists, almost invariably in a jargon that explains the latter fact. Modern academia, on the non-science side, thus reprises the position of Renaissance universities uncomfortably closely. Contemporary intellectuals inhabit journalism, the media, publishing, non-governmental organisations; they are writers or artists, commentators, or independent entrepreneurs in forms of business related to the media and arts. While many of these intellectuals contribute substantially to the shaping of cultural life, their academic contemporaries pass their time obscurely multiplying footnotes to unreadable, unread, and soon-forgotten papers to add to the great number published in recondite journals. If there is a justification for this, it is that flowers require compost to grow, and indeed real advances occasionally happen as a result. But much of it – probably most of it – has little value, either instrumental or intrinsic.

Renaissance humanism was purveyed not through the universities but through secondary schools. It was only later in the

Renaissance that the universities began to adopt parts of the humanistic curriculum. Some of the secondary schools, meanwhile, became famous for the quality of their teaching in the classical languages and literatures (especially Latin), and children were sent to them from all over Europe. One such was the school run by Vittorino da Feltre in Mantua; another was the school of Guarino in Ferrara. The motivating belief of these teachers was that a classical training disciplines the mind and furnishes it with excellent materials for developing a civilised outlook distinguished by taste, insight, and a cultivated sensibility. The intended beneficiaries of such an education were future leaders, civil servants and professional men – not clerics, for whom a quite different training was required: one that would lead to a capacity for drawing subtle distinctions in theology.

Texts and treatments

In order of importance, the first fruit of humanism was the rediscovery and proper editing of ancient texts. Petrarch and his close contemporaries at the beginning of the humanist adventure were keen collectors of manuscripts, travelling widely to search for them in monasteries and castles. They found not only older and better versions of known manuscripts, but manuscripts that were thought lost, and manuscripts by forgotten writers. Many of the manuscripts were copies made in Carolingian times, some four or five centuries beforehand, and so were not in the literal sense lost; but many of these many had certainly been lost to view. Different copies were of differing accuracy and completeness, and the collection, collation and editing of improved versions of them was a major advance. But there were also genuine rediscoveries, including many of Cicero's works, and – most notable of all – the works of Tacitus and Lucretius. These were major finds. Later, and chiefly as a result of the fall of Constantinople in 1453, the small number of Greek manuscripts in European collections was greatly supplemented, almost all the ancient Greek literature we now know being recovered during this time. Among the works then first translated (into Latin, to make them more widely available to the Renaissance world) were many works of Plato – who had hitherto been known almost exclusively through his late dialogue the *Timaeus* – all of Plotinus, Epictetus, Marcus Aurelius, Lucian and Plutarch, and almost all of the Greek commentators on Aristotle. This was an extraordinary haul, a treasure trove. It takes no imagination to see what an impact it had on the eager, alert sensibility of the Renaissance, thirsty to drink it all in.

It was not just the careful editing but also the annotating of ancient works, and the writing of commentaries on them, that fuelled humanism's growth. As the fame of the works spread, a demand grew for vernacular versions so that merchants, women, even labourers – all classes of people who in the conditions of the time received only a rudimentary education – could read them. They duly appeared in Italian, French, English and Spanish versions, increasingly so from the sixteenth century. The lingua franca of educated people remained Latin, and one of the ambitions of humanists was to restore that language to its classical purity after the barbarisms introduced in medieval times. A rage for writing pure Latin swept the Renaissance world, including the Church, to the extent that affectations of classical vocabulary and Ciceronian mannerisms of style gripped even theological writing. Some churchmen went so far as to call the Christian god 'Jupiter'.

The dignity of man

But the chief fruit of attention given to the art, literature and philosophy of classical antiquity was the impetus it gave to Renaissance interest in man for his own sake. An immediate expression of this was the flurry of essays, starting with Petrarch and continuing throughout the Renaissance, on the dignity of man. Their point was to contest the standard medieval view (the religious view) that man's life is one of durance vile in a vale of tears, a brief and agonising exile in the flesh before – if the temptations of the devil and his own weakness do not defeat him – a man is able to escape into bliss. In the medieval outlook each age of man was represented as full of woe, from infancy to the decay of old age. The torments of the flesh, of disease and injury, of anxiety and terror, of the malevolence of devils, of blindness, poverty, hunger and oppression – all were painted with ghoulish relish by the medieval mind, to frighten people into church and to keep them there.

All this was part of a long tradition of Christian *contemptus mundi* literature. The humanist response was to praise man's reason and the beauty of his body. His reason makes him godlike, able to commandeer the world to his will; unlike the animals, who are tied to one kind of food in one kind of place, man can live in the hills or on the plains and can take as his food the creatures of the sea or the sky. He is not as strong as the ox, but the ox draws his plough; he is not furred like the fox, but he wears the fox's skin in winter. And this is not yet to remark how man talks, can accumulate knowledge, and can see into the past and the future.

Inspired by the classical authors, the humanists likewise praised the body. This was certainly a new departure, in the light of a long Christian tradition in which the body was to be feared for its proneness to rebel against the soul's interests, needing to be mortified to be kept under control. Ascetics flagellated themselves; Origen went so far as to make himself a eunuch for the kingdom of heaven (he later regretted it) – all to subdue the flesh.

The humanists would have none of this. They sang the beauty, symmetry and proportion of the body, and in a literal application of Protagoras's dictum that man is the measure of all things, some of them argued that everything should be designed to conform to human proportions – buildings, temples, ships – just as (so said Henry Agrippa) Noah's Ark had been. Modelling themselves on writings by Lactantius and Cicero (the latter in his 'On the Nature of the Gods'), humanists examined and applauded each of man's parts, from his limbs to his lights, and especially his posture – for alone in creation man stood upright and gazed at the stars, which was taken to be proof of his higher nature and general excellence.

The humanists of the Renaissance thought and wrote by reflex in religious terms, and among their grounds for rejoicing in man was the 'fact' that a god had taken human form to complete his intentions for creation. Moreover, he had made man in his own image, going so far as to make man a little god in his own right, for, as stated in Genesis, man had been given dominion over the earth and all things in it. More than this: through his combination of body and soul man was evidently the lynchpin of creation, for he thereby combined both the mortal world of time and matter with the eternal world of spirit and truth. This was a Neoplatonist view dating from a thousand years before, but the humanists revived it with enthusiasm, chief among them Marsilio Ficino (1433–99). In addition to seeing man as the knot tying the earthly and divine halves of the universe together, Ficino saw man as thereby representing in himself the whole of creation – which was why, he said, god had incarnated himself as a man, because by so doing he could be united with all aspects of his creation.

The idea at work in this is of man as microcosm – as the universe in little. It was a conception already present in Plato's *Timaeus* and much employed since, but which now acquired greater significance. One argument given for construing man as microcosm was that he is composed of the same elements as the macrocosm, namely, earth, air, fire and water. Paracelsus said that man linked earth and heaven by reason of the fact that to these he added a fifth – but this time divine – element, the 'quintessence'.

In a famous extension of the idea of man as microcosm, Pico

della Mirandola, in his *Oration on the Dignity of Man* (1486), said that because man contains all things within himself he has the potential to become anything he desires. This removed humanity from the median position in the great Chain of Being, conceived as stretching on either side of man from the lowest form of existence to god himself, and made man instead a free, self-creating agent. Pico adduced as evidence for this view god's licence to Adam to do and be what he would. Pico's view was immediately influential, and persistently so; one of its longer-term consequences has been the idea of the autonomy and existential solitude of the individual, a notion that has played a powerful role from Romanticism to the present.

Although humanism naturally and readily reached for the religious ideas that formed the mental environment of its existence, its focus upon things that concern man in this life, not least the body and the senses, meant that its attitude to sexuality was markedly different from medieval attitudes. Boccaccio's *Decameron* (1350), especially the tales of adultery in its Seventh Day, and two centuries later the bawdy tales of Pietro Aretino's *Ragionamenti* (1534), were public works whose like would have been unthinkable to the medieval mind. The often pornographic poems of Catullus (84–54 BC) had survived the Middle Ages in textually degenerate form, and were translated into Italian in the fourteenth century. A century later, in 1472, they were published in a carefully researched *editio princeps*, a fact that by itself says much about the new liberal atmosphere of the Renaissance, and the large distance that separated it from the closed morality of the Gothic world view.

The humanist interest in man and man's circumstances quite generally explains the examination and celebration of the human world in art, poetry, architecture, prose and music that is distinctive of the Renaissance. Portraits, cityscapes, landscapes, still lives, mythological subjects, many paintings of a more or less explicitly erotic connotation, abounded alongside the religious subjects that were produced in industrial quantities owing to the patronage of the Church and the pious. An example – very many offer themselves – of the new genres in art is Francesco del Cossa's *April*, one of an astrological series of the months, painted in 1470 as frescoes in the Este country retreat of Schifonoia. It shows a group of handsome young men and pretty young women, several of the latter carrying musical instruments, in a landscape dotted with rabbits – symbols of the fecundating ebullience of the season – and with what appears to be a 'Judgement of Paris' proceeding in the background. A couple kneel in the centre of the canvas, embracing; his right hand slips down her décolletage, his left between her thighs. Not since Pompeii, one imagines, had many commissions been issued for quite such frescoes.

Cicero in the Renaissance

One of the largest influences in the formation of Renaissance humanism was the work of Cicero, both for its manner and matter. The great Erasmus said that whenever he read Cicero's *On Old Age* he felt like kissing the book, and saw no reason why that distinguished Roman should not be called 'St Cicero'. Cicero was Petrarch's greatest love; so admired was his style that some took oaths never to use a word or linguistic form unless it was found in his pages.

The most notable among these pledgers was the famous and occasionally scandalous Pietro Bembo (1470–1547). He and a fellow Latin secretary to Pope Leo X, Jacopo Sedaleto, led the movement known as 'Ciceronianism', which aimed to standardise Latin according to the Ciceronian model. Later critics saw this as an endeavour to extend Rome's authority over permissible language, but it is hard to imagine Bembo ever having censorious ideas in mind, and certainly not before receiving his cardinal's hat late in life. What mattered to him was the elegance and precision of Ciceronian Latin, and in the period between serving Leo X (who died in 1520) and returning to active life in the Church in 1539, Bembo retired to Padua where he was kept comfortable by a magnificent library, the friendship and admiration of all the leading literary figures in Italy, and his beautiful mistress Morosina. He wrote exquisite Latin and Italian, and dedicated a dialogue on Platonic love to his friend Lucrezia Borgia, modelled on Cicero's *Tusculan Disputations*.

What the Renaissance valued in Cicero was his belief in the human individual. He believed that individuals are autonomous, at liberty to think and decide for themselves; that they have rights, and that rights carry correlative responsibilities; and that all men are brothers – 'There is nothing so like anything else as we are to one another,' he wrote in *On Laws*, adding that 'the whole foundation of the human community' consists in the links between person and person, whether foreigner or member of one's own family, and that these links are 'kindness, generosity, goodness and justice'. His justification for this view is that all men have a divine spark of reason in them. Possession of reason confers on human beings a duty to develop themselves to the full as civilised, educated individuals; and the fact that everyone has reason forges unbreakable ties between us, which is what imposes the duty on us all to treat each other with respect and generosity.

It was not lost on his Renaissance admirers that Cicero advanced these views during a terrible period in Roman history – the last years of the Republic, as it collapsed into a civil war that culminated first in the dictatorship of Caesar and then, after further internecine agonies, the empire under Augustus. Cicero saw any form of autocracy as equivalent to slavery; when Caesar became dictator, Cicero left Rome for his estate in Tusculum, and there wrote some of his greatest works, among them the *Disputations*, *On Duty* and *On Friendship*, all within a matter of months.

Cicero was a widely read and reflective man, who made a lifelong study of the Greek philosophers and adapted them to the conditions of contemporary Rome, 'popularising' them, as we would now say, so that his contemporaries could have in accessible form the fruits of the thinking of the best philosophical minds. He was modest about his aims; he did not wish to reproduce the technicality and rigour of the originals, since those features of them would be of interest only to close scholars, and his desire was to convey what was useful to the practice of living. (This does not mean that he could not, when he chose, get among the minutiae himself; his *Academics* and *The Nature of the Gods* demonstrate this side of his work.) But he was not a mere transmitter. He was an adapter, who selected eclectically ('as all the wise do', according to Einar Lofstedt) from the works of the Greek thinkers, and wove together – in elegant and striking form shaped by his own extensive experience of life and his thereby matured judgement – the best of their ideas for his contemporaries. In the event he did this not just for his contemporaries; as the Renaissance admiration for him shows, he thereby created a body of writings with value for all time.

There had been admirers of Cicero even in medieval times, though they were mindful of the proscription of his writings by Pope Gregory I (590–604) who thought that their beauty of style and their beguiling interest were too likely to distract the young from their study of scripture. Nevertheless, medieval philosophy owed much of its technical terminology to Cicero, who in his adaptations from Greek had laboured to find translations of technical terms (accordingly we owe to him the English words, derived from his Latin coinings: 'appetite', 'comprehension', 'definition', 'difference', 'element', 'image', 'individual', 'induction', 'infinity', 'instance', 'notion', 'morality', 'property', 'quality', 'science', 'species', 'vacuum', and more). With no less a mind than Dante acknowledging his indebtedness to Cicero, not just to *On Duties* for the list of sins in the *Inferno*, but to the *Dream of Scipio* for the very idea of an educational journey through hell, purgatory and heaven, it is not surprising that the fresh new world dawning at the beginning of the fourteenth century AD should find him a general inspiration.

Petrarch began by thinking that Cicero was the model of one who makes active use of a retired life to cultivate his mind ('We educate ourselves to make noble use of our leisure,' Aristotle had said), and then he discovered that the writings he admired had been written by a man who had lived a hectic political life. Cicero's belief in the duty to engage in public affairs greatly recommended itself to Renaissance Italians; the idea of the refined, civilised man who divides his time between active politics and private intellectual pursuits was very congenial. Such an individual is now called a 'Renaissance man' for his all-round character, but 'Ciceronian' would be as apt a label.

So comprehensive did Cicero's influence become that the school of Guarino at Ferrara set only two fixed texts, *On Duties* and the *Disputations*. Editions of Cicero's works multiplied and became best-sellers; they were among the first to come off the new printing presses in the 1460s when this instrument of Renaissance enlightenment appeared. Because of his influence in Italy, Cicero became a beacon to the rest of Europe as the Renaissance spread across it. An English pupil of Guarino, John Tiptoft, translated *On Friendship* into English and published it in 1481, but Cicero in his native Latin was already becoming central to the school curriculum in England. Later scholars, beginning with Theodor Mommsen in the nineteenth century, disdained Cicero because he was not (and expressly did not claim to be) an original thinker, but rather a syncretist and broadcaster. This later snobbery does him injustice. Humanists of the Renaissance would have been unable to understand such a limited view of a figure whose graces of style and thought gave them so much.

Erasmus

A figure on whom Cicero had a profound effect, and who himself sums up much that is distinctive of Renaissance humanism, is Desiderius Erasmus of Rotterdam (1466–1536). This is especially so because Erasmus remained faithful not just to Christianity – making him, in the fullest sense, the exemplar of Christian humanism – but to Rome, even as the first earthquakes of the Reformation occurred.

To understand Erasmus, and in particular the fame he enjoyed in his own lifetime – he was a Renaissance superstar, admired to distraction by literate men, and actively sought out by kings and universities all over Europe, who wanted his presence, his erudition and his wisdom – it is necessary to remember two things. First, the secular, or 'pagan', character of much fifteenth-century humanism was not congenial to orthodox churchmen, who therefore resisted it. Secondly, the prime movers of the Reformation were of the same mind. Like the humanists, they too looked back to the deep past for their inspiration; but to the New Testament, not to Cicero and the pagan authors. Their intention was 'evangelism', as it has since been called, that is, a reliance on the 'evangel' of the gospels, apostolic acts, and Pauline letters, the original religion of the New Testament scriptures. A growing split was already evident between those humanists who looked with disdain on theology, and those theologians who were suspicious of pagan classicism. The example of writers who had tried to bridge the divide – St Augustine, St Thomas Aquinas, Dante – was luminous but insufficient, at least in the climate of the first decades of the sixteenth century, when matters were coming to a head in the Church.

Erasmus saw himself as making a further effort to bridge that divide. His chosen means was education. He thought that the mutual fertilisation of classical and religious writings would multiply the good in both, and that the study of them together would forge a new kind of human being – more tolerant, more peaceful, of wider imagination and deeper insight. Like the reformers, he believed that the Church required cleansing and renewing. He especially disliked its corrupt practices, the laxity of its morals, and its cruel pursuit and punishment of 'heretics'. But although this meant he had much in common with the inspirers of the Reformation, he could not follow them into schism.

If the expression is not too much an oxymoron, Erasmus is best described as a 'vigorous moderate'. He disliked the jargon and obfuscation of Scholastic theology. He thought many humanists went too far in their devotion to the pagan classics, thereby compromising their Christianity. He also disliked what he called the 'pharisaism' of certain of the pious, especially some of the religious orders, in their rigid adherence to outward forms of ritual, dress, fasting and vigils. But what most characterises his contribution to the debate of the times was his advocacy, from a Christian standpoint, of the classics and their value.

An undoubted influence in the formation of Erasmus's moderate outlook was his early education at the hands of the Brethren of the Common Life at Deventer in his homeland, the Netherlands. Perhaps the most famous member of this movement was Thomas à Kempis, author of *The Imitation of Christ*. The Brethren stressed inwardness, placing no importance on outward forms, and certainly not on any kind of compulsion. There were, for example, no lifelong vows for members.

One wing of the Brethren, the wing to which Thomas à Kempis belonged, shared with other religious movements a suspicion of learning as a thing harmful to prospects of salvation. This attitude had deep roots in the Church Fathers and the medieval Church, and its supporters could quote St Paul to great effect on the folly of the wise. But another wing was liberal in this respect, some of its most influential senior members being much attracted to the classical authors, not least Seneca and Cicero. Erasmus had the good fortune to be educated by votaries of the liberal wing; but true to form, the piety of the more austere wing made its mark on him too, and therefore both aspects of his intellectual constitution can be seen as a legacy of the Brethren.

Still, a large part of his task in formulating an educational programme to humanise religion and keep the faith alive in humanity was, as he recognised, to defend the value of pagan literature against attacks by theological conservatives. 'Whatever is pious and conduces to good manners ought not to be called profane,' he wrote in his tract *Against the Barbarians*:

> The first place must indeed be given to the authority of the Scriptures; but nevertheless I sometimes find things said or written by the ancients, even by the heathens, even by the poets themselves, so chaste, holy and divine, that I cannot but think they were divinely inspired when they wrote them, and perhaps the spirit of Christ diffuses itself farther than we imagine, and that there are more saints we should enrol in our calendar. To confess it freely among friends: I cannot read Cicero on old age, on friendship, or on duties, without kissing the book, and venerating his divine soul. When I read some of our modern authors on politics, economics and ethics, good god! how frigid they are in comparison! So I had rather lose one Scotus or twenty such subtle doctors, than one Cicero or Plutarch. For I find that when I read one of these latter, I become better; but when I rise from reading one of the others, if I am not coldly affected towards virtue I am certainly hotly affected towards cavil and contention.

Erasmus saw himself as a liberal Catholic, and not as a fomenter of splits and factions. He wished to liberalise the Church, to purify its doctrines, and to educate a class of men able to administer the Church humanely, and to diffuse into society at large the generous and mature spirit of an attitude to life enriched by all that the ancient world had to teach. He wished to see the faith based on textually correct editions of the scriptures – his own edition of the Greek New Testament, dedicated to Pope Leo X, showed that there were a number of important errors in the Vulgate. He advocated toleration, and genuine moral commitment in place of the outward show of ritual and pomp. His satires on the follies and corruptions of the Church were biting, and intended to prompt internal reform; but his views in these respects were appropriated by Protestants of various stripes, so that at the time of his death and in the decades following it, both his writings and his influence were effectively disowned by Catholics. The Counter-Reformation was very far from Erasmian in spirit – he would have been appalled at the founding of the Roman Inquisition in 1542, and he would have been even more dismayed to learn that his own friend Carlo Caraffa placed all Erasmus's writings on the Index of Forbidden Books in 1559 after becoming Pope Paul IV.

What makes Erasmus a humanist, albeit a Christian humanist, is not simply his love of the classics and his application of them in his life and thought, but more importantly his belief in man's rationality and his ability to take moral responsibility for himself. This is a crucial matter. Neither of these commitments was congenial to the orthodox Christianity that split apart at the Reformation. In the orthodox Christian view, man is fallen; his reason is weak and gives the devil a handle to lead him astray. Only by mortification, discipline, works and assiduous observance of the sacraments can a man be saved from sin – which shows that he is certainly not in a position to exercise moral autonomy. The Protestants took the opposite view. Each man is his own priest before god. He does not need priests, saints or rituals to mediate his relationship with god. He is capable of reading the scriptures for himself, and finding his own route to salvation. Such views strike at the very root of the Church of Rome, of course, which would lose its client-base entirely if everyone were to accept such tenets. Unfortunately for Erasmus's reputation with his fellow Catholics, his views were far too congenial to the Protestant outlook. Protestants accordingly embraced him, his own Church disowned him. When the city of Basle, where he was then living, joined the Protestant cause in 1529, Erasmus left in order to live in a Catholic community; but six years later he returned and, as far as is known, from that time until his death he had no contact with his own Church. What that signifies is anyone's guess.

As the example of the fate of Erasmus's thought shows, the relationship between humanism and the Catholic Church was fated never to work. Erasmus and like-minded fellows hoped that properly edited and widely available scriptures would usurp the technicality-laden, jargon-obscured, scholar-owned theology of the schools, thus refreshing the Church in the minds and lives of its members, who (they hoped) would read the scriptures for themselves and live the purer, de-institutionalised religion they taught. They also thought that many of the Church's practices and privileges were spurious, and that critical study of the arguments – and the documents – in support would help to clear away a great deal of dust. Naturally enough, neither the scholars in the universities nor the priests in charge of Church documents were at all happy about the threat to their positions represented by this attitude, and so they contested it vigorously. This fact is one of the explanations of the Reformation, for when it became apparent that the Church was not interested in reforming from within, it was inevitable that many would leave. They did so; and the bloody history of the Counter-Reformation began.

A principal feature of the Counter-Reformation is censorship. The Index of Forbidden Books *officially* came into existence in this troubled period (it had unofficially existed ever since literacy began to increase in the twelfth century), and that fact by itself was the single largest blow to the hopes of Christian humanists who wished to remain loyal to the

Church. The Index placed obstacles in the way of historical and philosophical research; and most of all, it entrenched the theology of the universities, whose Scholastic masters insisted that, as a highly complicated science on which the safety of human souls depended, theology should only be taught by carefully trained professionals, and only from carefully vetted texts.

Erasmus was chief among those who challenged this view. The philosophy of Christ could, he said, be studied by any literate person with access to a reliable edition of the scriptures. By the same token, he and other humanists challenged Aristotle's domination of university curricula by saying that Stoics, Epicureans and others should be studied too, for their writings enlarged the conception of the good. One of the most eloquent claims in this regard was made on behalf of Plato by Marsilio Ficino, the leading Platonist of the Renaissance period.

The Index of Forbidden Books was no light matter. Anyone who published or read a text on the Index suffered automatic excommunication. A Congregation for the Index was founded in Rome to supervise matters, reading everything in order to decide whether it should be banned or not, and issuing authority for publication of acceptable works. By the time the Index was officially abandoned in 1966 it was very long indeed, including on it, among many others, works by Abelard, Erasmus, Machiavelli, Calvin, Montaigne, Bacon, Hobbes, La Fontaine, Descartes, Pascal, Milton, Spinoza, Locke, Berkeley, Hume, Oliver Goldsmith, Condillac, d'Holbach, d'Alembert, Defoe, Swift, Montesquieu, Swedenborg, Sterne, Mme de Staël, Helvetius, Diderot, Voltaire, Rousseau, Gibbon, Kant, Heine, J. S. Mill, Alexandre Dumas, Flaubert, Victor Hugo, Balzac, Stendhal, Bergson, André Gide, Zola, Maeterlinck, Pierre Larousse, Anatole France, and Jean-Paul Sartre – in short, most of Western culture in the last thousand years. One wonders what was taught by way of literature and culture in Catholic schools.

It was not only the Counter-Reformation that repudiated humanism. In the most influential sources of Protestant thought, the views of Luther and Calvin, humanism's optimistic and positive belief in man's worth met with cold hostility. Luther's view of man rests on the doctrine of the Fall. Because of the disobedience in Eden, he said, man's only hope is redemption through Christ; human nature is corrupt, infected by original sin; there is nothing man can do on his own account to save himself. Likewise Calvin held that unless men see how wrong is their overweening sense of self-importance, recognising instead their fallible, impotent and degenerate state, they will not be saved. A chief result of the debacle of Christendom in the early sixteenth century was therefore a Counter-Enlightenment from both sides of the religious quarrel. If the votaries of both sides had had their way, another Dark Age would have supervened. But the Counter-Enlightenment did not wholly succeed: too much had been set in motion in the hearts and minds of men, and it was only a matter of a century before science, and two centuries before an Enlightenment shrived of religious affiliations altogether, brought the modern world to birth.

Morals and the good for man

Since Augustine, who claimed that the pagan schools between them had produced nearly three hundred different definitions of the highest good, it had been the reflex Christian view that nothing attainable on earth could compare with what was truly the supreme good for man, namely, gaining access to heaven after death in order to enjoy the eternal vision of god. The idea of a supreme good – a *summum bonum* – was derived from Aristotle, as was his view that the end and aim of ethical enquiry is to identify the supreme good and the means to attain it. An alternative way of putting this is to say that ethics is the enquiry into the meaning of life, for by identifying the greatest good it thereby uncovers the purpose of living.

Specifying the greatest good comes easily to Christianity, but it presented a problem to the Scholastic philosophers of the medieval universities, whose great authority outside the Church and the scriptures was 'the Philosopher', Aristotle. How could his identification of the supreme good – *eudaimonia*, or happiness – be reconciled with the Christian one? A widely accepted answer was that Aristotle identified the supreme good for man on earth, but that this was only a relative or imperfect version, and that the true good waits upon post-mortem entry to the divine presence itself.

In earlier phases of Christianity's history Aristotle had not been so prominent. Among Patristic writers the favoured pagan philosophies were Stoicism and Platonism, although the relationship of the Fathers with them was an uneasy one, the ever-present fear being that pagan thought might seduce the believer away from the true path. 'No one comes to the Father but by me,' Jesus had said, describing himself in exclusive terms as 'the way, the truth and the life', implying thereby that no other route is valid.

For the humanists, however, the free exercise of reason showed that the ethical teachings of the pagans were often consistent with Christian teaching, and therefore to be welcomed. Such was Erasmus's opinion. Before him Petrarch argued that although pagan ethics was mistaken in thinking that virtue is itself the goal, nevertheless the road to heaven leads through virtue, so we can accept the ancient writers as guides for at least part of our journey. Some humanists, among them Coluccio Salutati of Florence (1331–1406), recognised that there was a significant difference between pagan and Christian morality in one respect, namely, that the latter emphasised inner conscience whereas the former emphasised overt behaviour and its effects. But they did not think this impugned the value of the pagan writings wholly.

Others disagreed. For those who thought that only the light of Christ could illuminate the way, even the most plausible-seeming and agreeable aspects of pagan teaching were a potential snare. The Church walked in that light, whereas the pagans groped in the dark. If they said anything that accorded with Christian teaching, it was by luck. In any case – and such was the emphatic view of Lorenzo Valla – the faith had rendered obsolete everything that went before, and had ushered in a new dispensation based on a new arrangement between god and the world. The teachings of those who lived before the incarnation of god among men had no relevance.

For some among Protestant thinkers, whose ethical conceptions turned wholly on the doctrine of the Fall, the pagan authors were an irrelevance because they had not taken the Fall into account. Not only did they not know that man is born in sin, and carries its stain throughout life, but they also did not know that the Fall had corrupted man's reason, so the instrument they used in devising their ethical views is flawed. Pagan ethics in its entirety, therefore, is on this argument useless.

Fortunately for the Protestant world, these hard views were countered by no less a person than Philipp Melancthon (1497–1560). Before turning to theology under Luther's influence, Melancthon had taught the pagan classics at Tübingen University, and knew them thoroughly. He accepted the doctrine of the Fall and all its implications, including its infection of human reason; but he argued that god had allowed human reason to remain sufficiently robust for it to understand the laws of nature, and the results in the world of human actions – thus allowing men to judge how to act in the sublunary realm, where alone considerations of ethics apply. Accordingly, the teachings and example of the best pagan authors, providing they are kept strictly apart from, and subordinated to, the gospels, are a permissible resource in the business of life in the flesh. 'Christ did not come to earth to teach morality, but to forgive sins and to convey the Holy Ghost to those who accepted him,' Melancthon wrote in a discussion of Aristotle's ethics. His distinction between ethics as applicable to the earthly realm and theology as applied to the heavenly realm readily won adherents among many Protestant humanists, enabling them to continue editing and commenting upon classical works, and encouraging their study in the secondary schools.

Still, the doctrines people read in their pagan sources presented a number of challenges to their Christian views. The chief of the pagans for the Renaissance period was, of course, Aristotle. His dominance in the universities had already been absolute for centuries, and almost every educated man had been bred upon his texts. Apart from the enormous influence given them by St Thomas Aquinas, Aristotle's writings were excellent pedagogical instruments, for they were written as systematic treatises, and were much easier both to teach and to study than the more difficult, complicated, circuitous and sometimes ambiguous writings of Plato. As a result, Aristotle's works were standard, and attracted any number of commentaries, both of the technical Scholastic kind and of the more accessible and up-to-date humanist kind. Versions of both the texts and the commentaries were produced for all educational levels, from secondary school to university, and for use in private study.

An immediate result was that Christian commentators had to address the fact that Aristotle, in characterising *eudaimonia* as what accrues to anyone who uses his reason in accordance with the virtues, said that certain goods of body and fortune are also required for the full flowering of happiness. To a Christian, health and wealth are incidentals, and wealth – a degree of which Aristotle claimed to be necessary for the best life – was especially problematic. Money, let alone the pride and avarice it can prompt, was regarded by Christianity as a source of sin, and for that reason poverty was regarded as one essential of most forms of monastic life. It took the Protestant shift to make the getting of money, by honest endeavour in trade and commerce, a respectable sign of god's favour, even if such a life was not quite the best that could be envisaged.

Another point of disagreement was Aristotle's claim that since reason is the highest of man's qualities, the best life for man is the life of contemplation – by which Aristotle meant philosophical enquiry. Among the many objections to this were, first, that the finitude of man's reason meant that he could never discover the truth about most things, since there are infinitely many truths to be known, and therefore a life of contemplation would be a frustrating and not a happy one; and secondly, that since the causes of things are hidden, they cannot be known in this life. Others objected that it is anyway a mistake to think that knowledge is the right goal for man, since his true happiness lies not in hoping to know the greatest thing there is, namely, god – an impossibility given the infinitude of god – but in enjoying god's presence. And naturally, Aristotle was accused of inconsistency in saying that man is a political animal who must play his part in the affairs of society, while at the same time holding that the best life for man is the life of contemplation.

Among many Christian Renaissance thinkers the ethics of Plato seemed far more congenial than those of Aristotle. Two aspects of his views made him attractive. One was his claim that the Form of the Good is the highest being, and that the supreme good consists in contemplation of it. Naturally, Renaissance admirers of Plato such as Marsilio Ficino identified the Form of the Good with god, and Ficino himself went further and argued that since we grow to be like the things we contemplate, meditation on god will make us godlike. Encouraged by Plato's own writings, his Renaissance adherents claimed that the proper contemplation of god can only be effected when the soul has quitted its muddy vesture of flesh, a view consistent with what had by then become a standard view about death and post-mortem existence.

The second attractive feature of Plato was his account of love. His idea that the greatest good can be attained by means of love proved especially influential among his Renaissance admirers. In the *Symposium* Plato has Socrates recount a discourse by a prophetess called Diotima, who describes an ascent through several increasingly rarefied stages of love, from passion for an individual beautiful body to love of beauty wherever manifested in the physical world; thence to love of the beauty of souls, as something higher than physical beauty; and then, by way of love for life, law, and different kinds of knowledge, to love of the eternal and perfect Form of Beauty itself, from which all beautiful things get their nature. This notion was adapted by Ficino in a widely read commentary on the *Symposium*, in which he described beauty as a ray emanating from god, and beauty in things as the influence (in the literal sense of this term, to mean 'in-flowing') of god in them: 'In bodies we love the shadow of god; in souls, his likeness; in angels, his image. So in this present life we love god in all things, so that in the next life we can love all things in god.'

Despite these attractions, there was strong resistance on both sides of the religious divide to annexing Plato as a kind of Christian doctor before the event. It tempted commentators into adapting Christian doctrine to Platonism rather than the other way round, and it obscured important differences of view, not least the large difference in the Platonic and Christian conceptions of the soul. Plato said that the soul had always existed, that it certainly existed before its first incarnation, and was periodically thereafter reincarnated. Christianity held that the soul is created with its individual body, and is not reincarnated. Moreover, Christians believed that god created all things, whereas Plato believed that the sublunary realm, including therefore the human bodies in it, was created by demons (not things of evil in his ontology, as they were for Christians, but a species of minor deity or spirit). Protestants, again because of the importance they attached to the Fall and original sin, were opposed to the Platonic view that evil is ignorance, and that the good is to be attained by gaining knowledge – in particular, knowledge gained by the exercise of reason. Indeed, all

Christians were opposed to any reliance on reason, and still more to the exaltation of reason for securing the good (which in their moral theology is equivalent to salvation); in its essence Christianity, in common with the other Religions of the Book, is a non-rational and in many ways anti-rational view, which means that conflict with the pagan philosophies is inevitable at some point.

Even Stoicism fell foul of this difficulty, despite being the classical outlook in many ways most congenial to Christianity. Known chiefly through the writings of Cicero and Seneca, but during the fifteenth century also in rediscovered works of Diogenes Laertius and the *Enchiridion* containing Epictetus's doctrines, Stoicism was admired by many from Petrarch onwards, even when they felt that it was too demanding and austere as a viable *lebensphilosophie*. Stoicism's indifference to material goods had been criticised by St Thomas Aquinas, whose Aristotelian leanings taught him that a degree of physical comfort is a great aid to living virtuously, and this theme was repeated often by commentators in the Renaissance. One chief point of objection, however, was Stoicism's doctrine of 'apathy', which means control of the feelings in the face of external fortune, especially misfortune. It seemed bizarre to some that pain, loss, grief and hardship could be a matter of indifference to a human being, so destructive are they of happiness. Moreover, the example of Christ showed that feelings are acceptable and appropriate: Christ had wept at the death of Lazarus, felt anger at the money-changers in the temple, suffered fear and despair in the Garden of Gethsemane, and pity for the repentant thief. If it was in order for Christ to be 'pathetic', it was wrong for man to try to be 'apathetic'.

But most of all, Christian commentators objected to Stoicism's view that the virtues constitute the good, and that living in accordance with them is sufficient of itself. Erasmus pointed out that this doctrine meant that man has his happiness in his own hands, whereas Christian doctrine denies this, claiming that man can do nothing without god, least of all attain security and felicity – if he merits them, whether by faith or works (depending on which side of the religious divide he stood). Calvin said that people should seek god's glory, not their own glorification by claiming to be virtuous; and in voicing this view he was joining all those who thought that the Stoic's self-reliance and moral self-creation was arrogant and prideful, contrary to the Christian teaching of humility, which requires abasement before god and belief in one's own insufficiency and weakness.

Defenders of the Stoic outlook were not without a reply. A 'Neostoic' movement began at the end of the sixteenth century under the inspiration of the Dutch scholar Justus Lipsius. In extolling the Stoic virtue of steadfastness in the face of misfortune, Lipsius cited a number of Church Fathers who had written favourably about Stoicism, and with their help sought to prove that Seneca and Epictetus pointed the way to central Christian sentiments, not least in their love of the divine and their repudiation of the world. At the time Lipsius wrote, the Low Countries were engaged in their independence struggle against Spain, so it was a time of tumult, and his Neostoical views found a welcome among contemporaries. From there, not least as the Wars of Religion engulfed most of Europe – representing Catholicism's attempt to regain by fire and the sword what it had lost in the Reformation – the Neostoic outlook spread, aided by the popularising works of William du Vair, who wrote in the French vernacular and whose work was quickly translated into English. His Christianised brand of Stoicism had its most vigorous English proponent in Bishop Joseph Hall, 'England's Seneca', who nevertheless agreed with most of his Renaissance forerunners in abandoning the full Stoic doctrine of 'apathy', for, he said, any man who could not feel anger when god's honour was impugned was surely likely to feel god's anger in response.

Despite the criticisms levelled by Christian commentators,

Stoicism fared far better than Epicureanism in the Renaissance. In promoting pleasure as the highest good, and in being the source of Lucretius's atheistic *De Rerum Natura*, which had been rediscovered in 1417 after languishing forgotten for six centuries, the teachings of Epicurus were little likely to be received otherwise. Mainly they were caricatured, and Epicureans were condemned as voluptuaries and sinners. The excellence of the *De Rerum Natura* as poetry, and the power of many of its teachings, were not lost on humanists; Ficino could not resist making use of it in his famous commentary on Plato's *Symposium*, and several of the poem's editors and commentators mounted vigorous defences of its merits. But Epicureanism's denial of the soul's immortality and of providence was too much for the time to stomach. The Church Fathers long before had condemned Epicurus; Dante put him and his followers in the sixth circle of hell along with heretics; and poems appeared 'on the immortality of the soul' in Lucretius's style but of opposite doctrine. Among Protestant writers the Epicurean view that men naturally seek pleasure was emphatically rejected; they took this as a mark rather of man's fallen nature. For them, as for Melancthon, pagan ethics were to be kept as far away from Christian doctrine as possible.

Faith and reason

Nothing shows better than these last sketches how entangled with religion the enlightenment endeavour of the Renaissance was. To the alert intelligence of many humanists there was a glaringly obvious tension between an interest in man in this world, and in his soul in the next; between faith and reason; between the scriptures and the classics; between the urbane, mature and civilised outlook of the writers of antiquity, and the attitude towards man's earthly existence taught by a Church whose corruptions largely consisted in a venal enjoyment of those same alleged sources of misery. No doubt, the attitude of

Christian humanists who tried to reconcile these matters was sincere, but there is equally no doubt that the humanists (without the adjective) of the fifteenth century would have made earlier gains on behalf of reason and the advancement of man's interests on earth, if the other great current of the time, which led to the Reformation and its ensuing century-long upheavals throughout Christendom, had not temporarily derailed the project. The derailment was only temporary, however; there was no putting the rediscovered classics back into obscurity, despite the Index of Forbidden Books; and the humanities themselves had opened avenues of enquiry that made the next stage of enlightenment inevitable, this time far less hampered by the rusted drag-anchors of powerful religious loyalties and their hold on the mind of man.

One major reason for this was that the Renaissance had opened a Pandora's box (from the Churches' point of view) of enquiry and scepticism, and had revived confidence in man's own powers, especially the powers of his intellect. The result was added impetus to science, and a growing movement towards liberty, both in the political sense and in the sense of a concomitant liberty of thought. Science and such liberties are fatal to religious orthodoxy – as the events of the next centuries proceeded to prove.

6

THE THIRD ENLIGHTENMENT

After the century of science

In his novel *Les Bijoux Indiscrets* Denis Diderot, editor of that great monument of the eighteenth-century Enlightenment, the *Encyclopédie*, recounts a dream. In it there is a building without foundations, whose pillars soar upwards into a fog. A crowd of misshapen and crippled old men move about among the pillars. The building is the Palace of Hypotheses, and the old men are makers of theological and metaphysical systems. Then an energetic little child appears, and as he draws near the building he grows into a giant. The child's name is Experiment, and when he arrives at the building he gives it a mighty blow, and it shatters to the ground.

The dream encapsulates one important aspect of the eighteenth-century Enlightenment's source: the rise of science in the seventeenth century. That century began, in scientific respects, with Galileo seeing the moons of Jupiter through a telescope, an observation adding powerful support to the Copernican view of the universe. Galileo was put under house arrest by the Vatican for saying that the Earth moves, contrary to the definitive pronouncement in scripture that god had 'laid the foundations of the earth, that it should not be removed for ever' (Psalm 104, verse 5). The century ended with Newton. It contained a spectacular army of genius in the natural sciences and mathematics, whose work laid the simultaneous foundations of science and the modern world: Hooke, Boyle, Wren, Huygens, Wallis, Descartes, Roche, Kepler, Napier, Leeuwenhoek, Fermat, Pascal,

Leibniz – the names resound. It was also a miraculous century in philosophy and literature, to say nothing of the arts and music, for it also contained Hobbes, Spinoza and Locke in philosophy; Shakespeare, Cervantes, Donne, Corneille, Racine, Molière, La Fontaine, Marvel and Milton in literature; painters too remarkable and numerous to mention, among them Poussin, Claude, Caravaggio, Bernini, Rembrandt, Hals, Vermeer, Rubens and Velazquez; and in the century's last quarter the composers Vivaldi, Telemann, Handel and J. S. Bach, inheriting a tradition that earlier in the century had witnessed the first of their great tribe, Claudio Monteverdi.

Alongside this litany of genius one would need to add the dramatic histories of the religious wars that began the century; the Netherlands' golden age, which occupied most of it; the high point of what had for long been Europe's superpower, namely France, in the reign of Louis XIV towards the century's end; and England's Civil War in the mid-century, and its constitutional settlement of 1688 – events of great political significance for the future history of Europe and the world.

The character of the extraordinary seventeenth century explains the difference between the enlightenment of the Renaissance and the Enlightenment of the eighteenth century. The key is, obviously, science, and specifically the use of observation and reason, experiment and quantification, to penetrate the appearances of the world, and to provide powerful ways of describing natural phenomena and predicting their behaviour. When it became demonstrably clear that the mind of man can discover the secrets of nature, other doctrines – for a prime example, that of the divine right of kings – began to lose intellectual respectability, even if in more or less indirect ways. It would have been unthinkable for an English writer of Elizabethan or Jacobean times to argue that the Crown should be subject to Parliament; but by 1688 that principle was not merely established but operational. The change is a symptom of a massive reassembling of views about the universe in general and mankind in particular. By the end of Elizabeth I's reign Shakespeare could represent regicide as a matter of cosmic significance – in *Macbeth*, for just one example, the night of Duncan's murder is described as full of strange portents: 'Lamentings heard i' the air; strange screams of death... the earth was feverous, and did shake'; and Duncan's horses went wild and ate each other. Half a century later the beheading of Charles I was not regarded as subversive of the divine order. A rapid diffusion of a new and remarkably different sentiment had begun; an example of how it reached beyond the closets of philosophers is the use of mathematical and scientific metaphor even in poetry, as in the work of John Donne:

> And as no chemic yet th'elixir got,
> But glorifies his pregnant pot,
> If by the way to him befall
> Some odoriferous thing, or medicinal...

Little could better indicate how a new way of looking at the world had supplanted the world view of the Middle Ages, whose grip on the human mind had at last begun to be loosened in the Renaissance.

Yet even in the seventeenth century this process was still in its early stages, and patchy in its reach. Witches continued to be hunted and burned, ignorance and superstition were still the main condition of the majority of men, and – a fact that makes the seventeenth century's giant strides in science and the arts astonishing – it was a century plagued by wars, with scarcely a decade in which peace reigned over Europe as a whole. The eighteenth century lost fewer years to war, and in its relative peace and growing prosperity its thinkers were able to address questions that their predecessors had shelved: the implications for views about man and society of the triumph of scientific method.

This indeed is the key to the eighteenth-century

Enlightenment. It consisted in the application to wider regions of thought – and the spread of these, as a result, into wider public cognisance – of the new attitude of mind made possible by the seventeenth century's intellectual advances.

What enlightenment is

'Enlightenment', wrote Immanuel Kant in his seminal *What Is Enlightenment?* (1784), 'is man's emergence from his self-imposed immaturity. Immaturity is the inability to use one's understanding without guidance from another. This immaturity is self-imposed when its cause lies not in lack of understanding, but in lack of resolve and courage to use it without guidance from another. Sapere Aude! (Dare to Know) – "Have courage to use your own understanding!" – that is the motto of enlightenment.'

It is essential to note that neither Kant nor any of his contemporaries – and certainly not those intent, as he was, on disseminating the gospel of self-governing reason – believed that enlightenment had actually been attained. Their applause, rather, was for the progress being made towards it. As Kant put it, 'If it is now asked, "Do we presently live in an enlightened age?" the answer is, "No, but we do live in an age of enlightenment."'

Although Kant began by describing the immaturity of the intellect as the state in which it needs guidance from another, he also attacked the various hegemonies which keep the human mind shackled to that need. In order to mature, the intellect needs liberty; but in all spheres, he wrote, that is precisely what is lacking: 'Nothing is required for enlightenment except freedom; and the freedom in question is the least harmful of all, namely, the freedom to use reason publicly in all matters. But on all sides I hear: "Do not argue!" The officer says, "Do not argue, drill!" The tax man says, "Do not argue, pay!" The pastor says, "Do not argue, believe!"'

The officer and the tax man represent authorities who might

dislike anyone's questioning the political and social status quo, but the pastor represents authority which dislikes questioning *tout court*. Kant, enough of a creature of his times not to assault this most jealous hegemon directly, found it convenient not to overemphasise his criticisms of religion, but it was his primary target nevertheless. The project that occupied one of the chief places in the eighteenth century's progress of mind, the *Encyclopédie* of Diderot and D'Alembert, declared its emphatic war on religion on the grounds that it had always been a barrier to intellectual advance, and that it had signally failed to provide a satisfactory basis either for morality or a just society. In this the Encyclopedists were following the lead given by Voltaire, who with his battle cry of '*Écrasez l'infame*' had persistently attacked superstition and priestcraft with all the weapons of logic, satire and ridicule. Voltaire had, of course, circumspectly claimed that criticising superstition was not the same thing as criticising faith, and that criticising the Church was not the same thing as criticising religion. But it was faith and religion that felt the blows; like Kant, Voltaire was boxing clever.

In common with many who took the same view, whether or not they publicly acknowledged doing so, Voltaire claimed to be a deist, that is, one who does not believe in any revealed religion such as Christianity or Islam, but nevertheless believes that there is a supreme being who created the universe. Most deists take it that this being has no personal interest in the affairs of mankind, and does not intervene in what happens in the world, leaving it to the operation of natural laws alone. Diderot had no time for deism, seeing it as a mere fudge; it had, he wrote, cut off a dozen heads of the Hydra of religion, but from the remaining one all the rest would grow again. 'In vain, oh slave of superstition,' says Nature to Mankind in his *Supplement to Bougainville's Voyage*, 'have you sought your happiness beyond the limits of the world I gave you. Have courage to free yourself from the yoke of religion ... Examine the history of all peoples in all times and you will see that we humans have always been subject to one of three codes: that of nature, that of society, and that of religion – and that we have been obliged to transgress all three in succession, because they could never be in harmony.' The result is, said Diderot, that there has therefore never been 'a real man, a real citizen, a real believer'.

Perhaps one of the most swingeing eighteenth-century assaults on religion occurs in Baron d'Holbach's *Natural Politics*, which concludes with the remark that religion, by teaching people to fear invisible despots, thereby teaches them to fear earthly ones, and consequently prevents them from seeking independence and choosing the direction and character of their lives for themselves. As this suggests – and this is crucially important for understanding the Enlightenment – the repudiation of the hegemony of religion over thought is, although central, not the sole concern, but just the starting point for what really counts: the project, to be undertaken by each individual, of relying on reason and applying the lessons of science as the chief guides to building better lives and societies. The Enlightenment project is accordingly a creative one, a reforming one, premised on the promise of freedom – most especially intellectual freedom – to deliver a new and improved world.

Peter Gay is careful to point out, in his magisterial *The Enlightenment: An Interpretation*, that the Enlightenment has always had its simplistic admirers and its vehement detractors, among the latter those who blame it for those aspects of modernism that exemplify 'superficial rationalism, foolish optimism, and irresponsible Utopianism', including the excesses of the French Revolution and the failed experiments, terribly costly in human terms, of the twentieth century's various upheavals. The reminder is a salutary one. But as Gay and before him Ernst Cassirer remark, even though such strictures have point, the Enlightenment as a cultural climate, as a complex movement of thought, and as a set of aspirations for the improvement of mankind's lot, remains eminently worth understanding – and not least because it represents a key moment in the quest for the good life.

Gay also lends support to the principal idea at work in the present argument, namely, that the quest for the good has, in all the epochs of intellectual advance, primarily taken the form of a conflict between humanistic and transcendentalist perspectives.

The philosophes' experience [Gay writes, speaking of the thinkers of the Enlightenment collectively by the French label they applied to themselves] was a dialectical struggle for autonomy, an attempt to assimilate the two pasts they had inherited – Christian and pagan – to pit them against one another and thus to secure their independence... theirs was a paganism directed against their Christian inheritance and dependent upon the paganism of classical antiquity, but it was also a *modern* paganism, emancipated from classical thought as much as from Christian dogma. The ancient philosophers taught the philosophes the uses of criticism, but it was the modern philosophers who taught them the possibilities of power.

In these remarks, as in those of Kant and the philosophes quoted, a key notion is that of 'autonomy', by which is meant self-government, independent thought, and possession of the right and the responsibility to make choices about one's own life – not least moral choices. Autonomy is self-direction in the light of reason and the lessons of nature; its opposite, heteronomy, means direction or government by someone or something outside oneself; it means subjection of one's own will to the will and choices of an external authority, typically a deity or some other abstraction. Of course, the conditions of social life mean that an individual is subject to many constraints made necessary by the fact of living in community with others. But the autonomy in question is autonomy first and foremost of thought and moral responsibility, and it is the progress towards increasing autonomy, in this sense, that Kant and his eighteenth-century contemporaries saw as 'enlightenment'.

The *Encyclopédie*

If the aim of enlightenment is to think for oneself and choose for oneself – this autonomy conceived as essential to the life worth living – then it is essential that one should be equipped to think fruitfully and to choose wisely. That requires information; and not just information, but information organised into knowledge; and not just knowledge, but knowledge interpreted into understanding. The monument of the eighteenth-century Enlightenment is a work that set out to answer this need. It was a work of education, designed as a tool for the illumination and thus liberation of the mind. It was the *Encyclopédie, ou Dictionnaire Raisonné des Sciences, des Arts and des Métiers*. Edited by Denis Diderot with the assistance of Jean Le Rond D'Alembert, its aim was – as Diderot put it in his introduction –

> to collect all the knowledge scattered over the face of the earth, to present its general outlines and structure to the men with whom we live, and to transmit this to those who will come after us, so that the work of the past centuries may be useful to the following centuries, that our children, by becoming more educated, may at the same time become more virtuous and happier, and that we may not die without having deserved well of the human race.

The most significant part of this statement is Diderot's assertion that education is the route to the good life – education, not faith or some variety of submission to past pieties or present tyrannies; and, moreover, education in the sciences and humanities, as evolved in the centuries since the beginning of the Renaissance – which D'Alembert, continuing the theme, pointedly characterised in his own 'Preliminary Discourse' as a radical break with the outlook of the Middle Ages. The philosophes were thus self-confessed propagandists for a secular and rationalist view of the world. At the same time they were self-confessedly and proudly popularisers and publicists for the advance of learning in all fields, claiming to be neither less nor more. This iterates a point worth bearing in mind about the eighteenth-century Enlightenment: it was a period of application rather than invention, when the previous centuries' innovations were put to work, and introduced to wider audiences.

As a fertile field for controversy among historians, even so clear-cut a programme as the one implied by Diderot's claims for the *Encyclopédie* has been interpreted differently. In *The Heavenly City of the Eighteenth-Century Philosophers* Carl Becker argued that the Encyclopedists' thought was permeated with Christian tropes and assumptions. His view has been eloquently refuted by Peter Gay and others; but one does not have to turn to the commentators to see how far Becker was from the mark. A persistent theme of the *Encyclopédie*'s articles, especially those on method and enquiry – as the very titles of articles on 'Observation', 'System', and 'Hypothesis' indicate – is that the empirical method and the use of reason are keys to knowledge, and that these are not only inconsistent with appeals to the authority of scriptures or revelation, but actually controvert them. In the 'Preliminary Discourse' D'Alembert begins his account of the organisation of knowledge by defending empiricism, and then accepts the implications of this commitment: that the fundamental concepts of morality and justice have to be derived from facts about mankind's experience, not from supposed metaphysical or theological foundations.

Still, the eighteenth century was far from being a secular age, which meant that the philosophes could not afford to be too cavalier in attacking their contemporaries' sensibilities. One way of advancing a secular line in a still clerical and therefore largely hostile era was to use irony. In his article 'Atheism' the Abbé Yvon pretends to attack the sceptic Pierre Bayle while, under this camouflage, showing that the pagan philosophers of antiquity were better men than most self-professed Christians:

'From these examples [of the pagan philosophers] M. Bayle concludes that religion is not as useful in repressing vice as people claim and that atheism does not cause the evil that people assume,' Yvon remarks, as if disagreeing. In the course of his article he cites Bayle's examples of people – and whole peoples – whose ethics did not rest on a supernatural basis, and yet who were superior to those whose ethics do so rest:

> Diagoras, Theodorus, Euhemerus, Nicanor, and Hippon, [were] philosophers whose virtue appeared so admirable to Clement of Alexandria that he wished to adorn religion with them, although antiquity recognised that they were determined atheists. He then goes back to Epicurus and his followers, whose conduct, according to their enemies, was irreproachable. He cites Atticus, Cassius and Pliny the naturalist. He finally ends this illustrious catalogue by praising the virtue of Vanini and Spinoza. This is not all, for he cites entire nations of atheists discovered by modern travellers on the continents and islands of Africa and America. The morals of these people far surpass most of the idolaters who surround them. It is true that these atheists are savages without laws, magistrates, and police, but from these circumstances he derives even stronger arguments to support his views; for if they live peacefully outside civil society, they would be even more inclined to do likewise in a society where general laws would prevent particular individuals from perpetrating injustice.

By this means Yvon subtly abetted the project Bayle had undertaken in his *Dictionnaire historique et critique* (1696) to insinuate 'free thought' under the guise – in Bayle's case rather a transparent one – of supporting religion. Bayle, and before him Montaigne and Pascal, far anticipated Kierkegaard in arguing that faith, to be genuine, must have no aid from reason. Montaigne and especially Pascal thereby sought to protect religion from the encroachments of sceptical enquiry, whereas Bayle, cheekily, sought by the same means to protect free-thinkers from Church attack. In his *History of Freedom of Thought* Bury reports Bayle's adaptation of the argument as follows:

> The theological virtue of faith consists in believing revealed truths simply and solely on God's authority. If you believe in the immortality of the soul for philosophical reasons, you are orthodox, but you have no part in faith. The merit of faith becomes greater, in proportion as the revealed truth surpasses all the powers of our mind; the more incomprehensible the truth and the more repugnant to reason, the greater is the sacrifice we make in accepting it, the deeper our submission to God. Therefore a merciless inventory of the objections which reason has to urge against fundamental doctrines serves to exalt the merits of faith.

But of course, as Bayle well knew, a 'merciless inventory' of reason's objections to religion is far more likely to have exactly the opposite effect.

As telling an expression of the *Encyclopédie*'s aim as Yvon's 'Atheism' is Diderot's charming essay on 'Enjoyment', in which the philosophe sets out to recalibrate his contemporaries' moral sense on the subject of sex. As with Yvon's quotation of Bayle's anticipations of the 'noble savage' ideal, certain auguries of Romanticism are discernible in aspects of Diderot's argument; Rousseau's prize essay *Discours sur les sciences et les arts* had not long since been published, purveying the 'noble savage' myth, and he had just been enrolled among the *Encyclopédie*'s contributors, so this is no surprise.

Diderot's 'Enjoyment' merits quotation at length.

Among the objects that nature everywhere offers to our

desires, you who have a soul, tell me if there is anything more worthy of your pursuit, anything that can make us happier than the possession and enjoyment of a being who thinks and feels as you do, who has the same ideas, who experiences the same sensations, the same ecstasies, who brings her affectionate and sensitive arms towards yours, who embraces you, whose caresses will be followed with the existence of a new being who will resemble one of you, who will look for you in the first movements of life to hug you, whom you will bring up by your side and love together, and who will protect you in old age, who will respect you at all times, and whose happy birth has already strengthened the tie that bound you together?

... [If] there is a perverse man who could take offence at the praise that I give to the most noble and universal of passions, I would evoke Nature before him, I would make it speak, and Nature would say to him: why do you blush to hear the word pleasure pronounced, when you do not blush to indulge in its temptations under the cover of night? Are you ignorant of its purpose and of what you owe to it? Do you believe that your mother would have imperilled her life to give you yours if I had not attached an inexpressible charm to the embraces of her husband? Be quiet, unhappy man, and consider that pleasure pulled you out of nothingness.

The propagation of beings is the greatest object of nature. It imperiously solicits both sexes as soon as they have been granted their share of strength and beauty. A vague and brooding restlessness warns them of the moment; their condition is mixed with pain and pleasure. At that time they listen to their senses and turn their considered attention to themselves. But if an individual should be presented to another of the same species and of a different sex, then the feeling of all other needs is suspended: the heart palpitates, the limbs tremble; voluptuous images wander through the mind; a flood of spirits runs through the nerves, excites them, and proceeds to the seat of a new sense that reveals itself and torments the body. Sight is troubled, delirium is born; reason, the slave of instinct, limits itself to serving the latter, and Nature is satisfied.

This is the way things took place at the beginning of the world, and the way they still take place in the back of the savage adult's cave.

Diderot's account of sexual affection and infatuation has several notable features. It did not, of course, tell anyone anything they did not know, but it cast the familiar facts of puberty, sexual attraction and reproduction in what was then a daring light. Contemporary readers doubtless witnessed the reproductive activities of farm animals or (in town) domestic pets, and accepted that their behaviour represented obedience to biological laws; but to bring mankind explicitly into the same naturalistic mould, to accept and discuss puberty and early sexual awakening as continuous with the phenomenon of animal reproduction, and yet to put a high value on the intimate affections as a central amenity of the good life, is to place it all into a startling new perspective. In conformity with the *Encyclopédie*'s general tenor, there is not the faintest tincture of theology in the account: where a deity might have been, nature sits; the seamless connection of humanity with the rest of the natural order exempts the facts about sexual desire and its natural outcome from the need for moralising or disguise. If one could recover the freshness and candour of the essay in its first effect, one would better appreciate the demand it made on Diderot's contemporaries to see things anew from the perspective of what the Enlightenment premised in all its workings – science and reason.

The quarrel of the Enlightenment

The *Encyclopédie* was published between 1751 and 1772 in seventeen volumes of text and eleven of illustrations. The writing of its seventy-two thousand articles was distributed among a hundred and forty authors, among them some of the most eminent minds of eighteenth-century France – in addition to its editors they included Voltaire, Rousseau, Marmontel, d'Holbach and Turgot, to name a very few. They shared Diderot's aim not just of collecting and, in clear and accessible prose, diffusing the best of accumulated knowledge and its fruits, but of deploying this formidable mass as a machine of war to propagate 'Light'. The *Encyclopédie* therefore faced considerable opposition, not least from the censors, whose objections and interference caused many delays in publication. The first seven volumes appeared annually between 1751 and 1757, the last ten appeared in 1766. Six years later the last of the volumes of illustrations were published, completing the original plan. By that time reprints of some of the articles were already in existence, and works inspired either by agreement or opposition had begun to appear; the *Encyclopédie* had become an institution, and remains a monument to what the most optimistic intellects of the time aspired to.

Although the *Encyclopédie* is in this way a concrete expression of the Enlightenment spirit, for all its significance it represents just one thread in a larger and longer story. Part of that story concerns the contemporary opposition to the Enlightenment project, chiefly from the defenders of the religious and political status quo threatened by the practical implications of its message. A larger part of the story concerns the Enlightenment's historical critics – those who see it as responsible for the excesses of the French Revolution, those who see it as meriting the reaction represented by Romanticism, those who see it as the ultimate source for both Stalinism and Fascism in more recent times, those even more recently who see it as ultimately responsible for 'liberal' values, where this is understood pejoratively in the American sense as destructive of 'family values' – and all those who see it as embodying the antithesis of all that matters most richly to the human spirit in its encounters with the mystical, the ineffable, the numinous and the divine.

The earliest opponents of the Enlightenment fall into two broad classes: those who would now be described as occupying the political or ideological right – ranging from clerics contemporary with the philosophes to somewhat later thinkers such as Edmund Burke and Joseph le Maistre – and those we now label Romantics, who championed nature, imagination and the emotions against what they saw as the reductive and mechanistic world view of Enlightenment rationalism.

Burke and others who shared his conservative political orientation identified the Enlightenment attack on tradition – and especially tradition as a source of moral and political authority – as the direct cause of all that was worst about the French Revolution. In fact their objection targeted a longer impulse of thought, stemming at least from Locke, which argued that the source of authority in society is not tradition or a monarch ruling by divine right, but the *people*, whose consent is required for all things affecting the common weal, and who have rights, some of them inalienable in that no form of government is entitled to abrogate them. The philosophes of the Enlightenment adopted this view as a matter of course, and it has been (despite Burke, because later conservatives adopted it too) the source of the Western evolution of liberal democracy and internationalism, both currently in the global ascendant. But in Burke's day 'democracy' was a word of horror, and 'the people' was an unruly and anarchic entity not to be trusted. From Burke's perspective the philosophes were *sans-culottes* before the fact, and he regarded all their principles as despicable accordingly.

Romantics interpreted the Enlightenment's championship of science as amounting to the claim that scientific development is synonymous with progress itself, which if so would mean that history and human experience can only properly be understood in mechanistic, even deterministic terms. As a way of recoiling from this degree (as they saw it) of rationalism and mechanism, the Romantics asserted instead the primacy of emotion over reason, and accordingly celebrated the subjective, the personal, the visionary and the irrational. They gave a privileged place to moods and passions as sources of insight and as arbiters of truth, and they exalted such experiences as the individual's response to natural beauty. Whereas Enlightenment attitudes might be supposed (and are typically so supposed) to be natural concomitants of the neoclassical preference for order, balance and harmony in music, architecture, art and poetry (a view that gets much support from the applied aesthetics of the eighteenth century), Romanticism is by deliberate contrast spontaneous and various, trusting to the emotions rather than the rules and principles discovered, or asserted, by reason.

It scarcely needs saying that we would not now willingly be without either the neoclassicism of the eighteenth century or the Romantic music and poetry of the nineteenth century, so the point here is not to take sides between the best of both styles, nor – having agreed that both have their worst sides and consequences too, as with the harsh and mechanical reductivism of the one, and the irresponsible thinking of the other that led to such catastrophes as nationalism and racism – to choose which did most harm. If there is one salient difference, it is that the amorphous embrace of Romanticism gave unreflective house-room to many of the shibboleths that the Enlightenment worked hard to extirpate, given their negative effects on human flourishing – for a chief example, superstition; and in this respect a preference might be justified as follows: the good life for human individuals certainly requires the best of both traditions, but arguably it least requires the worst aspects of Romanticism, if these come down to yielding authority to such things as race, the Hero, the Genius, the Leader, tradition, nature, untutored emotions, visions, supernatural beings, and the like.

The crux of the argument here is, as this of course shows, the place of reason in the good life. On the Enlightenment view, reason is the armament of ideas; it is the weapon employed in the conflict between viewpoints. This suggests that reason is an absolute that, responsibly used, can settle disputes and serve as a guide to truth. But reason understood in this uncompromising way has always invited opposition. One main opponent – as a matter of historical fact, *the* main opponent – is religion, which claims that revelation, in any form from mystical experience to dictation of scriptures by a deity, conveys from outside the world of ordinary experience truths undiscoverable by human enquiry within it. Another opponent is relativism: the view that different truths, different views, different ways of thinking, even those that compete with or contradict each other, are all equally valid, and that there is no authoritative standpoint from which they can be adjudicated. In this sharp contrast the Enlightenment's weight lay emphatically on the side of the argument which says that reason, despite its imperfections and fallibilities, provides a standard to which competing standpoints have to submit themselves. Its votaries accordingly reject any outlook which says that there are authorities alongside or even more powerful than reason, such as race, tradition, nature, or gods. The rationalists' defence of reason does not have to be, and of course had better not be, unqualified, not least given the fact that answers to questions about what human beings are (or, what human nature is) are now more ironic and conditional than ever they were, and less entitled to confidence. This, though, was something that promoters of Enlightenment in the eighteenth century themselves understood very well. Consider Voltaire's satire on the excessive adherence to a rationalist optimism as exhibited by Dr Pangloss in *Candide*, a work that gives the lie to anyone who thinks that the philosophes were unselfcritical or unreflective about the extent of human rationality. And as we shall shortly see, the leading philosophers (not philosophes) of the period –

Hume and Kant – were likewise careful not to overrate reason, while yet using it to describe its own limits.

Consider a later critical reaction to the Enlightenment, which serves as an example of how its optimistic, almost certainly over-optimistic, outlook came to be seen as self-destructive. In *The Dialectic of Enlightenment*, which allegedly began as a New York kitchen conversation between Max Horkheimer and Theodore Adorno during the darkest days of the Second World War, the idea is mooted that the Enlightenment's principles and themes have metamorphosed into their opposites. Individual freedom was sought by the philosophes, but became a form of enslavement to economic powers for those who came after them. Science was seen as the rational alternative to religion, but scientism – itself taking the form of a salvation myth, in which science will answer all questions and solve all problems – simply came to replace religion and to exert as malign an influence.

Their criticism of scientific rationality mattered greatly to Horkheimer and Adorno, because they believed that they were witnessing the moment at which its promise had turned fully toxic. Adopted as the philosophical method of Enlightenment, scientific rationality not only promised to bring progress in all fields, but simultaneously to undermine the dogmas of religion and with them the hegemony of priesthoods. It could do this, the original philosophes believed, because of its objective character and its obvious pragmatic success. In its promise both of progress and of liberation from ancient superstitions, scientific rationality was supposed to serve the interests of freedom and tolerance. But scientific rationality has a dynamic of its own, Horkheimer and Adorno argued, which gradually made it militate even against the values responsible for its own rise. In so doing it turned from being a weapon *against* repression into a weapon *of* repression. Believing its own dreams of progress, intoxicated by the successes of rational method, triumphant in its increasing mastery over nature, the humanistic dream of the philosophes eventually turned into a nightmare, and the shibboleths it attempted to destroy all reappeared in new disguises – chief among them, so Horkheimer and Adorno held, Fascism.

This analysis was immensely influential in the Frankfurt School, and occasioned a vigorous debate after the Second World War. But reflection on the transitions Horkheimer and Adorno suggest does not substantiate their view. The quickest way to see why is to note the implausibility of their equation of scientific mastery over nature – for the Enlightenment, a mastery intended to liberate mankind – with the mastery over the majority of mankind exercised by those who, as a result of the material progress made possible by the Enlightenment, came to control the levers of economic and political power in succeeding centuries. In the crisis of the 1940s the oppressive power Horkheimer and Adorno had foremost in mind was Nazism, which they thus saw as the self-fulfillingly paradoxical outcome of the Enlightenment: as they put it, 'instrumental rationality' had transmuted itself into 'bureaucratic politics'. But this is implausible. Nazi ideology drew its strength precisely from the peasantry and petit bourgeoisie who felt most threatened by capital's advance to power; so it is not the latter that has to be seen as the source of the new oppression, but instead the former, viewed as latter-day representatives of the groupings who had most to lose from the Enlightenment and therefore constituted the reaction to it – namely (and literally) the reactionaries. The embracers of Nazism would, had they inhabited the eighteenth century, have defended the traditions of absolute government, whether in heaven or Versailles, against the 'instrumental rationality' which in the eighteenth century expressed itself as a set of secularising and democratising impulses. Horkheimer and Adorno accordingly got matters the wrong way round. Nor is it clear that the alternative form of tyranny available for study in that same era – namely, Stalinism – would admit of any better a genealogy to the Enlightenment, and for similar reasons.

The most famous aspect of *The Dialectic of Enlightenment* is the authors' attack on what they saw as the repressive nature of the 'culture industry'. They took mass culture to be another long-term outcome of the Enlightenment's instrumental rationalism, and rejected it accordingly; but here too their view, with its oddly misplaced elitism, invites disagreement. Mass culture is by no means incapable of producing things of great value, whether in the form of art or knowledge; and the technologies designed to serve the interests of mass culture are equally capable of producing art as refined as any elitist could require – as witnessed by the best work in cinema and television. So the pessimism of these two critics of the Enlightenment has not been borne out, which, chief among other reasons, calls their criticism into question.

The philosophers in the age of the philosophes

It is, of course, not in the least coincidental that the seventeenth and eighteenth centuries should have seen, after fifteen hundred years in which questions of morality were regarded as settled by the articles of the Christian faith, a revival of philosophical debate not just about moral questions but about the very basis of morality itself. Among a distinguished collection of contributors to this revived debate two figures stand out: David Hume and Immanuel Kant.

Hume regarded his chief work on ethics, the *Enquiry Concerning the Principles of Morals*, as 'incomparably' his best book. Given that he wrote the even more celebrated *Treatise of Human Nature*, an admired history of England, and essays of great beauty and penetration, this judgement has seemed surprising to some among those who have studied his work. But it shows the importance Hume attached to it, unsurprising in light of the fact that his chief aim in philosophy was to settle the question of what he called 'the general foundation of morals'.

The background to Hume's interest in this question is the

controversy that arose as soon as philosophers again felt free to examine the basis of ethics. This was the controversy over whether the principles of morals are derived from reason or from the emotional responses of agents. As Hume put it, the question that must be asked is whether 'we attain the knowledge of [moral principles] by a chain of argument and induction, or by an immediate feeling and inner finer sense; whether, like all sound judgement of truth and falsehood, they should be the same to every rational intelligent being, or whether, like the perception of beauty and deformity, they be founded entirely on the fabric of the human species'. One school of thought among Hume's immediate predecessors in philosophy held that moral truths are apprehended by reason. Another school taught that the only basis any rational agent could have for acting one way rather than another is self-interest, which, however, can be 'enlightened' in that it recognises kindness or concern for others as being in the agent's own long-term interests. A third school – and this is the one closest to Hume's position – held that there is an innate human moral sense that determines what we think is good and bad. Two of the proponents of such a view were the third Earl of Shaftesbury and Francis Hutcheson, both of whom Hume quotes in his *Enquiry*, saying of the latter that he 'has taught us, by the most convincing arguments, that morality is nothing in the abstract nature of things, but is entirely relative to the sentiment or mental taste of each particular being; in the same manner as the distinctions of sweet and bitter, hot and cold, arise from the particular feeling of each sense or organ'. Endorsing this view summarises Hume's own conviction, that 'Moral perceptions, therefore, ought not to be classed with the operations of the understanding, but with the tastes or sentiments.'

This theory is known as 'moral subjectivism', and Hume had given it a classic statement in his earlier *Treatise* as follows:

Take any action allowed to be vicious: wilful murder, for instance. Examine it in all its lights, and see if you can find that matter of fact, or real existence, which you would call *vice* ... You can never find it, till you turn your reflection to your own breast, and find a sentiment of disapprobation, which arises in you, toward this action.

The key notion here is that of a 'matter of fact, or real existence', by which Hume means something objectively in the world, which therefore exists independently of human sentiments. Put in these terms, Hume's claim is that morality is not something objectively in the world, existing independently of anyone's private choices and preferences, but is a product of these latter. The fact that there are no objective moral facts is, says Hume, one reason why the claim of the 'Rationalists' – in this connection 'rationalist' is a term of art denoting those philosophers who think that all truths, including those about moral principles, are discoverable by reason alone – has to be rejected. He added another argument: even if there were indeed objective moral facts, the mere recognition of them would never motivate anyone to act one way rather than another; action can only be prompted by emotion, and therefore it would still be necessary for us to *feel* something in order for us to be moved to *do* anything. He put the point in a way that has since prompted much philosophical debate, by saying that you cannot derive a prescription from a description – that is, you cannot derive a statement telling you what you ought to do from a statement describing some aspect of the world.

One objection typically urged against subjectivism is that it makes moral judgement an arbitrary matter, dependent upon the whim of the individual, whose subjective responses might vary widely from those of others. But Hume thought that human nature is generally the same everywhere for everyone, and that it is fundamentally benevolent. This optimistic view means that there will be wide agreement in moral responses, just as there is in judgements of beauty. Of course he acknowledged that differences of opinion arise both in the ethical and aesthetic spheres, but he explained them by claiming that one or some of the parties to the disagreement must either be insufficiently well informed, or confused or deficient in their moral sense. Comparing moral sense to skill in literary criticism, Hume argued that we can refine our abilities as judges, and grow more competent – provided that we avoid what he called 'the illusions of religious superstition and philosophical enthusiasm'.

For Hume, our moral judgements are principally directed at the virtues and vices of the human character. In his view there are two kinds of virtues, the natural and the 'artificial', the latter in the sense of being dependent on social conventions. Artificial virtues consist in conformity to socially adopted norms, and include justice, chastity and the observance of various kinds of duty – as, for example, adhering to laws and agreements. Whereas the artificial virtues depend on the conventions that specify their content, the natural virtues are found widely diffused among human beings because, as their label implies, they are part of the innate human endowment. They include friendship, faithfulness, generosity, courage, mercy, fairness, patience, good humour, perseverance, prudence and kindness; and Hume saw them as also including the sociable virtues of good-nature, cleanliness, decorum, and being 'agreeable and handsome' enough to 'render a person lovely or loveable'.

These last 'virtues' invite criticism, on the grounds that they do not depend on an individual's will. One cannot choose to be or not to be handsome, and it might even lie outside one's power to be charming, witty and generally good company. How then, asks the critic, can these be virtues? Nevertheless it is clear what Hume intended: he was thinking of fellowship and the pleasures of society as counting among the chief goods for mankind, and saw it as a virtue if an individual possessed – and perhaps cultivated – the required characteristics. One might not be able to will oneself into being handsome, Hume might say, but one can endeavour to be, and succeed in being, presentable and clean.

Hume significantly remarked, in a letter to Francis Hutcheson, that his favourite author on morality was Cicero. In the same letter he recalled being made to study, when a boy, a Protestant tract called *The Whole Duty of Man*, a staple for school children of his day; and he told Hutcheson that even then he rejected its outlook. The contrast between the Ciceronian and Christian views taught him that virtues are what bring pleasure to their possessors or to others, or are genuinely useful in the promotion of good fellowship, whereas 'celibacy, fasting, penance, mortification, self denial, humility, silence, solitude, and the whole train of monkish virtues', are, he said, horrible: 'They stupefy the understanding and harden the heart, obscure the fancy and sour the temper.'

From this and his list of virtues one readily grasps Hume's conception of the good life. It was an outlook whose development began early; in a letter written at the age of twenty-three he wrote,

[I] read many books of morality, such as Cicero, Seneca and Plutarch, and being smit with their beautiful representations of virtue and philosophy, I undertook the improvement of my temper and will, along with my reason and understanding. I was continually fortifying myself with reflections against death, and poverty, and shame, and all the other calamities of life.

The Stoicism that forms part of this early view did not survive whole into Hume's mature work; its self-denying, self-disciplining aspects yielded to a more cheerful allegiance to the sociable virtues. And Hume practised what he preached, for he was universally liked, meriting well his sobriquet of 'le bon David'.

In common with other thinkers of the Enlightenment,

Hume was adamant that philosophy – here in the generalised sense of enquiry and reflection – belonged to the world at large, and not to the academy or the scholar's study alone. The 'great defect of the last age', he wrote, thinking of the period of Scholastic philosophy which the Renaissance had brought to an end, was that it separated 'the learned from the conversable world'; the latter had lost much as a result, while the learned 'had been as great a loser by being shut up in colleges and cells'. The result had been that philosophy had become 'as chimerical in its conclusions as she was unintelligible in her style and manner of delivery'. The reason for this was that the scholars had lost touch with the world; they 'never consulted experience in any of their reasonings, [nor] searched for that experience, where alone it is found, in common life and conversation'. Hume rejoiced that in his own day men of letters and men of the world were conversing together again – among other things reprising the debate about the good life, as had once been done under the shade of the olive trees in ancient Athens.

Reason in action

Hume is one great exemplar of the Enlightenment and its values. The other giant of eighteenth-century philosophy, Immanuel Kant, was, however, nothing like Hume's ideal of a man engaged in accessible and civilised conversation with his fellows. Kant's philosophical writings are ferociously difficult and highly technical – but for a good reason, which is that he was a thinker of originality and power who had to find a new vocabulary for the expression of his novel ideas. His *Critique of Pure Reason*, a classic of modern philosophy, is one of the most difficult of all philosophical texts to master. As with Hume before him, Kant's main philosophical aim was to solve the fundamental problem of the foundations of morality, and for this the *Critique of Pure Reason* is, for all its importance to discussions in metaphysics and the theory of knowledge, just a starting point. In a series of following works, the two most important being the *Critique of Practical Reason* and *The Groundwork of the Metaphysic of Morals*, Kant set out his austere views about the 'supreme principle of morality'.

If there is to be such a thing as morality, Kant argued, then its laws must apply to a realm of free-willed action, and not to the realm of deterministic causality – that is, the empirical realm governed by natural causal laws. This means that the task in moral philosophy is to show how reason by itself ('pure' reason, unmixed with empirical factors) governs and directs the will. The will, in turn, when truly autonomous – when it obeys only laws it makes for itself – thereby expresses the highest good there can be, which is freedom. 'The *summum bonum*', he wrote, 'is freedom in accordance with a will which is not necessitated to action.' Free-willed beings are the most valuable things in the world; they are 'ends in themselves' which should never be treated instrumentally as means to other ends.

In Kant's view, moral value resides in the good will of an agent who acts not out of inclination or the desire to achieve some particular end, but out of a sense of duty – specifically, a duty to obey a moral law which reason recognises as the right one for the circumstances. The law in question will not take the form of a 'hypothetical imperative' advising that if the agent wishes to achieve a certain aim he should do so-and-so. Imperatives of this kind – for example, '*If* you wish to protect your health, *then* you must give up smoking' – are such that if you do not desire the end (as specified in the 'if' part), you do not have to obey the command (as specified in the 'then' part). Rather, a genuinely moral law will take the form of a 'categorical imperative' bluntly asserting 'do so-and-so'. It is absolute and unconditional.

Kant arrives at this view by distinguishing between action-guiding principles which are subjective, in the sense that they apply only to the agent himself, and those that are objective, in the sense that they apply to all rational beings. Subjective principles are called 'maxims'; objective principles are called 'laws'. If there existed perfectly rational beings, without appetites and passions to interfere with their reasoning, they would invariably act in accordance with objective laws. Animals never act in accordance with such laws, because they do not possess reason but only appetites and instincts, so their behaviour is wholly governed by the laws of nature. The big difference between rational and non-rational beings is summarised by Kant in the *Groundwork* thus: 'Everything in nature works in accordance with laws. Only a rational being has the power to act *in accordance with his idea* of laws – that is, in accordance with principles – and only so has he a *will*.' Human beings are, figuratively speaking, halfway between the animals and the angels, in the sense that they have both reason and the full complement of animal appetites and instincts. They are therefore in the unique position of being able to act in conformity with objective principles identified by reason, but they do not always do so. So they alone are in need of concepts of duty and obligation, and therefore of imperatives unconditionally stating what they ought to do.

The general form of the categorical imperative is: 'I ought never to act in any way other than according to a maxim which I can at the same time will should become a universal law' – that is, which I regard as applicable universally, to everyone and not just me. The most famous formulation of the categorical imperative is: 'Act in such a way that you always treat humanity, whether in your own person or in the person of any other, never simply as a means, but always at the same time as an end.' Kant thinks of the moral community of persons as a 'kingdom of ends', a mutual association of free beings, in which each individual seeks to realise freely chosen goals compatibly with the freedom of everyone else to do likewise.

In stating these views Kant had to traverse some very hard terrain. He argued that the supreme principle of morality is the principle of autonomy, and that the 'determining ground of the moral will' is the purely formal concept of *lawfulness* as such, which is a concept of pure reason. Kant claims that the very possibility of morality depends on there being free-willed beings who obey laws of reason they apply to themselves. He therefore had to give an argument to show that there is freedom, and he had to explain how laws can be valid just in virtue of their formal properties and not in virtue of what they enjoin. The details of these knotty arguments belong in a different kind of book; but for all their complexity they were intended by Kant to underpin something quite familiar and practical, namely, the ordinary morality of ordinary people.

Kant did not agree with those, whether among the ancients or the moderns, who thought that morality is only accessible to an educated elite. Moral principles apply to everyone, and therefore everyone must be capable of understanding the obligations and ideals that govern their moral lives. He believed that in fact all ordinary folk have a basically correct grasp of morality, even if a detailed and technical philosophical treatise is required to spell out both its details and its justification. He took his own task to be that of explaining and analysing what is 'inherent in the structure of every man's reason', which includes the supreme principle of morality itself, namely autonomy or freedom, together with the categorical nature of true moral laws. He was criticised by contemporaries for not having introduced anything original in this respect, to which he replied, 'Who would wish to introduce a new principle of morality and, as it were, be its inventor, as if the world had hitherto been ignorant of what duty is or had been thoroughly wrong about it?'

According to one of his biographers, Friedrich Paulsen, Kant's view was consciously democratic, in that he understood (not least from his own experience, as the son of a poor father) that whereas those born into wealth and leisure might have a variety of pleasures and opportunities to choose among – which nevertheless did not make them conspicuously more moral; rather the contrary – poorer folk had not much else to expect than a life of hard work for little reward, or perhaps no other reward than the sense that they had performed their duties conscientiously. Morality does not exempt or privilege the rich, but holds for everyone – and, by the same token, gives the same rights and dignity to everyone. This is what Kant means when he insists that no one has a moral entitlement to use others as means to their own ends. And this further means that there are no grounds for discriminating negatively between one person and another. Individual worth is not a matter of wealth or birth, luck or fortune, but rather is inherent in the possession of free will and reason. Moreover, actual experience shows how human beings struggle because of the competition between the animal and the rational aspects of their natures. Indeed, says Kant, it is because of this struggle between our desires and our duty that we grasp the reality of morality in the first place.

Commentators and biographers alike are apt to make much of Kant's Pietist upbringing as a source of his stern morality of duty. The Pietists were numerous and highly influential in eighteenth-century Königsberg, where Kant was born and lived all his life. His parents were strictly observing members of the movement, so he attended a committedly Pietist school, the Collegium Fredericianum, and then the city's university, a centre of Pietist theology. Pietists believed in Original Sin and its concomitant, the human tendency to evil; but this had a further concomitant in the form of a doctrine of salvation through spiritual rebirth, good works, and the unremitting pursuit of moral perfection. Kant deeply disliked the obligatory pieties of Pietism, and by extension religion in general, but he carried from his experience of it the idea of inner dutifulness and discipline.

The most potent influence on Kant was not Pietism, however, but something opposed to it both temperamentally and in principle: the Enlightenment itself. He saw himself as a votary of it, even a custodian of its values. For much of his teaching career at the University of Königsberg he lectured on the subjects that all the proponents of Enlightenment sought to make more generally known – physics and astronomy included – and he championed the ideal of making progress in the condition of mankind through the application of science and its methods. For this, as noted, Kant argued that the necessary condition is freedom – freedom from external constraints on debate and the diffusion of knowledge, and freedom internally from the timidity and uncertainty which inhibits independent thought. The enemies of progress are those who impose censorship or conformity, whether of a political or religious kind. Such abuses of power, Kant wrote in *What is Enlightenment?*, 'trample on the holy rights of mankind'. Elsewhere he added, 'Religion through its sanctity, and law-giving through its majesty, might seek to exempt themselves from [criticism], but they then awaken rightful suspicion, and cannot claim the sincere respect which reason accords only to that which has been able to sustain the test of free and open examination.'

Despite thus holding that religion is not just irrelevant but harmful to morality, Kant did not think it theoretically possible to justify morality as a whole without invoking metaphysical concepts of a deity and the immortality of the soul. These notions, together with that of the freedom of the will, constitute a trinity of concepts that, although they cannot be proved to be valid, are necessary to make sense of the practice of morality as a whole – for if, he said, we assume that there is a deity and that we survive our earthly existence, and moreover that we are fully accountable, as a result of having free will, for everything we have done in life, then we can think of ourselves as being liable for reward or punishment in a posthumous dispensation. And this, in large, is what in his view confers overall point on morality for the ordinary man.

In Kant's terminology, the concepts of god, immortality and

freedom are 'postulates of pure practical reason'. His argument for them is that the moral law requires us to attain the highest possible good, and that we do this by conforming the will wholly to the moral law. But success in this amounts to 'holiness', a state not attainable in the empirical world, where the senses will always offer temptations to disobey the moral law. If holiness is possible and is required by the moral law, yet is not attainable in this world, it follows that we must entertain the possibility of another dispensation, a non-physical one, where the supreme moral goal of holiness can be reached. 'Thus,' said Kant, 'the highest good is practically possible only on the supposition of the immortality of the soul.'

Similarly, said Kant, it is necessary to postulate the existence of a god to make sense of the idea that virtue will receive its merited reward of happiness. Man is not the cause of nature and he is therefore not able to will that nature should reward the deserving. Given that the idea of moral law requires that such reward should be possible, we have to postulate that there is a being capable of ensuring that merited rewards are enjoyed.

Although these are not proofs of immortality or deity, as Kant readily acknowledged, but only 'postulates' or assumptions required by the idea of morality, nevertheless they can be 'rationally believed'. It takes very little to see why most commentators on Kant do not agree that this is so. We might for example ask, they say, why we cannot think it an obligation to try to attain the highest good without assuming that it has to be attainable. We might think that it is only attainable by a few; or that we might more or less closely approximate it without actually ever attaining it. So much for the need for immortality. As for the need to reward virtue: there are those who hold that virtue is its own reward, and those who think that virtue is still worth pursuing even if there are no guarantees of a reward – so once again the concept of morality does not collapse without the aid of the concept of a deity. On the contrary, the idea that striving for the good, and living according to a best conception of virtue, without the inducement of either guaranteed success or guaranteed rewards, seems to be a finer thing than Kant here offers.

Some find it odd that Kant believed both that religion is harmful to morality, and that nevertheless the concepts of deity and immortality – the two fundamental concepts of religious metaphysics – are required to give morality point. His meaning is that religion, which is the organised worship of a deity and submission to (what priests say is) its will, is harmful to morality; but that the idea that one has an immortal soul which is answerable for everything one does to a supreme judge is, in effect, a useful postulate or fiction for rounding off what one might say to justify morality to any sceptic who asks 'Why should I be moral?' Unfortunately, the idea preserves the kernel of the *argumentum ad baculum* discussed in chapter 4 above, and fails on that account too.

Kant was not a personally religious man, and his 'postulates' for making external sense of morality share the notional, deistic character that (for example) Voltaire's views have. The significant fact is that the content of Kant's moral theory is thoroughly humanistic, in arguing, first, that morality's most fundamental presupposition is the autonomy of the will, meaning that the will obeys laws it imposes on itself and not those prescribed by an outside source such as a deity or sovereign; and second, that the law such a will thus obeys must be shown to be valid on purely formal grounds – as a matter of logic. In this respect Kant's theory is a paradigm of Enlightenment thinking.

The lights

The French term for the Enlightenment means literally 'the lights'. Once they had been switched on, it was impossible for their opponents – chiefly the forces of reaction in Church and state (especially, then, when the latter took the form of an absolute monarch) – to hide in shadow the true nature of their claims to authority. Too many of the shadows were dispelled for that, and although neither religion nor tyranny has since been vanquished, they have at least had to change their grounds – and arguably have suffered diminishment, despite egregious examples of both in the centuries since. Certainly in the century that followed the epoch of Enlightenment, thinking about the good for man proceeded in a significantly different key – a shift that would have been impossible without it.

7

THE CRISIS OF OUTLOOKS

A time of prophets

The nineteenth century was a fertile age for a new breed of prophet, each trying to describe a future that had become open and plastic as a result of the ever-burgeoning consequences, especially in science, of the intellectual revolutions of the preceding centuries. Whereas it had once been possible to believe that the universe and history were both fixed and stable orders, this was emphatically no longer so. The new prophets were thinkers and discoverers who, in highly individual ways, contributed to forging a world view radically different from the one that had been common, in many essentials, to minds as far apart in time as Augustine and Shakespeare, but which since the latter's day had been dwindling in viability despite the best efforts of orthodoxy to preserve it.

The nineteenth century's need to think about possible futures was made especially acute by the important scientific discoveries it witnessed, most notably those of Darwin and his scientific contemporaries, and by the revisionings of the political and ethical possibilities for humanity offered by Mill, Marx, Nietzsche and others – indeed, many others, for a full story of that intellectually dramatic century would have to explore the thought of Herbert Spencer and Auguste Comte, John Henry Newman and Matthew Arnold, Thomas Carlyle and Ralph Waldo Emerson, the German biblical scholars and Walter Pater, the French realist novelists and the Romantic composers, the physicists whose work later made Einstein's theories of relativity possible, the geologists who measured the age of the Earth, and the biologists who reintegrated mankind into the animal creation, to name only a few. Here the task of identifying materials from which ideas about the good life emerged in this epoch is best done by selecting three striking contributions – those made by Darwin, Mill and Nietzsche – and by noting the outlines of the titanic struggle which raged in that century over the fate of the Christian faith.

Darwin and the reinvention of humanity

Charles Darwin is a more important figure than any other seminal thinker of the last two centuries apart from Einstein – and this includes Marx and Freud – because his work has effected a more radical change in human self-perception than anything before it in recorded history. The consequences of it are still, and with increasing significance, infusing themselves into the life of mankind through the biological sciences, most notably in the form of genetic medicine.

Summarily put, before the Darwinian revolution humans thought of themselves as special beings, occupying the summit of a divine creation, which – according to one influential reckoning of the Bible's time scale – occurred about six thousand years ago. After Darwin this perspective became utterly different. Life, he taught us, is the product of long, slow, blind struggles for survival, taking place over aeons. The prior belief that the world was created on a Sunday morning in 4004 BC put mankind (especially, as some in that period believed, white European males) at the top – and not just figuratively speaking – of the tree of nature. Imagine what it felt like to be assured of the truth of this proposition; among many other things it explains the long-standing sources of racism, colonialism, sexism, speciesism and a host of other '-isms' that have bedevilled the history of the last several centuries and now seem intolerable.

But when humans see themselves as an evolving part of a

long and tortuous natural history, as apes who descended from the top of a real tree, intimately close in genetic endowment to other mammals and behaving just like them in conflicts over resources, territory and dominance, they no longer have grounds for quite the same opinion of themselves. From the point of view of ruling hierarchies, the supposed threat to religion is even worse, because nothing has ever been so effective in controlling people than the belief that an invisible policeman is watching them everywhere and always. Darwin's views called all aspects of these beliefs into question.

The truth is, though, that Darwin's revolution would have happened even if there had been no Darwin. He was the right man in the right place at the crucial time; his gifts as an observer and reasoner were by no means incidental to the shape that evolutionary theory took, but if he had not sailed round the world on the *Beagle*, someone else in the scientific circles of the day would, sooner rather than later, have brought those same ideas to light. Someone else almost did: Alfred Russel Wallace, a self-taught naturalist who collected wildlife specimens first in the Amazon basin and then in the East, in the 'land of the orang-utan and the bird of paradise', as he called Malaya in his most famous book. Here he brought to completion the ideas about natural selection that he had long been considering. He sent a letter to scientific colleagues in England outlining his theory – and thereby galvanised Darwin into publishing his own views, which he had been concealing for fear of the public outcry that he rightly expected they would provoke.

To say that Wallace or indeed any other well-placed biologist would have discovered the objective facts about evolution does not belittle Darwin's achievement. After his voyage on the *Beagle*, during which he collected the data that prompted his version of evolutionary theory, Darwin hesitated and fretted many years before publishing it. The facts he had observed plainly indicated evolution, yet to Darwin it felt – as he put it himself – that by publishing the theory he would be 'murdering

God'. When at last *The Origin of Species* appeared he found, as he had guessed, that many others shared that view, and a violent controversy flared. Darwin was ill for much of his life – a tropical illness acquired on the voyage, or anxiety? – and shunned both publicity and conflict. He left the task of championing his views to redoubtable allies, chief among them T. H. Huxley, who easily rebutted critics such as Bishop 'Soapy Sam' Wilberforce. But Darwin's theory hardly needed help: it was its own defence, and it completely redrew mankind's intellectual map.

Many before Darwin had hypothesised that evolution is what explains the emergence of species. Among them was his grandfather Erasmus Darwin, a physician and poet as well as a naturalist, who advanced one of the first formal theories of evolution in his *Zoonomia, or, The Laws of Organic Life*, published in 1796. It premised the idea, elaborated by his grandson sixty years later, that all life evolved from a single common ancestor, forming 'one living filament'. Jean-Baptiste Lamarck, who died in 1829 while Darwin was afloat in the *Beagle*, had arrived at similar ideas, offering a statement of the idea of heredity which, although not now accepted because it hypothesises the heritability of acquired traits, had an important influence on the thinking of nineteenth-century biologists. Darwin wrote of him, 'Lamarck was the first man whose conclusions on the subject excited much attention. This justly celebrated naturalist first published his views in 1801 ... he first did the eminent service of arousing attention to the probability of all changes in the organic, as well as in the inorganic world, being the result of law, and not of miraculous interposition.'

Darwin's own special contribution was to give an account of the *mechanism* by which evolution occurs, namely, 'natural selection', a process involving the success of organisms whose random mutations prove best-adapted to their environments so that they have a better chance than rivals of surviving and procreating, thereby passing on their adaptations. Darwin generalised to all nature the lesson long taught by stockbreeders and pigeon fanciers, who improve breeds by working on the random variations which occur in them. This is artificial selection; Darwin saw that the same process occurs in nature, but as a product of the competition for survival. Even slight advantages confer a better chance of surviving and reproducing; even slight disadvantages typically prove too great. Selection means an increase in frequency of individuals with the successful adaptation, diffusing it through the population until it becomes the average characteristic of the species.

Seeing all life as familially related through a process of 'descent with modification', in which tiny changes accumulate into major divergences between species and genera, thus giving rise to the variety of life – including the extinct life evident in the fossil record – demands thinking in terms of immense tracts of geological time. Controverting the hitherto accepted view of the seventeenth-century Archbishop of Armagh, James Ussher, that the world had come into existence in 4004 BC, Charles Lyell's *Principles of Geology* (1830) settled beyond dispute the great age of the Earth, and gave Darwin the framework required.

Darwin's *Origin of Species* was published in 1859. At a meeting of the British Association at Oxford in the summer of the following year its revolutionary thesis was attacked by the Bishop of Oxford, Samuel Wilberforce, and defended by the naturalist and physician T. H. Huxley. Huxley was one of Darwin's most eloquent and redoubtable defenders, and had a large part in disseminating Darwinism and promoting its acceptance. For that reason he came to be known as 'Darwin's bulldog', which underestimates not only his independent stature as a scientist, but the fact that his astute criticisms of Darwin's views helped the latter improve them. Soon after the *Origin* was published Huxley wrote to Darwin,

I finished your book yesterday...no work on Natural

History Science I have met with has made so great an impression on me & I do most heartily thank you for the great store of new views you have given me ... As for your doctrines I am prepared to go to the Stake if requisite ... I trust you will not allow yourself to be in any way disgusted or annoyed by the considerable abuse and misrepresentation which unless I greatly mistake is in store for you ... And as to the curs which will bark and yelp – you must recollect that some of your friends at any rate are endowed with an amount of combativeness which (though you have often and justly rebuked it) may stand you in good stead – I am sharpening up my claws and beak in readiness.

The debate between Wilberforce and Huxley was a crucial one, for it resulted in an emphatic victory for Darwin's theory and thus for science. Wilberforce's attack took the mistaken form of an attempt to ridicule the idea that mankind is descended from apes. Huxley's defence invoked intellectual responsibility to scientific evidence and logical argument. It was easy enough by that means to vanquish the a priori position adopted by Wilberforce, but Wilberforce's defeat took with it religion's claim that the authority of its dogma should trump the investigations of science. To many commentators, the debate marks the point at which the hitherto rising tide of Victorian evangelicalism began to ebb; even contemporary churchmen recognised the occasion as a signal defeat.

Years later a witness recalled the momentous debate in *Macmillan's Magazine* in these terms:

I was happy enough to be present on the memorable occasion at Oxford when Mr Huxley bearded Bishop Wilberforce. There were so many of us that were eager to hear that we had to adjourn to the great library of the Museum. I can still hear the American accents of Dr

Draper's opening address, when he asked 'Are we a fortu-
itous concourse of atoms?' and his discourse I seem to
remember somewhat dry. Then the Bishop rose, and in a
light scoffing tone, he assured us there was nothing in the
idea of evolution; rock-pigeons were what rock-pigeons
had always been. Then, turning to his antagonist with a
smiling insolence, he begged to know, was it through his
grandfather or his grandmother that he claimed his
descent from a monkey? On this Mr Huxley slowly and
deliberately arose. A slight tall figure stern and pale, very
quiet and very grave, he stood before us, and spoke those
tremendous words – words which no one seems sure of
now, nor I think, could remember just after they were
spoken, for their meaning took away our breath, though
it left us in no doubt as to what it was. He was not
ashamed to have a monkey for his ancestor; but he would
be ashamed to be connected with a man who used great
gifts to obscure the truth. No one doubted his meaning
and the effect was tremendous. One lady fainted and had
to be carried out: I, for one, jumped out of my seat; and
when in the evening we met at Dr Daubeney's, everyone
was eager to congratulate the hero of the day. I remember
that some naive person wished it could come over again;
and Mr Huxley, with the look on his face of the victor
who feels the cost of victory, put us aside saying, 'Once in
a life-time is enough, if not too much.'

Sir Joseph Hooker described Huxley as having 'saved a great
cause from being stifled under misrepresentation and ridicule'
and described how it was Huxley to whom, 'thus marked out
as the champion of the most debatable thesis of evolution ... the
Bishop addressed his sarcasms [asking whether Huxley was
descended from apes on his grandmother's or grandfather's
side], only to meet with a withering retort ... [the] battle over
the "Origin" loomed all the larger in the public eye, because it

was not merely the contradiction of one anatomist by another, but the open clash between Science and the Church.'

The religious crisis

Darwin's views – more accurately, the outcome of work in geology and biology that reached its emblematic point in Darwin's views – would have had a seismic impact on religious belief in the Victorian era even if in other respects the Churches and their various versions of the faith had been enjoying a period of quietness and stability. But the religious outlook was enjoying nothing of the kind: on the contrary, in other ways and as a result of other pressures it was already in profound turmoil.

There were a number of reasons for this. In England, opposing tendencies of activity in the established Church were threatening to pull it apart. On the one hand there was the Tractarian or Oxford movement, which sought to 'renew' the Church of England by reviving certain Roman Catholic practices, and which soon enough led some of its members, most famously John Henry Newman, to the logically inevitable result of converting to Catholicism. On the other hand there was the modernising and quasi-secularising movement represented by the 'Seven Against Christianity', the authors of the controversial *Essays and Reviews* published almost at the same time as Darwin's *Origin* and imbued with a spirit that owed everything to the same legacy of rational enquiry. Moreover, in continental Europe both biblical scholarship and sociological theory were making deep inroads into old certainties – among the most notable of such contributions were Strauss's *Life of Jesus* and Feuerbach's *Essence of Christianity*, both translated into English by George Eliot.

It was not surprising that George Eliot should be the translator of these works. She and her consort G. H. Lewes, an historian of philosophy and disciple of Auguste Comte, are paradigm nineteenth-century secular intellectuals. Long before her distinguished career as a novelist began George Eliot was already the *Westminster Review*'s resident heavyweight, abreast of the latest developments in science and philosophy and a maker of opinion about them. Frederick Myers recalled an evening walk with her in Cambridge during which she made clear to him her perspective:

> she, stirred somewhat beyond her wont, and taking as her text the three words which have been so often used as the inspiring trumpet-calls of men – the words *God, Immortality, Duty* – pronounced, with terrible earnestness, how inconceivable was the *first*, how unbelievable the *second*, and yet how peremptory and absolute the *third*. Never, perhaps, have sterner accents affirmed the sovereignty of impersonal and unrecompensing Law.

These views were inculcated into George Eliot by the transforming experience of reading Charles Hennell's *Inquiry Concerning the Origin of Christianity* in her early twenties. Her brilliant, questing, widely self-educated mind was ripe for Hennell's exacting enquiry, which he had undertaken with the aim of seeing whether it is possible to separate fact from fiction in the gospel accounts. His hope at first was to find by this means a secure basis for the Christian faith; but his scrupulous investigations led him to conclude: 'The true account of the life of Jesus Christ, and of the spread of his religion, [contains] no deviation from the known laws of nature, nor [requires], for their explanation, more than the operation of human motives and feelings.' Naturally enough, Hennell himself, being a man of his time, could not bear to leave the pill so unsweetened. 'Many of the finer thoughts and feelings of mankind find a vent in fiction,' he wrote, 'expressed either by painting, poetry, or the poetic tale; and the perception of historical inaccuracy does not prevent our sharing the thoughts and feelings which have embodied themselves in this manner.' He accordingly recommended that even though we have to free ourselves from belief in the fables that wrap it about – the virgin birth, the resurrection, indeed the whole supernatural framework – we can still regard Christianity as a 'system of elevated thought and feeling'. Later this attitude, shared by many in the nineteenth century, came to be satirised as Moldavianism:

> There was a young man from Moldavia
> Who could not believe in the Saviour
> So he erected instead
> With himself as the head
> The religion of decorous behaviour.

George Eliot became a member of Charles Hennell's circle, and it was this connection that led to her becoming the translator of Strauss's *Leben Jesu*. This seminal work had been written before Hennell's *Inquiry*, but Hennell did not know of it until later. Nevertheless there was such an affinity between the two books that Strauss had the *Inquiry* translated into German, and contributed a preface to it, noting that although the great progress in German biblical scholarship had been unknown to Hennell, who had therefore been obliged to depend upon his own resources, he had independently arrived at much the same critical vantage – a fact that showed how much agreement was produced by unrelated exercises in biblical criticism.

Strauss's *Leben Jesu* is a far broader and more profound work than Hennell's, and is one of the major achievements of the nineteenth-century debate about religion. Strauss had the advantage over Hennell of a half-century of erudite German biblical research to draw upon – the ignorance of George Eliot's Casaubon in *Middlemarch* captures the gulf between the German and English scholarly worlds at the time – and he made excellent use of it. After absorbing surveys of the development of religious thought and the history of biblical scholarship, Strauss offered his conclusion about how the Bible is to be interpreted, namely, as myth. For example, the scriptural stories of miracles, designed to establish that Jesus was indeed endowed with divine authority, are not to be thought of as deliberate fictions or exaggerations of natural events, but as imaginative symbols, expressing the feelings and hopes of the people who recounted them from tradition, usually some length of time after the miracles had supposedly occurred. Myths come naturally as a way of expressing religious sentiment, especially for people living in historical periods when superstitious attitudes and scientific ignorance are jointly prevalent, working together to make it seem obvious that almost everything that happens in the world is the work of gods. The modern distinction between fact and fiction, prosaic truth and poetic fancy, was not known in earlier periods, Strauss argued, and this explains how religious traditions began.

At the end of his book Strauss acknowledges that his conclusions must pain many to whom it would seem that 'the boundless store of truth and life which for eighteen centuries has been the aliment of humanity, seems irretrievably dissipated; the most sublime levelled with the dust, God divested of his grace, man of his dignity, and the tie between heaven and earth broken'. Unable, like Hennell, to leave his readers in this pass, Strauss resorted to saying that, nevertheless, Christianity has a philosophic although not a literal truth, which is in essence the same as the insights of Hegel. (Few of his English readers would have been much comforted by this claim.)

Several years later George Eliot translated Feuerbach's *Essence of Christianity*, and there found an attitude still more appealing to her own outlook. Instead of trying to salvage something elevating from the wreck of Christianity, as Hennell and Strauss had done, Feuerbach argued that it distracts attention from the real task in life, which is to focus upon helping one's fellow men and improving the world. While George Eliot was in the process of translating the *Essence* she wrote to a friend, 'Heaven help us! said the old religion; the new one, from its very lack of faith, will teach us all the more to help one another.' The sentiment is pure Feuerbach.

Marx described Feuerbach's work as 'the dissolution of the religious world into its secular basis'. The remark exactly summarises Feuerbach's view:

> He who says of me that I am an atheist says and knows nothing of me. The question as to the existence or non-existence of God, the opposition between theism and atheism, belongs to the sixteenth and seventeenth centuries, but not to the nineteenth. I deny God. But that means for me that I deny the negation of man. In place of the illusory, fantastic, heavenly position of man which in actual life necessarily leads to the degradation of man, I substitute the tangible, actual, and consequently also the political and social position of mankind.

To Feuerbach is owed the thesis that religion makes man 'alienate' himself from himself, by worshipping a ghost he has himself created. Rather than attributing love, justice and wisdom to this projected fiction, man should see that these concepts apply to the best of himself. Religion turns everything on its head by pointing the good things towards a transcendent abstraction, said Feuerbach, whereas they really belong to mankind, at least in potential. We have only to 'invert the religious relations...to destroy the illusion, and the unclouded light of truth streams in upon us'.

The joint effect of these influences on George Eliot's thought was to bring her to a view of the good life that she made central to writing:

> My books have for their main bearing a conclusion [she wrote to a correspondent] without which I could not have cared to write any representation of human life –

namely, that the fellowship between man and man which
has been the principle of development, social and moral,
is not dependent on conceptions of what is not man: and
the idea of God, so far as it has been a high spiritual influence, is the ideal of a goodness entirely human (i.e. an
exaltation of the human).

Such is one, although highly intelligent, nineteenth-century
view formed on the back of the revolution in science and
scholarship that made it impossible, without a deliberate choice
to ignore the evidence and the arguments thus provided, to see
the world in anything like the medieval way. As an expression
of a basis for thinking about the good life it is, as George Eliot's
very choice of terminology shows, a repeated statement of the
humanist outlook as here understood.

Although George Eliot's conception of the good life encapsulates the nineteenth century's best thinking about the matter,
it was left to the century's philosophers to try to state an explicitly practicable version of it. The chief of them in England were
Bentham and Mill.

Utility and Liberty

Jeremy Bentham bridged the eighteenth and nineteenth centuries with his giant appetite to reform the world, his secular
rationalism, and his amazing combination of impossible ideal-
ism and practical realism. He was determined to find solutions
to humanity's problems, and turned his hand to many schemes
in pursuit of that end, from outlining systems of legislation to
designing star-shaped prisons (the latter so that a single guard at
the building's centre could see down all its radiating arms; he
called such structures 'panopticons'). He believed in benevolence and truth, and had no time for poetry and religion. His
dismissal of the latter was fuelled in part by the fact that evan-
gelical Christians of his day were apt to preach that poverty was

ordained by God and therefore the poor must submit with patience – 'Their situation, with all its evils, is better than they have deserved at the hands of God,' wrote one. Such views enraged Bentham. He thought that the catechism of the Church of England taught children insincerity by making them promise what they did not understand, particularly as regards unintelligible things such as 'the devil and all his works' – 'Who, or what is he, and how is he renounced?' Bentham asked – and the fables of Christ's birth and death.

Bentham's robust dismissal of Christianity was an aspect of his desire to state a practical, down-to-earth ethical view that anyone could understand and apply. He took the 'first law of nature' to be the wish for happiness, to which the voices of prudence and benevolence jointly add: 'Seek the happiness of others; seek your own happiness in the happiness of others.' Happiness, in turn, is to be understood as the enjoyment of pleasure and the exemption from pain. Virtue is whatever maximises pleasure and minimises pain. The moral task facing us therefore is, in Bentham's view, to weigh the consequences of our actions, in order to estimate the value of pleasures and pains they will be likely to produce. He went so far as to suggest that a 'felicific calculus' could be devised to help in the reckoning of pleasures and pains, measuring them according to such properties as their intensity, duration and fruitfulness. 'Nature has placed mankind under the governance of two sovereign masters, pain and pleasure,' he wrote; 'it is for them alone to point out what we ought to do, as well as to determine what we shall do.'

Impelled by his philanthropic desire to make the world a better place on rational principles, Bentham did not pause to consider that not all of the rest of mankind might share his benevolent impulses, nor to ask how, in the absence of a guarantee that they will do so, it is possible to infer that everyone should promote general happiness on the basis of the fact that they wish their own happiness.

The thrust of Bentham's views was adopted and, with greater nuance and subtlety, adapted by the outstanding figure in nineteenth-century English philosophy, John Stuart Mill. Mill was the son of Bentham's chief colleague and coadjutor, James Mill, who gave his son such a rigorous education – the younger Mill was reading Greek and Latin at an age before other children go to school – as almost to induce a complete mental breakdown by the time he reached early adulthood. His extraordinary *Autobiography* tells us that he began the study of Greek aged three, and within five years had read Herodotus, Xenophon, Lucian and Isocrates – and (a poignant touch) 'some of Diogenes Laertius'. He was studying Aristotle's logic by the age of thirteen, and soon thereafter was engaged in a complete course of study in political economy. Every morning before breakfast he went for a walk with his father during which, consulting his notes, he recounted his previous day's studies. He did not regard himself as especially clever, and therefore took his education to be proof that any child could learn what he had learned, and at as early an age.

The effects of a rigorous home education, without the benefit of other children for fellowship, gave his nervous breakdown at the age of twenty the form of 'dry heavy dejection', as he put it, in which he was 'left stranded, at the commencement of my voyage, with a well equipped ship and rudder, but no sail; without any real desire for the ends which I had so carefully been fitted out to work for; no delight in virtue or the general good, but also just as little in anything else'. He was rescued by reading Marmontel and Wordsworth, both of whom taught him the profound importance of the emotions even to reason:

> What made Wordsworth's poems a medicine for my state of mind was that they expressed, not mere outward beauty, but states of feeling, and of thought coloured by feeling, under the excitement of beauty. They seemed to

be the very culture of the feelings, which I was in quest of... From them I learned what would be the perennial source of happiness, when all the greater evils of life shall have been removed. And I felt myself at once better and happier as I came under their influence... the cultivation of the feelings became one of the cardinal points in my ethical and philosophical creed.

These remarks provide one source of evidence about Mill's conception of the good life. Another comes from what he had to say about Harriet Taylor, the woman he loved from the age of twenty-four until his death. She was another man's wife, but her husband was obliging; Mill was permitted to stay with her when Mr Taylor was away on business, and she spent summer weekends with him. Their relationship seems, however, to have been entirely platonic, and remained so when at last they could marry after Mr Taylor's demise. They both stated in writing the reason for the chaste character of their relationship: it was that neither of them liked sex.

Mill and Harriet Taylor were co-workers as well as partners. Mill said that most of his major works were written with her co-operation, or at very least her advice and guidance. She confirmed him in his feminist principles (he had them before he met her), and represented his ideal of 'the most admirable kind of human being', namely, one who is generous, modest, simple and sincere, who loves learning, is passionate about justice, and burningly indignant about brutality and tyranny.

In his ethical theory Mill adhered to the basic principles of the utilitarian philosophy of Bentham and James Mill, the chief principle of which is that goodness is whatever produces the greatest happiness of the greatest number. And like Bentham and his father he retained a lifelong and 'deeply rooted trust in the general progress of the human race'. But although he believed that Bentham was right in essentials – 'There is hardly anything positive in Bentham's philosophy which is not true,' he wrote – he recognised that the great reformer's philosophical vision was profoundly flawed because it left out so much of importance to human life. The source of the flaw was Bentham's sheer inexperience:

> He never knew poverty and adversity, passion nor satiety: he never had even the experience which sickness gives; he lived from childhood to eighty-five in boyish health. He knew no dejection, no heaviness of heart. He never felt life a sore and weary burthen. He was a boy to the last. Self-consciousness, that daemon of the men of genius of our time, from Wordsworth to Byron, from Goethe to Chateaubriand, and to which this age owes so much both of its cheerful and its mournful wisdom, never was awakened in him. How much of human nature slumbered in him he knew not, neither can we know ... Knowing so little of human feelings, he knew still less of the influences by which those feelings are formed: all the more subtle workings both of the mind upon itself, and of external things on the mind, escaped him.

This is why, Mill concluded, Bentham never recognised that man is 'a being capable of pursuing perfection as an end; of desiring, for its own sake, the conformity of his character to his standard of excellence, without hope of good, or fear of evil, from other source than his own inward consciousness'. Bentham had justified the principle of utility on the ground that pain and pleasure are the two governors of human existence, but this was too crude an account for Mill: 'Human beings', he wrote, 'are not governed in all their actions by their worldly interests.'

The strength of Mill's views in these respects derives from the fact that his copious output of work covers a large range in philosophy and the social sciences. He wrote, among other things, about logic, mathematics, and the philosophy of science, about moral philosophy, about political economy, about representative government, about the place of women in society, about religion, and about socialism. From this rich background his significant nuancing and deepening of utilitarian ethics flowed. As noted, he remained committed to the maximisation of utility as the ultimate principle of morality, and he accepted Bentham's view that the good that the principle of utility seeks to maximise is happiness, defined as pleasure and exemption from pain. And he took it that the fundamental evidence that it is right to identify happiness, thus conceived, as the good, is that people actually desire it. To the objection that people desire many things other than happiness Mill answered that everything people desire is desirable because it brings happiness with it; it is, he said, impossible to desire something unless the idea of it is in some degree pleasurable. His most careful statement of this idea is this: 'Whatever is desired otherwise than as a means to some end beyond itself, and ultimately to happiness, is desired as itself a part of happiness, and is not desired for itself until it has become so.'

As Mill's quoted remarks suggest, his notion of happiness – pleasure without pain – as the goal of life, reminiscent as it is of Epicurus, is not the simple, quantifiable emotion that it seems to be in Bentham's view. What mattered to Mill was not the mere quantity but the quality of happiness, and he saw the quality of happiness as the product of a wide diversity of activities, states, relationships and aspirations, of the kind he had been taught to value by Wordsworth, Marmontel and Harriet Taylor. But this aspect of Mill's theory gave him difficulty, because it is impossible to avoid the elitist-sounding conclusion that some pleasures are of higher value than others (reading Aeschylus versus drinking a beer, say), and moreover that some people are better able to appreciate the higher pleasures – and, symmetrically, more likely to suffer because of their sensitivity – than others. 'Few human creatures would consent to be changed into any of the lower animals, for a promise of the fullest allowance of a beast's pleasures,' wrote Mill; 'no intelligent human being would consent to be a fool, no instructed person would be an ignoramus, no person of feeling and conscience would be selfish and base, even though they should be persuaded that the fool, the dunce, or the rascal is better satisfied with his lot than they are with theirs.'

Who is to tell which pleasures are higher than others? Mill answers, 'competent judges'. The man who has both read Aeschylus and drunk beer is in a better position to judge than he who has only drunk beer. But what if the man who has done both prefers drinking beer? And who is to say that the pleasure of the non-Aeschylus-reading beer drinker is any less, and not perhaps more, than that of the Aeschylus reader, on a Benthamite calculation of the quantity of pleasure? One has to accept two things in order to be comfortable with Mill's view: first, that some people have higher faculties than others, which make them better judges of the value of different pleasures; and second, that some pleasures have objectively more or less value than others. Both points may well be true, but it is at least contentious to say so. Mill was not, however, an elitist of an unrecoverable kind; he believed that anyone is capable of cultivating the 'higher faculties' and thus of living the best life in the best way.

As these points show, Mill introduced an important rider to the utility principle, which is that considerations of individual cultivation matter as much as the promotion of the greatest happiness for the greatest number, and ultimately form part of it. Two points arise in connection with this. One concerns the relation between the individual and society, and especially the need for the right kind of social setting for the moral life. Here Mill was led to a criticism of his eighteenth-century forerunners, namely, that they did not appreciate how important it is for members of a society to develop restraint, a shared allegiance to shared values, and a 'principle of cohesion', which jointly would make for a stable framework within which the moral sentiments can flourish. In throwing off the old framework of discipline and cohesion without replacing it with a new one, he thought, the Enlightenment moralists had invited the excesses of the French Revolution. But in its turn a society's institutions must protect the rights of its members, and ensure justice among them; indeed justice 'is a name for certain classes of moral rules, which concern the essentials of human well-being more nearly, are therefore a more absolute obligation, than any other rules for the guidance of life'. A just society, accordingly, will be a moral one.

The other point concerns individuals as such, and in particular the importance of individual liberty in the good life. One of Mill's most famous works is the essay in which he sets out this view: his *On Liberty*. If the best life is the happy life, and happiness is pleasure, and the best pleasures are those that are appreciated by man's higher faculties, and if anyone can develop the higher faculties, then it is essential to the best life that everyone should be at liberty to develop those faculties, and to seek the pleasures that will reward their exercise. There are many such faculties and many such pleasures, and no one can prescribe in advance what any individual might discover in the cultivation of his own talents and interest. For that reason, individual liberty is essential. Indeed it is a fundamental right, Mill argued, and therefore imposes an absolute restraint on political power:

> The only purpose for which power can be rightfully exercised over any member of a civilised community, against his will, is to prevent harm to others. His own good, either physical or moral, is not a sufficient warrant. He cannot rightfully be compelled to do or forbear because it will be better for him to do so, because it will make him happier, because, in the opinion of others, to do so would be wise, or even right.

In a society that observes this principle people can explore a diversity of lifestyles and goals, and from this will flow creativity, the exercise of talents, and progress both in moral and intellectual respects. Mill summarised his argument in *On Liberty* as affirming 'a single truth... the importance, to man and society, of a large variety of types of character, and giving full freedom to human nature to expand itself in innumerable and conflicting directions... The grand, leading principle, towards which every argument in these pages directly converges, is the absolute and essential importance of human development in its richest variety.'

But Mill warned that liberty of thought, expression and lifestyle are threatened not only by political tyranny, but by the tyranny of majorities. 'If the American form of democracy overtakes us first,' he commented, 'the majority will no more relax their despotism than a single despot would'; and the despotism in such a case would be that of 'collective mediocrity'. But that is not a reason to be anti-democratic; rather, it is a warning to take care to construct a democracy that will fully safeguard individual and minority rights. 'Our only chance is to come forward as liberals, carrying out the democratic idea, and not as conservatives, resisting it,' he wrote; and offered various proposals about how such a democracy might be constructed on the basis of proportional representation and equal rights for women. Above all, the institutions of society must be so organised as not to quell the free play of thought and freedom for individuals to make experiments in styles of life.

A state of things in which a large portion of the most active and inquiring intellects find it advisable to keep their general principles and the grounds of their convictions within their own breasts, and attempt, in what they address to the public, to fit as much of what they can of their own conclusions to premises which they have internally renounced, cannot send forth the open, fearless characters, and logical, consistent intellects who once adorned the thinking world.

This is a pointed passage; his remark about the 'premises which they have internally renounced' was intended to apply directly to Christianity and its morality, which he described as 'incomplete and one-sided'. Other ideas and feelings are needed for the truly good life, he said: magnanimity, high-mindedness, a sense of honour and personal dignity, a sense of duty to one's fellow men without thought of reward – in short, the 'pagan' virtues of antiquity.

The revaluation of values

Mill's thought is instinct with liberality and humanity, and it is significant to note that even though his philosophical writings are on the whole restrained and largely impersonal in manner, their content owes much to his sensitivity to the central importance of *feeling* to the good life. Even so, there could not on the face of it seem to be a greater contrast between the English proprieties of Mill's thought and the emphatic, idiosyncratic, dramatic outlook of Friedrich Nietzsche, one of the nineteenth century's most startling intellects.

Yet they are both products of that same century, both inheritors of the changes that led to it, and both passionately concerned to identify and describe the best life. And there are significant points of contact, despite the great difference in manner of expression. Mill rejoiced in poetry, Nietzsche in music. Mill realised through poetry the indispensability of emotion to the cultivation of the self; Nietzsche wrote, 'Without music life would be a mistake.' He was an accomplished pianist, and auditors of his playing admired his skill at improvisation. He composed also, and once claimed that a piece he had written early in life closely anticipated *Parsifal*, the creation of his friend and idol Richard Wagner, whom later he came to attack bitterly.

Mill and Nietzsche also shared a belief in the idea of exceptional individuals. Nietzsche's 'Superman' ideal is a familiar feature of his thought, even in caricature. It is a more decided notion than Mill's picture of a refined, reflective and high-feeling Aristotelian 'great soul', but the similarity is there, and the ideal of such an individual is required by each of their respective ethical outlooks.

Nietzsche's views at first seem shocking, because he attacked traditional morality and especially Christianity, and described himself as an 'immoralist'. Traditional morality, he argued, 'negates life'. His principal reason is that it requires people to be conformists and mediocrities, to live a life of avoidance – avoidance of suffering, and of risk – and to value safety, submission, and the small rewards given to compliant members of the aggregate. It is 'herd morality'. True morality requires 'overcoming' this impoverishing morality, and the first step in doing so is to understand how this impoverishing morality arose. In a way characteristic of his philosophical method, Nietzsche does this by sketching a 'genealogy' of morals, that is, a conceptual history of how notions of virtue, duty and value developed.

The concept of the good originated in antiquity as descriptive of the nobles who then ruled society, Nietzsche argued. They called themselves 'good' and 'virtuous' to distinguish themselves from the common people they governed: the inferior or simple folk and slaves. At this point the ideas of superior and inferior, good and simple, carried no evaluatory connotations, any more than did the notions of noble and common – like these latter they just denoted rank. But they acquired evaluatory significance in the now familiar sense of herd morality, said Nietzsche, when a 'slave revolt' occurred, prompted by resentment on the part of the weak, who in self-defence inverted the qualities associated with power into evils, and elevated their own experiences of dispossession, impotence, suffering and meekness into virtues.

The inversion effected by this revolt explains Nietzsche's ideal of the 'Superman'. This is the noble-minded individual who, in overthrowing the herd morality's pieties and life-denying inhibitions in order to live passionately and supremely, is harking back to the noble origins of the good. Nietzsche saw slave morality as rooted in the suffering of the Jews in exile, an experience that at length gave rise to the 'Beatitudes' of the Sermon on the Mount. A crucial aspect of Christian morality, the Beatitudes tell the feeble, the fearful, and those who weep and mourn that they are the good and will inherit the Kingdom. Nietzsche was contemptuous of this view, which he saw as profoundly undermining the quality of human life. Instead of thinking in these terms, he proclaimed, man should 'overcome himself' by expunging the weaknesses in his nature and aspiring to live heroically, powerfully and positively.

Nietzsche characterised his view as 'Dionysian' in allusion to the two fundamental principles he saw in Greek culture: the analytic, formal, rational 'Apollonian' principle, and the ecstatic, enthusiastic, instinctual 'Dionysian' principle. Whereas sculpture is the paradigmatic Apollonian art, based essentially on form and structure, music is paradigmatically the Dionysian art, speaking immediately to the deepest instincts. The Dionysian ethical ideal is one of affirmation of life, a great 'Yes!', even in the face of difficulties and sorrows. The one who cries 'Yes!' is the Superman – Nietzsche's own term is *Ubermensch*, literally 'overman' – characterised in Nietzsche's strange and powerful *Thus Spake Zarathustra*. The notion of the book is that the prophet Zarathustra (Zoroaster), having made the 'calamitous' mistake of introducing slave morality into the world, is returning to put things right. He announces that 'God is dead', and that humankind has now to strive towards its proper goal, which is to become a higher type of being, the *Ubermensch*; and that it has to do this by 'overcoming' itself, by asserting the 'will to mastery' or 'will to power', which is the fundamental life-affirming drive (sometimes Nietzsche suggests that it is the fundamental life force in all things).

In this connection Nietzsche introduces his concept of 'eternal recurrence', the idea that everything that happens will happen over and over again, repeatedly without end. This is not supposed to be a metaphysical doctrine about the nature of history or the world, but a heuristic device to illustrate the idea of self-overcoming to achieve *Ubermensch* status, thus: suppose you were told that you had to live your life over and over again endlessly. Would you rejoice or despair? If you lived as an *Ubermensch* does, you would rejoice. Nietzsche's moral ideal can accordingly be expressed as *the affirmation of eternal recurrence*. One who accepts the idea of recurrence with joy is one who loves the life he has forged for himself, even those aspects of it which forced him to struggle and suffer in the process of his self-overcoming.

The optimism and affirmation of nineteenth-century secular thought had, however, a powerful rival, born of the partial retreat of religion which secularism had forced. New gods were in process of being invoked: the nation, the race, military might, empire. Allowed to grow and thrive in the wealth and relative peace of the late Victorian age, these monsters were ready for birth in the womb of Europe as the twentieth century opened. They seemed for a time to obliterate the liberal optimism of Mill, and to give a sinister twist to the energetic individualism of Nietzsche; but both views have proved more resilient than seemed possible when these new gods first took power.

8

THE REDISCOVERY OF ETHICS

The shameful twentieth century

Moving from the history of ideas to more recent ethical concerns, we think with special shame of the twentieth century, which was bloody and brutal beyond imagination. The number of the dead in war, atrocity, and man-induced famine, of refugees, of orphans and mourners, is huge, and each of them accuses the rest of us for the failure of humanity that led to their suffering. The clamour of so many victims, demanding notice and remembrance and a guarantee that such things will never happen again, so deafens the survivors – us – that sometimes we hear only silence. It makes us think that we live in an age that is morally peculiar, and, in searching for reasons, some among us too readily scapegoat the very things discussed in preceding chapters: the Enlightenment, science, the loss of religion, and the 'philosophers of suspicion' (such as Marx and Nietzsche) who attacked and destroyed conventional morality. Such is the revulsion we feel at our age that reaction to it has varied from unvarnished pessimism about the moral future of humankind, to a desperate return to ancient faiths. Philosophy – by the twentieth century a fully professionalised pursuit, whose critics accuse it of being insulated in the academy, its salaried votaries teaching a curriculum made highly selective by the need to prepare young people for examinations within three years, the votaries themselves jostling for preferment and reputation by publishing scholastic superfluities of intricate jargon and technical refinement of use to no one but at best a few colleagues –

not only had little to say for most of the century, but in some influential quarters, notably English-speaking analytic philosophy, explicitly repudiated any responsibility for such saying. Its excuse was to say that philosophy's purpose is not to tell people what is right and what their obligations are, but to analyse – in microscopic detail – the concepts of 'right' and 'obligation' abstractly considered; to examine – with technical minuteness – the logic of 'practical reasoning', not least to determine whether prescriptive statements can be deduced from descriptive ones; and to expose by careful and circumstantial criticism the deficiencies of other and earlier ethical theories. Academic philosophers thus appeared to make themselves irrelevant to the great practical questions of ethics at the precise time that these were most pressing. Their real reason for doing so, said their critics, was – *pace* their nice justifications – timidity well justified by incapacity.

The twentieth century's moral horrors are staggering; but the truth is that the only really different thing about them, in historical terms, is their scale. Humans have throughout history committed mass murder, pogroms, exterminations, cruelties and barbarisms. Since the nineteenth century the technology for doing so on increasingly massive scales has developed at a frightening rate. The straws were in the wind as early as the American Civil War, and should have been learned – but were not – by the First World War, whose recipes for butchery included such traditional fare as infantry advancing, at walking pace in line abreast, towards such untraditional things as machine guns. The novelties also included the high-explosive shells dropping on them and the poison gas enveloping them. By the end of the Second World War even these innovations were outdated, for the age of weapons of mass destruction had dawned, along with long-distance missiles and the involvement of civilian populations in the front lines of violence.

It might be thought that even these facts about the advance of technology, for all the tens of millions thus killed, would not alone have given the century its special character of vileness. For that, so this thought might go, Hitler and Stalin and Pol Pot were required. Gas chambers for mass exterminations, machine-gunning and torching of kulak villages, slaughter of whole populations – all in the various names of ideology, racial hatred, or political purification, and all on a grand scale – add a dimension to the moral history of the century that previous centuries could not match. But if the point here seems to be that the twentieth century is morally special in its horror because of an historically unique concomitance of evil leaders, then the previous point is being misunderstood. The truth is that there have always been Hitlers and Stalins, in the form of various tribal chiefs, emperors, kings, popes and generals, in all periods of history; it is just that they lacked the means of their twentieth-century avatars to commit mass murder on a scale they could only dream about. If the atom bomb had been available in the fifth century BC, it would have been dropped. If Zyklon B had been available in the tenth century AD, it would have been used. If anything, the fact that most of history's genocides and atrocities have been committed with the sword, spear, axe, stones, wooden clubs, fire and rope, merely iterates the same horror, and not one whit more comfortably.

Those who think that modern times are wickeder than previous times are apt to identify the cause as the weakening of a sense of moral law, associated with the departure of religious traditions of morality as a social influence. Not everyone who takes this view is an apologist for these latter; what they regret is the passing of a culture of moral concern which, they believe, religious traditions once helped to foster. Such views give comfort to apologists for religion, who fasten on the implication that to revive a culture of moral concern people must be encouraged back into churches. But this reprises the usual muddle that getting people to accept as true (whether literally or in some unexplained higher metaphorical sense) such propositions as that at a certain historical point a virgin gave birth, that the laws of nature were arbitrarily suspended so that, for example, water turned into wine, that several corpses came to life (and so forth), will somehow give them a logical reason for living morally (according to the attached view of what is moral – e.g. not marrying if you can help it, not divorcing if you do, and so forth again). It is scarcely needful to repeat that the morality and the metaphysics here separately at stake do not justify or even need one another, and that the moral questions require to be grounded and justified on their own merits in application to what they concern, namely, the life of human beings in their social setting. That is the lesson taught by all the enlightenments of the Western tradition and their chief thinkers from Socrates to Nietzsche; and no argument or evidence has ever been able to confute them.

What this means is that promoting moral sensibility requires the continued humanisation of ethics – which means: rooting it securely in human needs and values. This is a task that requires reflection and continual negotiation; it is always a tentative, exploratory process, aimed at making the best of the sense of moral identity each individual implicitly has, and at exploiting properly the human responses, especially sympathy. These responses can fail, not least when insufficient moral imagination is brought into play – which shows how vital is the cultivation at both the social and personal levels of a capacity for moral imagination which works with the grain of human nature.

From evil to good

It is always a mistake to underestimate how long it takes for mankind to understand the traumas it has suffered, especially the self-inflicted ones. In the half-century since the end of the Second World War the facts of the Nazi attempt to exterminate Europe's Jews have become a matter of detailed knowledge, and the massive body of historical data relating to it has received meticulous analysis by scholars. So vast an event as the organised murder of millions, carried out on an industrial scale, is impossible to hide. The perpetrators' perverse sense of order, and the many witnesses and survivors inevitably left by a project of such ambition, have together worked to keep the evidence in existence. That is one reason why revisionist attempts to persuade us that the Holocaust did not happen, or was 'not as bad as is claimed', are futile: the mountain of facts is as huge as the event it records.

Yet in some ways the psychological task of grasping the Holocaust is made not easier but harder by the systematic analysis of the facts. The more we know, down to details of individual men on specifiable dates in precise locations shooting or gassing to death other human beings – men and women, the elderly, children, babies too small to walk; in dozens, or hundreds, or thousands – the more our sense of moral perplexity and disorientation grows, and our revulsion and pity interfere with the task of comprehension. Almost all commentators agree that one thing at least is clear: that the human community has to keep working hard at severing the Hydra's heads of racism, ethnic nationalism, and cultural and religious bitterness that everywhere relentlessly threaten. In the period since the Holocaust exactly the same dangers have continued to lurk, and even the same monstrosities occur, only on scales which do not quite compare with what happened under Hitler.

This is why – so optimists point out – the human rights movement exists, with its development of conventions having in many jurisdictions the force of law, spanning the range of human vulnerabilities and interests in an endeavour to protect the former and enhance the latter – and why there is a developing international criminal jurisdiction, with an international criminal court empowered to enforce the conventions agreed by the member states of the United Nations. To critics, the fact that the history of human rights endeavours, and the founding of an international criminal court, are stuttering and stumbling affairs, is taken as a troubling sign of mankind's short memory and blind self-interest – a shortness of memory and a blindness that even so gross an insult to humanity as the Holocaust seems unable to overcome. Optimists naturally see matters differently: in the longer view of history, they say, the fact that the United Nations Declaration of Human Rights came as an immediate response to the Holocaust, and that the International Criminal Court came into existence a mere half-century after the United Nations itself, are positive signs.

Yet it takes a continuing act of recall to keep the need for these developments at the forefront of moral concern. Here is one such act of recall. When Adolf Eichmann visited the death camp at Chelmno, where victims were gassed in sealed trucks, he found himself unable to watch the proceedings. 'I didn't stay to watch the whole manoeuvre. I couldn't stand the screams...I fled. I jumped into the car and for a long time I couldn't open my mouth.' Later he attended a mass execution in Minsk. 'My knees turned to water,' he said, recalling how he had seen a woman throw her arms out behind her as she was shot. 'I had to leave.' He went to Auschwitz. 'I preferred not to watch the way they asphyxiated people...They burned the corpses on a gigantic iron grille...I couldn't stand it; I was overcome with nausea.' And Eichmann reports that he was not alone among high Nazi officials who responded in this way. Himmler visited a death camp to inspect it, and had to leave; 'He lost his nerve,' Eichmann says.

Remember who Eichmann was. He was the self-styled 'Jewish specialist' in charge of Gestapo Department IV B4 for Jewish Affairs, responsible for keeping the trains moving across Europe to the death camps of the Final Solution. It is a ghastly fact that he could not bear personal witness to the mass murder he orchestrated. Grant that he was somehow incapable of imagining it from the quiet of his office; why did he not, when he saw what it meant in reality, cry out in pity and horror, 'Stop it! No more!' He merely fled, and let it continue. What explains such moral perversion?

That is one of the questions posed by Tzvetan Todorov in his powerful and thought-provoking book *Facing the Extreme* about life in the concentration camps. His question comes couched in a larger aim, which is to see the death camps of Nazism and the slave camps of the Soviet gulag as a magnifying mirror reflecting the moral character of man, in which one can witness, with an often burning clarity etched by the extremity of the circumstances they imposed, the nature of good and evil. Primo Levi, writing of Auschwitz, said that 'fundamental values, even if they are not positive, can be deduced from this particular world', and Todorov takes the remark as his cue, examining the moral universe of the camps to bring central questions of morality more sharply into focus.

It is a commonplace that the degradation of life in the camps turned people into animals. Victims themselves said so. Tadeusz Borowski, who survived Auschwitz only to kill himself in 1951, said that war utterly abolishes notions of humanity; 'there is no crime a man will not commit to save himself'. In the same vein Levi wrote that the struggle to survive in the camps was 'without respite, because everyone was desperately and ferociously alone ... It was necessary to throttle all dignity and kill all conscience, to climb down into the arena as a beast against other beasts ... it was a war of everyone against everyone else.' The Hobbesian terror of this debased existence was the consequence of conscious design: the oppressors stripped their victims naked, left them to live in their own filth and excrement, starved them, turned them into competitors for scraps of food, denuded them of their names and identities. Under such treatment, in such extremity, how could the camps not be nightmares of hell, in which the very idea of morality loses all content?

And yet, as Todorov shows, the reverse is true. In the camps there were acts of kindness, heroism, love and succour of the most moving kinds. The physician Ena Weiss, even though she claimed that her personal philosophy for surviving the camps was

'Me first, me second, me third – and then me again', spent every day helping others, at great personal cost. Robert Antelme, a survivor of Buchenwald, described a man and his son 'hungry together... offering each other their bread with loving eyes'.

Two theses are suggested by Todorov's examination of accounts given by survivors of camp life. The first is that survivors generally paint a bleaker picture of camp morality than the facts support. One reason is that they need to emphasise negative aspects of their experience because that is what made it unique – that is what specifies the absolute difference between camp experience and ordinary life. But another and perhaps deeper reason is that it expresses their remorse, even guilt, at having escaped while so many others died.

The second thesis follows from the first. It is that the survival of moral life in the extreme horrors of the camps disproves the view that morality is a thin, conventional, easily dislodged veneer on human life. It shows instead that morality is natural, a firm property of human social existence, which can only be distorted or obliterated in very extreme circumstances: it takes beatings, terror, humiliation, imprisonment, starvation, cold, suffering, misery, loss of hope and identity, to root it out – and even then it is not rooted out completely, or from everyone. That is a magnificently hopeful fact.

What these desperate yet optimistic themes confirm again is something that we all wish and need to believe: that moral heroism is no fiction, and that humans can cling to their humanity in the very worst of times, and survive. For if this is true in the extreme case, then it is excellent news for ordinary times, and the prospect in them of a good life for mankind.

The return of ethical concern: the example of medical ethics

A distinctive feature of the second half of the twentieth century is the proliferation of what, in the jargon of these things, are called 'discourses' of special ethical concern – medical ethics, business ethics, environmental ethics, and discussions about animal rights not least among them. These areas of debate did not put out their green leaves from the desiccated earth of academic philosophy, but from a felt need for examination of how we are to conduct ourselves in a rapidly changing and complexifying world, where advances in technology seem to outrun our opportunities to incorporate them appropriately and reflectively into our lives.

Medical ethics is a good example of this development. Some writers on medical ethics observe that until quite recently the two ethical injunctions by which medical practitioners lived were: do not advertise, and do not have sexual relations with your patients. There was, of course, an adherence, at least implicitly, to the professional code suggested by the Hippocratic ideal, which enjoined confidentiality and required the practitioner to cure where possible but to avoid doing harm at least. In that ideal the focus of attention is the relationship between practitioner and patient, and that of course remains so in the much more extensive set of considerations that now constitute medical ethics. In these, the questions about the practitioner–patient relationship are more complex and diverse. They concern patients' rights, their consent to treatment, the practitioner's duty to tell patients the truth, the degree to which paternalism is justified, and how the practitioner is to decide in cases of divided loyalties – as when public-health considerations arise, or when a patient would be suitable as an experimental subject in testing an important new treatment. From the beginning of life to its end – from abortion and withholding treatment from severely deformed neonates, to difficulties about providing the elderly with life-sustaining treatment, and on to euthanasia – ethical dilemmas multiply and press.

The ethical nightmares of contemporary technologised medicine were first prompted by the introduction of life-support systems and kidney-dialysis machines. Given that the number of dialysis machines was, in the early days, far outstripped by the number of patients needing them, committees had to be established to choose who would receive treatment. That difficult task was made harder by the result of early studies showing that the patients chosen for treatment tended to resemble the committee members themselves in respect of social and educational profile. Life-support technology introduced a related dilemma that is now distressingly familiar: as many much-publicised cases have shown, for patients in a persistent vegetative state the question of when life-support should be ended – and of who has the right to decide – is hard to answer, and still sometimes has to be settled on a case–by–case basis in courts of law.

Indeed, the medical profession finds itself confronted by thorny problems on almost every front. In paediatrics, neurology and psychiatry, practitioners find themselves dealing with patients who are not competent to participate in decisions about their own treatment. In all aspects of reproductive medicine there are familiar but very hard choices about fertility, surrogacy, parenthood, the fate and rights of possible future persons, and much besides. In every general practitioner's surgery, limitation of resources means rationing, which is to say, a choice about who will get treated, and who not, and for what; and why. It is hard enough for busy general practitioners that they are expected to make these difficult decisions; it is harder still on patients, whose chances of treatment, even of survival, therefore become a lottery.

All the problems mentioned are real–life difficulties that are readily recognisable as part of the atmosphere of concern in contemporary medicine. But behind them lie other questions, in one sense abstractly philosophical, but in another acutely close to the practical difficulties experienced on wards and in consulting rooms. Some of them might at first glance seem to be entirely practical, but a moment's reflection reveals their underlying conceptual content. Among them are the following.

What is a person? What do we mean by 'rights' when we accord persons rights? Is a foetus a person? If not, does a foetus have rights anyway? Is a frozen embryo a person? When does life begin? When does it end? How does one define 'benefit' and 'harm'? When does something count as 'treatment'? Are doctors always obliged to help their patients? Must doctors always save life? Is it not sometimes justified and humane to end life rather than to prolong it? Are young people more valuable – more entitled to treatment – than old or older people? What is the definition of a 'worthwhile life'? Is a person with a family more valuable than one without? Should one never experiment on embryos? Does a woman have an exclusive and total right to determine what happens in and to her body, including the right to choose continuation or termination of pregnancy? If a treatment for a given condition exists, does everyone with that condition have a right to such treatment? Who decides what treatment shall be given to individuals (such as those with dementia) who are without representatives or competence to share in decision making?

One could extend the list, but its purport is already clear. There are few sharp definitions, and few easy answers, in connection with the intimate, often invasive, vexed, and unequal relationship between the knowledge-and-technology-possessing doctor and his or her vulnerable, perhaps afraid, and usually less well-informed patient. Medicine is, for these reasons, one of the prime places where the dilemmas of ethics present themselves most acutely. It is fortunate that many of those who choose to work in medicine are, by inclination, among the best equipped to think them through with intelligence, generosity and compassion.

Paternalism and autonomy

It is relevant to emphasise at this juncture that, in line with the distinction between 'ethics' and 'morals' drawn at the outset of this book, it is no surprise that medical ethics is appropriately called *ethics*. This is because it concerns everything about a relationship – the relationship between doctor and patient – which can be especially sensitive, and which turns on conceptions of human nature, rights, interests and responsibilities, which are relative not just to certain types of behaviour in specified circumstances, but to persons in conditions that might affect the whole quality and character of their lives.

A central and characteristic example of ethical dilemmas in medicine is provided by cases where patients are not able to share in decisions about their treatment, and where therefore practitioners seem to have a duty to make their decisions for them. This is the problem of paternalism and the autonomy of the patient.

We might aspire, in ethically ideal circumstances, to accord respect to each individual we encounter, at least until he forfeits it in a way that genuinely merits forfeiture, and correlatively to treat each individual as autonomous, that is, as being in charge of his own life – as shown by the etymology of the term; it connotes the state of being a lawgiver to oneself. Kant, recall, placed autonomy at the very centre of the moral life as its supreme value. Of course, there are so many social, legal, moral and psychological constraints on true autonomy for each of us, owing in part to our membership of society and in part to the finitary character of our intellects and experience, that the concept of autonomy is an idealisation, as Kant himself well knew. But we have learned from him to insist nevertheless that the ethical goal is for each individual to have the maximum degree of autonomy consistent with these social and natural restrictions.

The notions of autonomy and respect are asymmetrically linked. We respect the needs, interests and concerns of a young child even though we do not think he is autonomous, or fully autonomous; and we recognise that autonomous agents might, in virtue of their independently chosen actions, forfeit respect.

But it is a principal part of according respect to individuals that we treat them as autonomous, and when in some respect we cease to treat them so, we are being what has aptly been called 'paternalistic' − as implied by the heteronomy of children, which justifies us in acting on their behalf, taking decisions for them and directing their lives in what we judge to be their interests, for as long as they are insufficiently equipped with experience, or knowledge, or the requisite powers of mind, to choose for themselves.

It is a familiar fact that medical practitioners are especially apt to feel the tension between respecting autonomy and being justifiably paternalistic. Few patients, however intelligent and informed otherwise, can really be held to know enough about their condition and its available treatments to be full partners in decisions about what should best be done. Sometimes patients are unconscious, and cannot take any part in making those decisions. When a practitioner knows what is in a patient's interests but the patient refuses to take the treatment advised, is he ever justified in administering the treatment nonetheless?

One class of cases can be left immediately aside: those that involve third parties. If a patient is carrying a serious communicable disease, the interests of third parties are at stake and a patient can justifiably be required to accept treatment for the disease, or at least be prevented from spreading it. This degree of paternalism was accepted by Mill, who otherwise was strongly of the view, as we have seen (and it is eminently worth quoting again), that 'the sole end for which mankind are warranted, individually or collectively, in interfering with the liberty of action of any of their number, is self-protection ... the only purpose for which power can be rightfully exercised over any member of a civilised community, against his will, is to prevent harm to others. His own good, either physical or moral, is not a sufficient warrant.' A powerful argument supports this liberal tenet: it is that if one granted that a given body such as the state were licensed to decide what is in others' interests, there would be no obvious limit to the authority it could exercise over them. As Isaiah Berlin put it, the state could

> bully, oppress, torture them in the name, and on behalf, of their 'real' selves, in the secure knowledge that whatever is the true goal of man (happiness, performance of duty, wisdom, a just society, self-fulfilment) must be identical with his freedom – the free choice of his 'true', albeit often submerged and inarticulate, self.

It takes no effort to see what is wrong with such a view – a view that held sway in the Soviet Union and Maoist China, to take just two recent examples.

Mill also, of course, allowed paternalism in the case of children and the mentally impaired, but – much more riskily, from the viewpoint of his principles – he conceded that it would be justified to stop a man from walking onto a bridge that he did not know was in a dangerous condition. This concession is exactly one that a medical practitioner might invoke in the case of a patient who does not, or seems not to, grasp the seriousness of his condition and the advisability of a given treatment. And he might do it on the basis of an argument to the conclusion that sometimes a paternalistic authority knows better not just what an individual's interests are, but what his preferences would be if he were properly informed or able to judge.

It has, for example, been argued that a competent official could well 'respect your own preferences better than you would have done through your actions'. Take the case of tobacco smoking: a superficial preference to smoke cigarettes conflicts with a deeper preference to stay alive and well. The latter is not only a deeper but also a more settled and relevant preference than the former. Consider a young person who smokes because he wishes to appear sophisticated, or to conform with the behaviour of his peers: on this view, an appropriate authority would be justified in preventing him, on the grounds that he will, in time, himself come to a stable view that smoking is harmful. He is currently distracted and misinformed about his real interests, and is therefore not able to protect them. This applies even more to a medical patient choosing or acting in ways inimical to his interests.

Even if one rejects the 'slippery slope' argument that might underlie Isaiah Berlin's view, however, one can say that autonomy is such a crucial value that even the clearest case of a patient's choosing or acting in direct opposition to his interests cannot justify a doctor in overriding his decision and acting against his wishes. Of course, where a patient is demented, comatose, or otherwise mentally incapacitated, and has no competent family to decide, a doctor, or perhaps a hospital ethics committee, can and must do it for him But the envisaged standard case is one where an ordinarily rational person, even if not able to understand every intricacy of his condition and the treatment options, rejects his practitioner's advice – and where only he is going to be affected by his decision. On this view, even if he pulls out his intravenous lines and walks out of the hospital, with the medical staff knowing that he is likely to die within hours, he has to be allowed to act as he chooses. Is such a view tenable, in the face of doctors' duties and vocation, and their belief that he might, if he let them help him recover, be grateful that they restrained him after all?

Principles of autonomy and liberty conflict with paternalism in some cases – one could convincingly and almost endlessly multiply them – where some form or degree of the latter appears justifiable. This is a crucial problem because proposed solutions (or compromises) affect almost everything else in medical ethics: it concerns not only personhood, consent, the aims of medical intervention, and even decisions about the quality of life that medical interventions can offer, but also raises questions about the duties and rights of medical practitioners – which is to say, the very point of their vocation. One way this is so is illustrated by what might at first seem a marginal consideration. In the sketch just given, no mention is made of considerations about the therapeutic value of the practitioner's assumption of authority, and the confidence this can generate in some patients. Before the advent of technologised and biochemicalised medicine, this and regimen were the physician's principal tools. Perhaps the psychological power once inherent in certified possession of theoretical and practical knowledge counts for much less now; we live in an age when professional authority, with the paternalism it once both licensed and required, is no longer what it was. Certainly, in the face of growing assertions of autonomy and individual liberty, paternalism is regarded as intrinsically wrong unless well fortified by arguments tailored to specific cases. In this way, questions about autonomy and paternalism affect the fundamentals of the doctor–patient relationship, and lie at the heart of the ethical dimension of medicine.

Ethical dilemmas in medicine assume different disguises, depending on circumstances, just as the problem of paternalism does. That is a function of the variety of human interests and concerns, and the way that context renders them unique. It does not follow that it is wrong to seek general principles in ethics, for at the very least principles can serve as a starting point, a guide, or a touchstone, in finding ways of dealing with specific problems. Ethical reflection does not promise solutions that are invariably – or even very often – neat or satisfying; most of the time they are likely to be the opposite, ending as messy compromises, or as the least bad among a set of unpromising alternatives, despite all the thought and negotiation we can manage. But that is just how it is in human affairs, which gives us all the more reason to try to think clearly about questions of principle when we have opportunities to do so: not in the rush of the emergency room or operating theatre, but in the spaces we give ourselves for study and thought. The lesson is: 'be prepared' – if not with answers, then at the very least with a clear awareness of the kinds of questions we are likely to face, and with some sense of the answers – even if they are competing answers – that others have offered.

The right to die

Mention of the promise implicit in discussions of human rights, and questions raised by ethical problems in medicine, suggest how some of the most vexing questions we encounter at their interface might be resolved. Take the case of 'the right to die', claimed by terminally ill sufferers and others who wish to end their lives or to choose when and how their lives end. In some legal jurisdictions this right is recognised, in others not. In the latter case, for the most part the reason is a practical or caution-ary one, whereas in the former, the reason is recognition of the underlying principles that support it: once again, the autonomy of the agent, the freedom to make choices about the character and quality – and therefore the duration and the ending – of life.

A debate about the right to die would have seemed odd to people in Imperial Rome. Suicide and assisted suicide were commonplaces, and often enough grateful ones, for the inhabi-tants of that epoch. If a slave held a sword for his master to fall on it, or if a servant or family member helped mix poison into wine for someone ready to depart – or required to depart, for emperors gave senior figures the option of ending their own lives in cases of capital sentences – there was no question of either the principal or the assistant in the case being blamed, either morally or at law. On the contrary, anyone who helped in such a task was more likely to earn his contemporaries' praise.

Christian ethics brought about a complete change in the acceptability of such practices. The idea that life is sacred because 'god-given' introduces a proscription on the taking of life that has been construed in blanket terms when viewed from the perspective of practices such as abortion, infanticide and euthanasia, although (and inconsistently) it has otherwise admitted of many exceptions, such as war, killing in self-defence, and the execution of criminals and heretics. Nor has there ever been a principled extension of the 'sanctity of life' thesis to non-human creatures (using 'creature' in the theological sense to denote something brought into existence, and in the case of animals given conscious life, by a deity), despite the fact that the grounds for proscribing killing in the human and non-human cases are identical – unless one adds theses about souls as inhabiting only human animals.

There is a continuity between Christian ethics and Jewish thought in this respect. According to orthodox interpretations in Jewish ethics, the preservation of life is such an important duty that it even justifies non-observance of the Sabbath and the avoidance of non-kosher food. The length and quality of life are irrelevant considerations, because life is of infinite value, and (as one source puts it) 'any fraction of infinity is infinite'. Individuals do not have unlimited personal autonomy, and cannot dispose of their lives and bodies as they will; both have been given by a deity for a purpose that it is not open to the individual to question or obstruct.

The idea that the individual is heteronomous with respect to his or her own life and body – that is, does not have a final authority to decide what will happen in it or to it – is key to the Judaeo-Christian view. The secular ideal of personal autonomy in these respects contrasts directly with it, and lies at the root of several of the core provisions of human-rights instruments now widely accepted. The problem of the right to die arises directly from the conflict of intuitions between the lingering Judaeo-Christian view and the secular morality underlying human-rights thinking since the eighteenth-century Enlightenment.

The importance of this debate is such that it merits further examination, as an example of how contemporary ethical debate unfolds. The question that needs to be asked is whether, from the perspective of ethics, the conception of human rights enshrined in human rights conventions – for convenience take a specific one: the European Convention on Human Rights (ECHR) – should be interpreted as recognising that individuals have the right to choose when and how to die, and further, the right to suitable assistance in cases where they are not able to carry out their wish to die on their own behalf (for example, when paralysed or similarly incapacitated).

The relevant Convention rights at issue are those that accord the right to life, the right to be protected from inhumane treatment, the right to privacy, and the right to freedom of thought and belief (respectively articles 2, 3, 8 and 9 of the ECHR). Arguably, articles 2 and 3 singly, and all four of these articles jointly, give individuals the right to choose when and how to die.

The grounds for this claim are that a right to life itself includes, when fully understood, a right to die. If an individual is denied the chance to end his life before it becomes intolerable, he would in effect thereby be subject to inhumane treatment, in violation of article 3. Moreover, an individual's rights to privacy and freedom of belief amount to rights of self-determination, that is, the autonomy to decide what to do with his own life, subject to the proviso that he does not thereby harm others in the enjoyment of their rights.

The first question is whether the right to life includes the right to die. Judges in the English courts concluded that it could not do so because 'death is the antithesis of life'. It is not clear whether they therefore took article 2 implicitly to deny a right to die, for they did not develop a jurisprudence of their 'antithesis' point; but it is at least clear that their intention was to say that a right to life does not include or imply a right to die.

This judgment raises a crucial point, and arguably involves a crucial error. It is important to distinguish between the state of death and the act of dying, to recognise that dying is a process that happens in the course of life, albeit in life's final stages, and to see that all an individual's rights are fully engaged, in this particular connection, with the manner, timing and circumstances of his dying. Once an individual is dead, only residual rights remain – for example, in relation to wishes expressed and testamentary depositions made prior to the individual's decease, as affecting his estate and such matters as the form and place of the disposal of his remains.

With this distinction – between death as a state and dying as a living act – in view, it can be noted that important errors follow from failing to observe it. Although death is indeed the antithesis of life, dying is not. As an act of living, dying is one of the most important events in life, and because it can be pleasant or painful, timely or untimely, tragic or desired, it is integral to the character and quality of a person's life as he himself experiences it. We do not experience death, which is not an activity but a state – a state of non-existence indistinguishable from being unborn – but we might very much experience dying; and just as we hope that most of our acts of living will be pleasant, we likewise desire that the act of dying should be so too – or if not pleasant, then at the very least not frightening, painful or undignified.

A closely allied point is that 'life' in the phrase 'the right to life' is not *mere existence*. It is existence with at least a minimum degree of quality and value. In the main meaning of ECHR article 1 it means a life in which an individual is protected from arbitrary power and threat, is free to seek opportunities and to exercise choices, to enjoy the rewards of his endeavours in peace, and to seek and foster personal relationships – and which, to the degree reasonably possible for anyone in this world, is free from distress and pain. But these protections are there to ensure that it is not enough for a state or another individual to fulfil its obligations under the article merely by providing enough food and water to an individual to keep him alive, if he is otherwise deprived of fundamental amenities, opportunities and decencies. Thus, if someone is kept chained in a box, but fed and watered regularly, this would not be regarded as sufficient of a life for article 2 purposes to be satisfied. That is one reason why article 3 exists, to reinforce the sense in which the life to which human beings have a right is a life of a certain minimal standard and value. The life to which a 'right to life' is accorded is thereby a life of a certain kind; and that point is central to the question of whether an individual has a right to terminate his or her own life when it has ceased to have, and to have a renewable potential for, that minimum standard.

As these points imply, mere existence is not automatically a good. If it were, no life-support machine would ever be switched off, and contraception would be outlawed because it limits the sheer accumulation of human numbers. There are indeed people, familiarly enough, who oppose contraception and euthanasia on precisely the grounds that (respectively) the generation and the continuation of life are of such importance in their own right that they are not outweighed by considerations of the quality of life involved. This is precisely the Judaeo-Christian point already mentioned. But it takes only a moment's thought to see the questionable character of this view. The tendency of any argument that does not qualify the concept of the right to life as the right to a life of a certain minimum value, is to place quantity of life at the same or a higher level of importance.

Moreover, the English judges mentioned appear to have assumed that death – the state of non-existence that follows the life-process of dying – is in itself an evil. Naturally, most healthy and reasonably happy people wish to avoid or at least delay death, so that they can continue to enjoy their avocations, their pleasures and their important relationships. But for those who suffer and wish to cease suffering, death is not an evil but a welcome prospect. A life genuinely worth living is one in which neither dying nor death is an evil, but comes at a time and in a manner that completes the value of that life. Since death is inevitable, treating it as an evil to be delayed at any cost is a further error – and it gives rise to the poor argument which says that no one could possibly disagree that considerations of the quality of life should be subordinate to those about quantity of life.

The second question is whether the idea of rights to privacy and freedom of thought amount to a right of self-determination – the right, in other words, to decide how one will live one's life (always granting that no one has a right to live and act in ways that interfere with the rights of others). Obviously enough, these rights do indeed amount to a right of self-determination, for they protect the autonomy of personal life, and leave the great questions of life to individuals themselves – whom to love, whether to have a family, how to behave in private (consistently with the interests of others), and the like.

The question of when and how to die is one of these questions, even though most people answer it by leaving the time and manner of their dying to chance. But in fact it did not take the recent advent of the ECHR in England for people there to acquire the right to choose in this respect, for it was already implicitly acknowledged. The passing of the Suicide Act in 1961, at last making it lawful for a person to end his own life, in itself implied an acceptance of an individual's entitlement to decide the time and manner of his life's ending. It did so by leaving to an individual's own free choice whether to continue to live or to die. A permission is not automatically the same thing as a right, but in this case the legalisation of suicide was premised on recognition of claims of autonomy – in short, that a suicide's own choice in the matter is an autonomous one – and this in itself constitutes attribution of a right.

The point is reinforced by the implicit granting of a right to die to patients who request that measures to sustain their lives be discontinued, as in the case of patients who request that their life-support machines be turned off. This, and the validity of 'living wills' requesting that aggressive life-saving or life-sustaining treatments not be used in certain cases of illness or accident, jointly constitute acceptance that a right to die exists on its own merits.

However, an anomaly created by England's 1961 Suicide Act, an anomaly that has particular consequences for cases in which a sufferer cannot end his own life, typically because he is paralysed, is that although it is lawful to take one's own life, it is unlawful for anyone to help one take one's own life. The anomaly in this connection, therefore, is that it is unlawful to help someone do something lawful. The reason is that the Suicide Act rightly seeks to prevent murder under the disguise of assisted suicide; but because it does so by a blanket prohibition, making the aiding, abetting or encouraging of suicide a criminal offence under any circumstances, it has put anyone unable to commit suicide without help in the impossible position that he cannot attain the lawful end he desires. In the light of the foregoing argument, this thereby denies such an individual one of his fundamental rights.

Many confusions surround the debate about assisted suicide and euthanasia, but the main one is that most people fail to distinguish properly between them. 'Euthanasia' literally means 'a good death', and in that sense everyone hopes for euthanasia in the end, usually, by preference, a naturally occurring easy and painless death after a healthy old age. A suicide or assisted suicide might go wrong, if not properly carried out, and result in suffering for the subject – and thus not count as euthanasia in the literal sense.

Euthanasia has come mainly to mean deliberate acts or omissions that result in someone's death, as when an elderly patient with pneumonia is not given antibiotics, or when a life-support machine is switched off, allowing someone in a long-term persistent vegetative state to die. This is called 'passive euthanasia' and is regarded as lawful and acceptable. Active euthanasia takes place when someone is given death-inducing treatment of some kind.

There is, in fact, no moral difference between the two kinds of euthanasia, because deliberately not doing something is as much an act as doing something. The concept in theological ethics of 'sins of commission and omission' embodies a recognition that equal responsibility attaches to deliberate withholdings and choices not to act, just as it does to failing to act when action is required. In that central respect passive and active euthanasia are the same. They both involve deliberate choices, and they both have the same outcome.

It is a matter of sentiment that passive euthanasia seems more acceptable. This point is more obvious when one recognises how often active euthanasia is in fact performed. Failure to shorten the suffering of a patient in agonising or terrifying terminal phases of an illness is so cruel that, in reality, few medical practitioners allow themselves to stand aside. To do so would be to treat people with less consideration than is typically accorded to animals, for we regard it as a kindness to animals to end their lives swiftly and easily when their suffering is otherwise unrelievable. Happily for human victims of pain or distress, in hospitals all over the world, every day, doses of painkillers are raised to fatal levels when needed, the legitimacy of the exercise protected by the 'doctrine of double effect', which says that because the doctor's primary aim is to alleviate suffering, the life-shortening side effect is inescapable and therefore acceptable.

But as with the distinction between passive and active euthanasia, this is a conceptual convenience. Stating that one's intention is to relieve pain rather than to hasten death in such cases is a sleight of hand, given the empirical certitude that the latter will result. In any case, hastening death is the ultimate form of pain relief, and is therefore comprehended in the treatment to relieve suffering.

In discussions of physician-assisted death, whether direct in the sense of passive and active euthanasia, or brought about by 'double effect', the point is frequently made that medical practitioners are bound by their professional code of ethics to seek to save, protect and promote life, or at least to minimise the suffering incident on accident or disease. In the United States appeal is still made to the clause in the Hippocratic oath which states: 'To please no one will I prescribe a deadly drug, or give advice which may cause my patient's death.' The principal meaning of this is that the practitioner vows not to bow to (say) family, political, or other kinds of third-party pressure to end the life of someone who does not wish to die. But some translations bear a reading that says a practitioner will not accede to a patient's request for death either, and this is the form of reading appealed to by opponents of medically assisted suicide. But clearly, a practitioner who refused to help a patient die who was in great, unrelievable and interminable (other than by death) pain would be failing in his Hippocratic duty to succour the patient; so the appropriate reading of the relevant clause in the Oath is arguably the third-party one alone.

Nevertheless, there is a real concern for medical practitioners, whose primary raison d'être is to save life, ameliorate suffering, and cure ills and injuries. For this reason a practical or institutional innovation might be suggested. This is that there should be a medical speciality of thanatology (I here coin a word from *thanatos*, death), and that thanatologists should work within a careful framework of law and under the supervision of a hospital ethics committee, so that every occasion of thanatological treatment is approved in advance, monitored during administration, and properly recorded afterwards. Since only thanatologists will be involved in the work of helping sufferers to die who have elected such treatment and show a stable and intelligent intention to carry their wishes through, all other medical practitioners will continue to work under the assumption that their sole concern is to save life, cure ills and palliate suffering. Apart from anything else, this will clarify the very grey area in which many medical practitioners now work, given the frequency with which they knowingly, and for compassionate reasons, administer life-shortening treatments.

In the Netherlands a careful law now exists to permit active euthanasia and assisted suicide, and in the American state of Oregon an equally careful law permits physician-assisted suicide. Every year in Oregon a report is issued describing the numbers and circumstances of those who have availed themselves of the law, and it makes instructive reading – not least because in the majority of cases it meant that sufferers were able to die at home, with their families and friends around them, in relative peace.

Those who object to voluntary euthanasia and assisted suicide point out that there is excellent hospice care for people with terminal illnesses, where they are looked after in ways that palliate suffering and allow death with dignity. It is certainly true that the hospice movement offers outstandingly good terminal care, and that modern medications greatly enhance their ability to provide it. But the existence of palliative care is not invariably the choice of clear-minded but terminally suffering individuals. They might wish to die when still alert, unaffected by palliative medications and therefore able to interact in full consciousness with their families – able, furthermore, to bid them farewell properly. They may not wish to endure the helplessness and distress of the last stages of their illnesses, whatever is available in the way of pain control, psychotropic medication and psychological support. Despite their afflictions, such sufferers are still persons with minds of their own, and rights, who wish to make choices about their own affairs, and above all to say when, where and how they will leave the life which, for all the satisfactions it might otherwise have brought in personal terms, is drawing to an end so cruelly. Natural justice says that this is their right; and so does the concept and institution of human rights on the interpretation suggested here.

The nature of man: a Case Study

The foregoing discussions concern aspects of a particular family of practical ethical concerns. As always, they raise far more general questions. One is the recurrent problem of the nature of man. Before one can get far with thinking about the good for humankind, one has to have a view about human nature, for the simple and obvious reason that a theory about the human good that drew only on considerations about what, say, dogs and horses are like (and what dogs and horses like) would be of exceedingly limited use. Theories of human nature abound, but the dominating presence among those who have offered such theories in the twentieth century is unquestionably Sigmund Freud. For a time at least, his impact on how people saw themselves was incalculable, and therefore it is instructive to consider his views and their once-great bearing on the question of the good life.

Freud was a scientifically trained physician. He saw human beings as part of nature, and human nature therefore as something explicable in purely naturalistic terms. He accordingly held a deterministic, reductionist and mechanistic view of human nature which proposes that the basis of the human psyche consists of a set of fundamental instincts or drives. The strongest drive is sexual, seconded by two others: aggression, and the 'death wish'. In the mature development of his theory Freud held that the psyche consists of the individual unconscious and the 'id' (the primitive instincts), which influence the 'ego' (roughly, the conscious self) and 'superego' (roughly, the conscience), the two latter in tension with the blind power of the underlying instincts. Forms of behaviour regarded as higher or more civilised – those associated with the superego – are not natural in the sense of being innate, but are either acquired or imposed.

Without doubt Freud was a visionary who helped the modern world re-imagine human nature and confront taboos, especially about sex. But sceptics say that his theories, offered as science, fail under scrutiny. Their criticisms take different forms. Early on, Freud's views met strong opposition from the medical establishment, but they later became fashionable and quickly evolved into an orthodoxy, despite fragmentation into opposing schools. In the last few decades Freudian theory has met renewed opposition, not least from feminists, who have objected to what they see as the misogyny and patriarchalism in it, and to the spurious scientific authority accorded the idea that women are inferior because they are *hommes manqués* – castrated, and therefore lesser, versions of men. Defenders of Freud respond by attributing feminist attacks to 'resistance' and sublimated penis-envy, both technical Freudian concepts behind which they readily claim shelter.

Criticism from science and philosophy is not so easily deflected by appeal to technicalities, however, because what they question is the very basis of the theory. Karl Popper, Frederick Crews and Adolf Grünbaum figure largely in this attack. Among other things they charge that the empirical basis of psychoanalysis is inadequate, that its central concepts are untestable, and that its aim – which is to give a complete theory of human nature – is overambitious. Its methodology is inadequate, they argue, because it rests on speculation and subjective insights, not on objective examination of public and repeatable phenomena. It depends on generalisation from single cases or very small samples – much of Freud's data is provided by a few Viennese women together with his own 'self-analysis' – and its reasoning relies on analogies, subjective associations, memories real or supposed, puns, and ('unconsciously intentional') mistakes and coincidences. It assumes that mental activity is causally deterministic, and a number of philosophers, among them Wittgenstein, note that Freud also conflates the concepts of an action's causes and the reasons why it was performed.

In all this a central and unquestioned role is assigned to the 'unconscious mind'. At base, Freud's theory rests on a claim that, expressed unadorned and without preamble, looks frankly absurd: that an infant sexually desires its parent of the opposite sex, and is therefore hostile towards, because jealous of, its parent of the same sex; and that because neither the desire nor the hostility is acceptable, these feelings are repressed into the unconscious, as a result of which internal conflicts arise; and that this – the Oedipus complex – is the key to human nature. It is not, note, the key only to pathological human nature, but to human nature as such.

Freud did not invent the notion of the unconscious. By the end of the nineteenth century it had become a fixture of psychological medicine, accorded prime clinical significance by such practitioners as Jean-Martin Charcot and Josef Breuer. Freud inherited an elaborate theory of the unconscious stating that many perceptual and cognitive processes occur at subliminal levels, and that what is consciously learned can become automatic and remain non-consciously effective. It also held that many memories and beliefs can be stored in the unconscious entirely without the knowledge of its possessor, but can be recovered by (for example) hypnosis. It further held that the unconscious has a creative, mythopoeic capacity responsible for dreams, stories, symbols and ideas, which when pathological is responsible for delusions and hysterical symptoms. Finally it held that the unconscious is the source of psychic energy, which can be inhibited, sublimated or transferred from one application to another, and that within it can coexist 'dissociated' (split-off) subpersonalities, which manifest themselves in dreams or trances.

Freud's predecessors had relied on hypnosis to gain access to the unconscious, but under the influence of Breuer's experience with 'Anna O' Freud adopted instead the 'talking cure' – the process of eliciting, by the technique of 'free association', experience that had been repressed into subliminal regions of the mind. The aim was to release patients from neurosis, conceived as the baleful product of suppressed and therefore unacknowledged trauma, by effecting a discharge, or catharsis, of the emotions involved. Freud was struck by the fact that most of his patients seemed to have real or imaginary sexual trauma at the root of their difficulties. When he found them reluctant to tell him about their early sexual experiences and masturbatory fantasies, he diagnosed 'resistance'. Notoriously, he early thought that his patients had indeed been sexually abused as children; later he decided that these were fantasies, expressing 'infantile wishes' as described in the Oedipus theory.

A dispassionate evaluator of these views is bound to question Freud's version of the 'unconscious mind'. Today's cognitive and neurological science agrees that much information is processed in the central nervous system non-consciously, and that learned routines can be performed in the absence of self-awareness, without needing a notion of an 'unconscious mind' to explain either phenomenon. The idea of non-conscious processes is very different from that of an 'unconscious mind' conceived as a source of psychological motivation. Ideas of repressed trauma, subpersonalities, psychic energies, mythopoeic functions and mental life unknown to its possessor constitute a speculative and highly questionable mixture; but it is precisely on these concepts that Freudian theory depends.

There are two reasons, one conceptual and one empirical, for scepticism about the unconscious. The conceptual reason is that the very idea of *mental* life – of motives, emotions, reasons and intentions – seems essentially conscious. It is true that we need a distinction between what philosophers call 'occurent' and 'dispositional' mental states, meaning by the former those that are currently at the centre of attention, and by the latter those that are not but could become so. But the Freudian unconscious is a different thing, a realm where emotions, beliefs and motives are in lively play, just as they would be in conscious mental activity, with the difference that if we ever come to know of them, it is only by their indirect effects. To some critics this is like saying that we suffer unfelt pains; hence, the expression 'unconscious mind' appears paradoxical.

The empirical difficulty is that the evidence for unconscious mentation is at best ambiguous, and that there is no rigorous empirical way of testing claims about it. The objection is not that unconscious phenomena are by definition unobservable, for science admits many unobservable entities, whose existence and properties can only be determined by such indirect means as inference or the detection of remote effects. In these cases, however, there is a principled correspondence between the indirect evidence and the postulated entities, which is repeatable, testable and predictable. In sharp contrast, in the 'laboratory' of the analyst's consulting room, where free association of ideas is the means of enquiry, where anecdotal and subjective material constitute the data, and where 'suggestion' by the analyst is an ever-present danger, no such empirical control is possible.

To doubts about the reliability of Freud's methods – free association, reliance on subjectivity, the dangers of suggestion – have to be added doubts about the characteristic style of Freud's reasoning, exemplified by his analyses of dreams, and by his claims to be able to recognise intuitively what something 'truly means'. For example, he reports that during self-analysis he recalled a childhood incident in which he snatched flowers from a girl. 'To take flowers from a girl', he states, 'means to deflower her.' In another case he diagnoses a patient's impulse to go for a run after each meal as a wish to kill a man whom he sees as a rival for his fiancée's affections. The rival's name is Richard; running after meals is a way of losing weight; *dick* is German for 'fat'; Dick is a diminutive of Richard; the runner wishes to get rid of *dick*/Dick; QED. Why should one accept that these speculative leaps have landed on the right place, or even that there is a right place to land, given that there are any number of competing interpretations one could give? Why might the runner not be wishing to kill *himself* by burning off more calories than he eats? Or making himself more athletic and therefore more attractive than his rival? Or finding that running after meals soothes his anxieties about his fiancée's loyalty? In the flower story, would the young Freud not have snatched what was in the girl's hand if it had not been a bouquet? What if it had been a stick, or an ice cream? If he had snatched either, what would it have 'meant'? Why is it not the snatching that matters, no matter what object is snatched, when deciding how to give an interpretation?

In a letter to Jung, Freud spoke of his 'serene confidence' in his methods; few critics can share it. One has only to remember the case of Emma Eckstein. Freud claimed to have discovered a 'nasal reflex neurosis' and linked it to excessive masturbation, and diagnosed Emma as suffering from it. He got his colleague Wilhelm Fliess to remove the turbinate bone from her nose. After her nose had bled and suppurated for many days, another surgeon found a mass of surgical gauze left in the wound. Its removal caused a near-fatal haemorrhage. The bleeding continued intermittently for months; Freud meditated on the problem, and concluded that Emma's bleeding was hysterical in nature, caused by her wish to bring him to her bedside.

That Freudian theory is not science is suggested by the important difference between giving a systematic account of it, and doing the same for any of the physical sciences. To explain Freudian theory properly one has to recount its origins and growth. The standard account proceeds by tracing Freud's thought from his early days as a neurologist, through his associations with Charcot, Breuer and Fliess, to his rejection of the 'seduction theory' (which postulated widespread child sex abuse) and its replacement by theories of the Oedipus complex and dreams (his *Interpretation of Dreams*, published in 1900, is regarded as his greatest book) – and thence to the later development of theory to include, for example, the ego–id distinction. The variety of further, and often diverging, developments in Freudian theory, carried out by gifted followers, commands extra volumes. But it is only recently that a better understanding of Freud's intellectual adventure has been gained, showing among other things its dependence on his women patients and collaborators. In view of feminism's strictures on Freud, a certain irony attaches to this fact.

Freud's earliest women patients effectively invented psycho-analysis, and the psychoanalytic profession owed its rise, spread, and in time some of its most decisive transformations, to women who began as his patients and later became analysts. The two women who should be central in his life, his mother Amalia Freud – born Amalia Nathanson, she was his father's third wife, and twenty years younger than his father – and his wife Bertha, are dim presences; Freud hid the former behind a screen of sincere but nevertheless conventional filial respect, and the latter behind an embargo on his papers that seals them for another century. But the shadowiness of these two is more than compensated by a number of other extraordinary women, who in their different ways are chiefly responsible for trans-forming psychoanalysis from an oddity on the medical fringe to an explosive force in twentieth-century consciousness.

Freud said that psychoanalysis began when his colleague Josef Breuer treated the wealthy and beautiful young hysteric Bertha Pappenheim, 'Anna O', who as noted above effectively created her own therapy by substituting what she called 'the talking cure' – Freud called it 'free association' – for Breuer's standard treatment of hypnosis. (Subsequent research has shown that she was not in fact cured by this means, but lingered in hospital long afterwards; it also shows that her symptoms, which involved partial paralysis, contractures and diplopia, probably stemmed from a physical complaint that was first mis-diagnosed and then mistreated – it is now convincingly believed to have been tubercular meningitis, caught while nursing her father as he died from a tubercular abscess. Her illness began soon after his death.) Freud's experience with the woman he called his 'teacher', another Anna – Anna von Lieben – confirmed for him that the route to a new under-standing of psychology (an aim more important to him than any therapeutic possibilities) lay this way. Anna von Lieben was his patient for six years, and taught him that it takes a talented patient to make a talented analyst.

These early patients helped establish the technique of analysis. The theory emerged more slowly. Its painful growth is reflected in the different paths from Freud's couch taken by women as variously brilliant as Helene Deutsch and Princess Marie Bonaparte when they became analysts in their own right. Deutsch was a qualified psychiatrist who, after emigrating to America, specialised in the emotional life of women. Marie Bonaparte established Freud's theories in France, and later engaged in famous battles with Jacques Lacan over Freud's legacy. She was the great-grand-niece of Napoleon, and very rich. Nicknamed 'Freud-a-dit' by French analysts, Marie was troubled by the question of vaginal versus clitoral orgasm, and had two surgical operations to move her clitoris closer to her vagina. When she was contemplating sex with her son she wrote to Freud for advice. Although in general hostile to incest ('In my private life I am a bourgeois,' Freud wrote) he diplomatically replied that incest is not always harmful. Marie was, after all, a wealthy and influential follower.

Freud sometimes likened himself to King Lear. In a major respect the comparison is apt, for his youngest daughter Anna proved crucial both to him and to his cause. Although her disputes with Melanie Klein about child analysis later split the analytic movement, Anna's tireless loyalty was central to the later flourishing of Freudian orthodoxy. Freud analysed Anna, discussing with her at great length her almost obsessive masturbatory life. The significance of this fact should not be misread: some oppose Freud because of the heavy and disturbingly foetid scent given off by his family life, rather than coming to evaluations of his theories and methods on their merits. Defenders point out that psychoanalysis has always laboured against a heavy weight of convention and prudery.

The swingeing attacks to which Freudian theory is subjected by feminists arise from their scorn for the claim that girls suffer 'penis-envy' and that vaginal orgasm supersedes clitoral orgasm in the mature woman. According to Freud, girls are dismayed to discover their genital inferiority to boys, and long to acquire a penis, first by sexually desiring their fathers and then by wishing for children, especially sons, who bring the coveted penis with them. As to sexual maturity, Freud identified the 'phallic phase' in girls as an infantile stage involving external genital pleasure, initiated by the nappy-changing mother (whom girls blame for their 'castration', hence mother–daughter conflict); so any woman who does not mature by developing a capacity for internal – that is vaginal – orgasm has remained in the infantile stage. In their robust response to these latter claims feminist critics have powerful ammunition: empirical research undertaken by, among others, Masters and Johnson, decisively refutes Freud, showing not only that the clitoris is the chief sensory focus in the female pelvis, but that women are capable by its means of indefinitely many orgasms in sequence, prompting some feminists to argue that women are restricted if they rely on men for their pleasure.

The theories of infantile sexuality and female penis-envy are incredible enough on the basis of mere human biography, but standard knowledge of endocrinology and mammalian reproductive ethology – the familiar story of reproductive maturation and behaviour in all mammals including humans – makes the Freudian view appear merely fantastical. If one were to compare the frequency and intensity of pre-pubertal interest in sex and ice cream in the normal child, one could confidently bet that, although the former might not be absent, it is beaten hands-down by the latter.

Freudian theory thus fares ill under critical scrutiny. What explains its power? When Auden described Freud as 'not a person but a whole climate of opinion', and Harold Bloom nominated him 'the central imagination of our age', there was little hyperbole in the claims. Freudian theory indeed took Western twentieth-century civilisation by storm. How so? The answer lies in four factors. One is Freud's genius as author and ideologue. Another is the immense attraction of any theory that offers to each individual an explanation of his own hidden secrets. A third is the promise that science has at last delivered what there has never before been, namely, a proper theory of human nature. And finally there is the fact that at the centre of the package lies the most delicious, anxious, and titillating of all taboos: sex. Such a combination can hardly fail.

Of Freud's powers as a writer and advocate of ideas, as an immensely fertile system-builder, and as a possessor of an extraordinary ability to weave together medical knowledge, some genuine insights into the human condition, and a powerful imagination, there can be no question. To read him is to be spellbound. He has the narrative skills of a first-rate novelist, and a knack for devising striking ways to describe the psychological phenomena he studied. It is a characteristic of highly speculative enquiries that the thinkers who most influence them are those who find the most compelling vocabulary – a vocabulary that offers a new way of expressing and articulating its subject. Freud himself once wrote, in commenting on a book by Jung, 'In it many things are so well expressed that they seem to have taken on definitive form.' This exactly describes Freud's own talent. He had a genius for analogy and metaphor, and his marvellous powers of imagination fed on both, annexing the austere terminologies of scientific medicine and psychology to them. This gave them authority. His case studies are highly organised narratives constructed from true-life gossip based on voyeurism – irresistible to human curiosity – and yet they go further: they add the deeply satisfying denouement of the kind one has in detective stories, where mystery is unravelled by clever and striking juxtapositions of clues.

The second attraction – that Freud offers each individual a revelation of secrets about himself that he does not himself know – is equally irresistible. The same compound of insecurity and curiosity, anxiety and desire that makes so many resort, against their better judgement, to fortune-tellers, is at work here – except that here the imprimatur of science makes the proceeding respectable, which is why people will spend far more on their analysts than on their astrologers.

The third attraction is the promised theory of human nature. Religious accounts of fallen man, of humanity as midway between beast and angel, of imperishable souls trapped in disgusting matter and therefore sinful from birth, had lost their grip with many, while at the same time Darwinian views offered no account of why evolution had made man as he is. In identifying sexual and aggressive impulses as the fundamental human drives, and in specifying their causes, Freud offered an inclusive philosophical psychology. Once again, the authority of the white coat and Latinate terminology helped. Humans struggle with conceptual bewilderments about themselves and their complex natures; one can see why the appearance of Freud's magisterial new insights seemed as welcome as rain in drought.

Finally there is the fact that sex lies at the core of the story. Freud performed a great service by liberating debate on the matter, but it is questionable whether the importance he assigns to it is correct. The hungry always think of food; the fed put eating in its proper place. Only consider that if, say, religious teachings had given us inflated anxieties about scratching our kneecaps, and threatened us with perdition for doing it, it is certain that we would develop itchy patellas. The accidents of social history are easily mistaken for the essentials of human nature, and this is surely what explains Freud's choice of sexuality as the well-spring of human nature. The surprise is that people do not see how, at most, sex can be only part of a far more complicated story.

Philosophies that capture the imagination never wholly fade. From Animism to Zorastrianism, every view known to man retains at least a few devotees. There might always be Freudians, and there will always be admirers of Freud's great imaginative and literary powers – these two, as the foregoing remarks suggest, are intimately linked. But as to Freud's claims upon truth: the judgement of time has gone against him.

The moral philosophers in the shameful century

At the beginning of this chapter it was remarked that twenti-eth-century academic philosophers, especially in the tradition of 'analytic' anglophone philosophy, turned away from practi-cal questions and focused almost exclusively instead on theoret-ical ones, thereby reinforcing the regrettable implication of the common phrase 'It's only academic', meaning, 'It does not matter', 'It's irrelevant'. Alas, this was largely true until the century's later part. Since then, as the foregoing sections show in connection with medical ethics and applications of debates about human rights, practical ethics has made a large resurgence and has generated newly specific areas of discussion such as business ethics, environmental ethics and animal rights.

The history of academic ethics in the twentieth century is not without interest, however; nor, in the century's later part, importance. A survey indicates the good and the 'merely' academic, as follows.

The first significant work of moral philosophy in the twenti-eth century was G. E. Moore's *Principia Ethica*, published in 1903. It exerted an influence on those of Moore's contempo-raries who formed the Bloomsbury Group – among them John Maynard Keynes, Virginia Woolf and Lytton Strachey – who liked Moore's identification of beauty and friendship as the most worthwhile goods. (This, less kind observers might remark, explains how they were able to economise morally: by having beautiful friends.) Moore adopted a version of utilitari-anism in the sense that he defined right acts as those that produce the most good; but the distinctive feature of his view is that he denied that the good can be identified with some natural property such as pleasure, arguing instead that it is a simple, unanalysable property, just as a primary colour is – and that just as we cannot explain what (say) 'yellow' is by means of a definition, but only by showing someone an example, so we can only explain what goodness is likewise. We are, he said, able to recognise the presence of goodness by direct 'intuition'. Any theory that attempted to identify goodness with a natural property he apostrophised as committing 'the naturalistic fallacy'.

In the first three decades of the century the debate in academic moral philosophy occurred chiefly between those who, like Moore, invoked utilitarian notions in which the consequences of actions determine their rightness (so-called 'consequentialist' theories), and those who were fundamentally Kantian in thinking that principles of duty determine what is good. A leading figure on this side of the argument was Sir David Ross, who characteristically wrote, when considering a conflict between keeping a promise and helping someone in distress, 'Besides the duty of fulfilling promises I have and recognise a duty of relieving distress, and that when I think it right to do the latter at the cost of not doing the former, it is not because I think I shall produce more good thereby but because I think it the duty which is in the circumstances more of a duty.' Ethics of duty are called 'deontological' theories.

The struggle between consequentialism and deontology received a jolt in the decade before the Second World War when a claim was dramatically advanced to the effect that when we talk about right and wrong and the good and the bad, we are merely expressing emotional states of approval and disapproval, and that our remarks are otherwise literally meaningless.

The jolt was delivered by A. J. Ayer in his *Language, Truth and Logic*, published in 1935. The argument of the book, briefly stated, is that there are only two kinds of meaningful statements: *analytic* statements, which are such that one can determine their truth or falsity just by understanding the terms that occur in them (for example, 'All bachelors are unmarried men'), and *synthetic* statements, whose truth or falsity can only be determined by going and looking at the world to establish the facts either way. Examples of analytic statements are the statements of mathematics and logic; examples of synthetic statements are the statements of science, history and ordinary life. The meaningfulness of synthetic statements resides in their 'verifiability', that is, the fact that we can go and check whether or not they are true. Any statement that pretends to be synthetic but which cannot be verified is, strictly and literally, meaningless. Thus all statements about god are literally meaningless, because nothing can count as verifying their truth or falsity.

But the statements of ethics are not verifiable either – there are no empirical facts that can be checked to see whether a given ethical statement is true or false – and therefore they are literally meaningless. They therefore have to be understood as merely giving expression to their utterers' feelings. In virtue of this last, this theory is standardly called the 'emotivist' theory of ethics.

A philosopher who gave a more detailed version of the theory is C. L. Stevenson, whose *Ethics and Language* was published in 1944 – thereby exemplifying magnificent detachment, worthy of a Stoic, in the midst of one of the world's largest ever moral crises. Stevenson drew attention to the fact that individuals have both beliefs and attitudes in the moral sphere, the former relating to how things are in the world, the latter to what the individual feels about them. Because of the former, when an individual makes a moral judgement he is not only, or merely, venting his feelings about some matter, he is trying to influence others' attitudes to it too.

Both Ayer and Stevenson premised their views on the 'fact-value' distinction, which, as Hume had long since claimed, makes it impossible to deduce a prescriptive statement – one that says what ought to be done – from a descriptive statement saying how things stand in the world. In the years after the Second World War this distinction was attacked, and efforts made, notably by R. M. Hare, to construct a view on the basis of an analysis of the logic of moral language. Hare sought to show by this means that moral language is *essentially* prescriptive; the chief role of moral judgements is to state what ought to be done, he argued, and such prescriptions are identifiable as essentially *moral* in being universalisable, that is – as in Kant's theory – they are not restricted in application to a given individual, but apply to any and all moral agents. This view, aptly enough, is called 'prescriptivism'.

The most significant event in moral philosophy in the later twentieth century was the publication in 1971 of John Rawls's seminal *A Theory of Justice*, which is in fact a contribution to political philosophy rather than ethics, but which could not help influencing ethical thought profoundly. In any case, for anyone of an Aristotelian persuasion politics and ethics are seamlessly connected if not indeed the same, their apparent differences being ones only of the scale of the concern: the collective and the individual respectively.

Rawls's theory turns on discussion of the two fundamental principles required, in his view, for a just and morally acceptable society. The first is that 'Each individual is to have an equal right to the most extensive total system of equal basic liberties compatible with a similar system of liberty for all'; the second is that social and economic inequalities are to be so arranged as to be to the greatest benefit of the least advantaged, and all associated offices and positions are to be open to all 'under conditions of fair equality of opportunity'. His thesis places liberty and fairness at the heart of views about the good life and the good society, making him quintessentially the philosopher of what, in contemporary terminology, is often called 'social democracy'.

Hopeful departures

The views just sketched are highly theoretical and abstract, but there is less of a contrast than might at first seem between them and the more recent developments in applied ethics – medical ethics, business ethics and the others – as now discussed in the academic setting, for these latter require theoretical exploration and justification too, and the academy is the appropriate place for it (because, remember, getting things wrong in academic discussions is happily 'only academic' – a luxury not afforded to, say, the members of a hospital ethics committee faced with a difficult actual case). It might be thought odd by some, and a scandal by others, that a new venture calling itself 'applied ethics' – a pleonasm, surely, so critics might say – had to come into existence at all, for it marks the abandonment of responsibility by those moral philosophers who disclaim all but theoretical interest in the questions of ethics. However one looks at it, though, the rise (or return) of applied ethics is a hopeful departure.

It is not the only hopeful departure in the moral philosophy of the last hundred years. At least two others might briefly be mentioned. One is the intellectually dramatic and, as it seems at present, short-lived phenomenon of Existentialism. The other is the emergence or re-emergence of 'virtue ethics' as a major movement in ethical debate.

Existentialism – a more diverse if not fragmented movement of thought than the label by itself suggests – enjoyed a blaze of interest in the two decades following the Second World War, and indeed for most of its adherents, if not for all of its major contributors, that event was a major motive for their interest in it. Commentators on Existentialism saw it as having its roots in Kierkegaard, Nietzsche and Edmund Husserl, and for its principal exponents they nominated Jean-Paul Sartre, Albert Camus, Karl Jaspers, Gabriel Marcel and Martin Heidegger. Of this group it was the first two who were by far the most influential on the young of the 1950s and 60s, not least because they expressed their respective versions of an Existentialist outlook in the literary forms of novels, plays and essays.

Existentialism would have historical interest only, as a symptom of a period rather than a contribution to an age-old debate about the good for humankind, if there were not enough intrinsic interest in its themes to suggest that aspects of them merit, and will doubtless get, renewed attention in time. A brief sketch of just one version (although a main one) of Existentialism might show why.

It is a concomitant of an atheist view that such meaning as there is in human existence is found or imposed by humans themselves, for on the very premise of atheism no purpose is established for mankind from outside. In their respective ways Sartre and Camus made this gratuitous aspect of human existence central, emphasising the fact that individuals simply find themselves thrown into the world, as it were, without external purpose or guide, as a result of the blind flow of natural events. They gave the name 'absurdity' to this gratuitousness, this accidental and purposeless brute fact of existence. Camus dramatised the philosophical conundrum that this brute fact represents by saying, at the outset of his celebrated essay 'The Myth of Sisyphus', that the great philosophical question is: Shall I commit suicide? For if the answer is 'no', it is because one has a reason to live; there are things one regards as valuable to have, to do or to be. Since these things are not given from without, they have been chosen in the only other way possible: by the individual himself; and in choosing them he has thereby conferred meaning on his existence.

This puts matters schematically. Even more schematically one might describe the net result of the views put forward by Camus and Sartre in terms of their nomination of four values that individuals, in creating themselves in the face of absurdity, can impose on the antecedent meaninglessness of existence to give it value: namely love, freedom, human dignity and creativity. Freedom is not only a value but a condition of being able to choose these values; Sartre describes the possession of a free will as an 'agony' because it forces us to make choices in the face of existence's emptiness. Indeed Sartre thought that choosing and deciding are stressful enterprises, and ultimately solitary ones, and further that the business of living one's choices is an effort, a painful endeavour; so his is not an especially reassuring view. But he saw the endeavour as inescapable if life is to have a meaning, for without it one would have no choice even of approximating its goal, namely 'authenticity' – which means living according to one's beliefs, taking responsibility for the consequences of one's actions, and accepting the agonies of one's freedom.

These suggestive views express a conviction first voiced long ago by Fichte in a letter to Jacobi: 'We philosophise out of need for our redemption.' The idea is to bridge the gap between thought and life, between intelligence and the problem of living. Analytic philosophers are impatient with the high-sounding notions of Existentialism – A. J. Ayer dismissed them as 'woolly uplift' – in part for the good reason that it is never enough just to list a string of alleged values such as 'love', 'dignity' and the others, for one has to justify their choice, and explain what one means by them. Consider love: there are many kinds, and some militate against each other. There is love of parent for child and child for parent; of friend for friend; of erotic partners; of old comrades; of human beings for animals, landscapes, inanimate objects, literary and musical styles, and much besides. Which is the love that gives, or best gives – or perhaps alone gives – meaning to life? And so for the other values.

This criticism is forceful. But the suggestiveness of the Existentialist view, at least in the form given by Camus and (parts of) Sartre, remains, especially as it raises and attempts to address the idea of how individuals can face 'absurdity' – the absence of any meaning provided by a supposed outside source – and infuse existence with aims and desiderata both rich and stimulating. It is an attractive hint and bears further investigation.

The other hopeful departure is the renewed interest in 'virtue ethics'. Most of the moral theories sketched in the pre- ceding section address moral concepts and the question of right action. Virtue ethics is instead interested in character, in what sort of people we should be, rather than what we should do on specified occasions.

Moral debate about what it is right or wrong to do on a given occasion turns on a notion of obligation, of what *ought* to be done. Its roots lie in the Judaeo-Christian tradition's premise of divine law. Where a votary of this tradition saw a divine command, the moral philosopher saw an obligation-imposing principle or norm. An interest in virtue ethics takes its rise from the quite different basis of Aristotle's ethical reflections. There the founding question is not, What ought one to do in such-and-such a case? but instead, What is the best life for man? Aristotle accordingly sought an account of the *virtues*, the excellences of character that, if one lives in accordance with them, make one's life good.

Of course there is a connection between virtue ethics and questions of right and wrong action. Right action can be defined as what a virtuous person does, say, which is a help if one has a good antecedent theory of virtue. This is an important point, for although the very notion of 'virtue' carries with it a positive connotation, different and sometimes competing lists of virtues have been proposed. Humility is a virtue in Christianity but it figures neither in Aristotle's nor Nietzsche's views. Practical wisdom is chief among the Aristotelian virtues but appears nowhere in religious ethics, where intelligence and knowledge are on the whole regarded as negatives, since they interfere with the simplicity that makes submission (unquestioningness) to a deity (a priesthood) more complete.

For these reasons academic discussions of virtue ethics chiefly focus on the nature of the virtues and their relation to the traditional concerns of moral philosophy – the questions of obligation and right action – and both are important matters. But the very existence of debate about the good life and the overall ethical character of individuals who live it is a wholesome departure.

It remains that the largest and richest store of reflection on all questions of importance about the good life for humankind is literature – the novels, poems, plays and essays that distil and debate the experience of mankind in its richest variety. It does not matter whether a literary work is tendentious or not, that is, urges a point of view or enjoins a way of life; from that point of view literature is a Babel of competing opinions and outlooks. For the earnest enquirer that is a good thing, because the more viewpoints, perspectives and experiences that come as grist to his mill through the medium of literature, the more chance he has of expanding his understanding, refining his sympathies, and considering his options. That is the great service of attentive and thoughtful reading: it educates and extends the moral imagination, affording insights into – and therefore the chance to be more tolerant of – other lives, other ways, other choices, most of which one will probably never directly experience oneself. And tolerance is a virtue which no list of virtues could well be without, and without which no human existence could be complete or good.

9

LAYING THE GHOSTS

Humanist values

Anyone influenced by the humanist spirit as understood here – the spirit common to classical antiquity, the Renaissance, the Enlightenment, and the modern scientific revolution – would most likely nominate individual liberty, the pursuit of knowledge, the cultivation of pleasures that do not harm others, the satisfactions of art, personal relationships, and a sense of belonging to the human community, as the elements of the good life. They will list them when asked what offers people their best chance of fulfilment and, equally importantly, the opportunity to live a life directed by knowledge and reflection; for 'fulfilment' can never be understood as meaning some thin, vacuous species of 'happiness' that could be produced by a pill, or by acceptance of a system of falsehoods and illusions, or by any other means of limitation and ignorance. In particular, such people believe that liberty, love and the rest can do this without the aid of belief in supernatural agencies or adherence to an organised religion.

For much of its history – indeed, ever since the rise to dominance of Christianity in Europe in the fourth century AD – humanism has felt itself obliged to defend its commitment to secularism against the religionists' charge that it carries an excessively high price – the price, so the latter allege, of destruction of values and relationships, and ultimately of the self itself. One way this charge can be dramatised is to allegorise it as the already quoted Tzvetan Todorov does in his book *The Imperfect Garden*

– as a devil's pact after the fashion of Faust. In this allegory the devil offers Modern Man free will, which means the power to choose how to live; but he hides from Man the triple cost of his gift, which is that it will separate him from god, from his fellow man, and finally from himself. God will vanish because there will no longer be reason to believe that there exists a being superior to man, and therefore man 'will have no more ideals or values – will be a "materialist"'. Fellowship will go because other people will no longer matter, and every individual's circle of concern will shrink from community to family and in the end to his own self. Finally the individual's self will go too because, once separated from his community, an individual will be nothing but a collection of impulses, 'an infinite dispersal', alienated and inauthentic.

The point of Todorov's argument is not, of course, to substantiate this picture, but the reverse: he aims to show that humanism does not have to purchase the freedom it takes as its fundamental premise – the freedom to choose for oneself – by forfeiting common values or social relations, nor by sacrificing the integrity of selfhood. He does it by looking at the statement of the humanist case in its inception, in the full vigour of its originators' thought, which in his view occurred in the period from the sixteenth to the nineteenth centuries, with Montaigne, Descartes, Montesquieu, Rousseau, Constant and Tocqueville in its vanguard. What these thinkers jointly suggest to Todorov is an interpretation of humanism as involving three principal theses: recognition of the equal dignity of everyone, altruism (the 'elevation of the particular human being other than me as the ultimate goal of my action'), and the preference for freedom of action. These are irreducible values in the sense that they cannot be explained in terms of each other – they may even indeed be inconsistent with one another at times. But what creates humanism is their interaction, principally through the way they constrain one another. My freedom cannot be enjoyed at the expense of your freedom or dignity; my autonomy is limited by considerations of the equality and fraternity of all in the community to which I belong. Citizens might be interchangeable as members of society, but as individuals they are indispensable; it is their differences that matter, not their equality; and the relations between them turn on free choices and interpersonal affections.

Todorov describes the human domain as an 'imperfect garden' because his humanism is practical, realistic, even a little world-weary. His humanism does not 'believe' in man or unqualifiedly sing his praises. It sees his flaws, his failings, his capacity for evil. But through his freedom man is also capable of choosing the good, and it is this that saves him. The values of community and relationship are voluntary, and at their best humans premise their lives on them. In this respect humanism has natural affinities with democracy, even if it does not single out one political persuasion rather than another; for the humanistic impulse towards community and fraternity reveals that its basis is the belief that other people, far from being hell, are our escape from hell – which, although it does not make the human realm heaven, at least makes it fully man's own.

There is much in these views to accept, as a pragmatic and fundamentally healthy version of the humanist outlook. They amount to an eloquent case for a sensible secular ethics without illusory ideals, positively Horatian in their experienced view of things human – and for that reason they recommend themselves as a corrective to the enthusiasms that strain towards utopian visions of the good, visions which find proofs of mankind's large capacity for evil – consider again the egregious example of the Holocaust – difficult to contain and assimilate.

But although one can sympathise with almost all of this, there is a cavil. This is that the supposed price paid for man's free will is, as Todorov describes it, immediately and obviously implausible. Yes, the notion of supernatural agencies evaporates when mankind attains his majority and assumes moral and intellectual responsibility for himself, because of course varieties of fatalism, and the subordination of the self to heteronomous direction of the kind most religions demand, lose all credibility. But this happens in conjunction with views of the natural and social worlds informed by science, among them observations of the essential sociability of humankind, so that at the very outset of accepting his individuality and asserting his autonomy, Modern Man recognises himself as inherently a community being also. That is why the humanist project of the Enlightenment immediately involved debate about institutions of law, government and education, of the kind required by a comity of freely though mutually engaged agents. So centrally is this fact placed in humanism that it is hard to see how opponents, suppositious or otherwise, could have failed to recognise the essentially democratic and contractarian nature of the ideal.

The real problem faced by the humanist project is the survival of religious beliefs and practices, and in particular their growth in parts of the world, especially Africa and Asia, where the fertile mixture of under-education, poverty, impotence and resentment makes the promises and quick psychological fixes of religion especially welcome. Fundamentalist forms of Christianity, of the Pentecostal and charismatic kind mixed with local superstitions, have flourished mightily from their missionary roots in ex-colonial Africa, and can be observed at full strength among the émigré West African communities of south London. Islam is readily seen by its votaries as radical because it is a simple and direct religion which easily lends itself to political and military applications, thereby offering the illusion of power and a sense of pride to otherwise disempowered communities. All these forms of religious expression are essentially regressive, oppressive and at best medieval, and their dissonance with the modern world is a continual and too often terrible source of conflict.

Religion and the public domain of morality

Religion has been given comfortable house room in liberal democracies, which protect the right of people to believe as they wish, and accept the wide variety of faiths brought into them by immigrants from all over the world. This has to be accepted, for freedom of speech and belief are essential values, and the very idea of democratic society is premised on the idea of liberty. (It should be, but alas it is not, needless to say: responsibly exercised liberty, something which is not always guaranteed by the enthusiasms and dogmatic certitudes of faith.)

As votaries of imported religions grow more assertive in seeking the same privileges as are enjoyed by religious organisations indigenous to those democracies, and as the tolerant democracies respond concessively, so the prospect arises of ever-increasing difficulty. It seems that Western governments do not fully appreciate this, because, for one example, they tolerate and in some cases encourage the spread of faith-based schools, whether Christian, Islamic, Jewish or Sikh, and legislate to protect people from harassment or discrimination if suffered specifically on the grounds of faith. Both developments seem innocuous, even (in the latter case) desirable; but in fact they dramatically increase the potential for problems, which when understood shows why the public domain needs to be completely secularised.

The reason lies in the fact that the world's major religions – especially Christianity, Islam and Judaism – are not merely incompatible with one another, but mutually antithetical. All religions are such that, if they are pushed to their logical conclusions, or if their founding literatures and early traditions are accepted literally, they will take the form of their respective fundamentalisms. Jehovah's Witnesses and the Taliban are thus not aberrations, but unadulterated and unconstrained expressions of their respective faiths, as practised by people who are not interested in refined temporisings or theological niceties, but who literally accept the world view of the writings they regard as sacred, and insist on the morality and way of life prescribed by them.

This is where the most serious threat lies, because all the major religions in fact blaspheme one another, and each by its principles ought actively to oppose the others – although not, one pessimistically hopes, as they did in the past with crusades, jihads and pogroms. They blaspheme each other in numerous ways. All non-Christians blaspheme Christianity by their refusal to accept the divinity of Christ, because in so doing they reject the Holy Ghost, doing which is described as the most serious of all blasphemies. The New Testament has Christ say, 'I am the way, the truth and the life; no one comes to the Father but by me.' This places members of other faiths beyond redemption if they hear this claim but do not heed it. By an unlucky twist of theology, Protestants have to regard Catholics as blasphemers too, because the latter regard Mary as co-redemptorix with Christ, in violation of the utterance just quoted.

All non-Muslims blaspheme Islam because they insult Mohammed by not accepting him as the true prophet, and by ignoring the teachings of the Koran. Jews seem the least philosophically troubled by what people of other faiths think about their own, but Orthodox Jews regard themselves as religiously superior to all who fail in the proper observances, for example by not respecting kosher constraints. And in general all the religions blaspheme each other by regarding the others' teachings, metaphysics and much of their ethics as false and even pernicious, and their own religion as the only true one.

It is a liberal hope that all religions might be viewed as worshipping the same deity, only in different ways; but this woolly-minded expedient is untenable, as shown by the most cursory comparison of teachings, interpretations, moral requirements, creation myths and eschatologies, in all of which the major religions differ and frequently contradict each other. History shows how clearly the religions themselves grasped this; the motivation for Christianity's hundreds of years of crusades against Islam, pogroms against Jews, and inquisitions against heretics, was the desire to expunge heterodoxy and 'infidelity', or at least to effect forcible compliance with prevailing orthodoxy. Islam's various jihads and fatwas had and have the same aim, and it has spread halfway around the world by conquest and the sword.

Where they can get away with it – as the Taliban did in Afghanistan – fundamentalists continue the same practices. The religious right in America would doubtless do so too, but it has to use television advertising and political lobbying to urge its version of the truth on America. It is only where religion is on the back foot, reduced to a minority practice, with an insecure tenure in society, that it presents itself as essentially peaceful and charitable.

This is the chief reason why allowing the major religions to jostle against one another in the public domain is dangerous. The solution is to make the public domain wholly secular, leaving religion to the personal sphere, as a matter of private observance only. Society should be blind to religion both in the sense that it lets people believe and behave as they wish provided they do no harm to others, and in the sense that it acts as if religions do not exist, with public affairs being straightforwardly secular in character. The constitution of the United States of America provides exactly this, though the religious lobby is always trying to breach it – while government grants of public funds for 'faith-based initiatives' actually do so.

To secularise society in Western democracies at least requires withholding public funding for, or removing the privileging (for example, by withdrawing charitable status) of, faith schools and related organisations and activities, and by ending religious programming in public broadcasting. In Britain it would mean the disestablishment of the Church of England, and the repeal of laws relating to blasphemy and sacrilege, leaving protection of private observance to the safeguards that already adequately exist in law.

As science and technology take the modern world even further away from the ancient superstitions in which religions consist, and as secular values continue to grow in influence, the resulting tensions between the new and old world views can only become greater. The science–religion debate of the nineteenth century was a skirmish in comparison to what is invited by allowing not just religion but mutually competing religions so much presence in public space. Mankind's future needs the public domain to be a neutral territory where all can meet, without prejudice, as humans and equals; and that requires the wholesale privatisation of superstition.

A case for the defence

If religion were removed from the public domain it would be harder, to some degree anyway, for organised faiths to maintain their numbers. One reason is that religions survive chiefly because they proselytise the very young, before they acquire the intellectual capacity to resist or question what they are being told. (In England over eighty per cent of Church of England schools are primary schools for this reason.) Committed parents and their churches would no doubt continue to propagandise the young, but the absence of public reinforcement, appearing to take the form of official endorsement, would be something of a counterweight.

For those whose psychological commitment to some form of religious faith is deeply rooted, the idea of a wholly secular society is anathema. But less committed people can feel the same, believing – often rather vaguely – that some conception of 'spiritual' values, or at least expressly non-materialistic ones, is required for human flourishing. As an eloquent example of a conservative view about the condition of man in modern society, one need look no further than an attack mounted by the philosopher Anthony O'Hear against what he says is the false promise of Progress, as embodied in science and the humanist values of reason, atheism, democracy and human rights. He thinks that acceptance of these notions in the contemporary world has degraded our experience, foisted shallow materialistic values on us, and banished the only thing that can bind humanity together, namely, a recognition of life's higher purposes as expressed by religion.

O'Hear devotes the bulk of his argument to examining the sources of what he describes as Progress's deleterious effects. They are, predictably, the scientific revolution of the seventeenth century, eighteenth-century Enlightenment theories about man and society culminating in the French Revolution, and the later progeny of these theories in nineteenth-century science, along with Darwinism, Marxism and Freudianism. Opposed to these successive tidal waves which, he says, have engulfed mankind in a swill of agnostic materialistic triviality, are the great figures of the counter-Enlightenment, and especially Edmund Burke, whose argument that tradition is the precipitate of historical wisdom O'Hear eagerly accepts as a defence of conservatism. And he describes as 'thinkers of loss' those writers – Plato, Augustine, Nietzsche, Spengler – who did not, in their speculations about man and society, accept assumptions of the kind that underlie the modern world. Despite occasional gestures towards the fact that not everything brought by Progress is bad (antibiotics and electric light, for example), O'Hear finds nothing but disenchantment in it otherwise – even literally so, using this word to describe the reductive effect that science has had, in his opinion, on our perceptions, by turning the world into a prosaic realm of mere fact.

What is wrong with O'Hear's case is not hard to see. His chief mistake is to accept the false and hackneyed claim that Western man is unhappy, empty and lost because material values have displaced spiritual ones. The opposite is the truth:

more people are happier now than has ever been the case. It is a mistake to think that peasants were happier in days of yore – scratching their lice in church on Sundays, which they attended despite the hectoring sermons and boredom because it was warm and provided a diversion from their daily routines (indeed, it probably provided their principal measure of theatre and art), and because anyway they had been indoctrinated from childhood into thinking they would suffer eternal damnation if they did not at least sometimes conform to the requirements of the faith they had been born into. It is a mistake to think that they were more fulfilled and content with their laborious days slogging about in muddy fields, and their illiterate candle-lit nights drinking home-made beer and chewing bread with grit in it, than their descendants who have television, football, bingo, cinema, shopping malls, theme parks, zoos, holidays in Majorca, sliced bread, and vastly more money and more things to spend it on than their forebears could even dream of. People are now, accordingly and as a rule, neither unhappy nor empty; to have the satisfaction of a good grumble they are obliged to complain about the weather or our national sports teams – barrel-scrapings by comparison to the harsh realities of life in the Good Old Days mourned by nostalgists.

Once one denies O'Hear's premise that contemporary humankind (or, at least, Western humankind) is unhappy and unfulfilled, the rest of his case fails. Many people have given up the older religious traditions and substituted a Babel of New Age religion and quasi-religion in its place, often a pick-and-mix involving some tincture of astrology, feng shui, herbalism, and much besides (usually in short-lived bursts, between the shiatsu and the low-fat diet) – because life has become lifestyle and the shopping-mall ethos applies as much in philosophies as in footwear. That is a fact; it is neither good nor bad except as taste dictates. Like O'Hear one might infinitely prefer to do nothing but very highbrow things – read Goethe, listen to Schubert, dine after the theatre with good conversationalists –

and one might be right to argue as Mill did (despite the imme-diate charges of elitism and pretension it would attract to do so) that such a life is richer both in content and meaning than the bingo-and-beer version. But the latter is a preference even for some who know about Goethe and Schubert, and it is a mistake to think that if only one closed the bingo halls and shopping malls (and for the O'Hears of this world, the science laboratories too) and got people back into church, they would all begin to read Goethe and listen to Schubert. They would not.

Moreover, O'Hear is wrong to think that High Culture is under threat from the reductivism of Progress. High Culture was always the preserve of a tiny minority; its tender candle flame has been kept alight among the gales of barbarism throughout history by little bands of devotees. The happy fact is that things are now far safer for High Culture than they have ever been. Far more people now than at any time in history visit art galleries, attend theatres, listen to classical music, read the great works of the literary canon, and make systematic study of the arts and humanities. Rather than being engulfed by Progress, High Culture has been given wings by it.

At the end of his book O'Hear writes vaguely of a 'higher power' through which salvation for mankind will come – salva-tion, remember, from Progress and materialism. We would fill up the alleged spiritual vacuum induced by too much wealth and enjoyment – we would overcome our human inadequacy, as demonstrated by the gulf between 'ancient wisdom' and the 'brashness of modern times' – if only we would be humble and 'cede to silence and waiting'. Such is O'Hear's solution to the deluge of woes he says have been brought by science and Enlightenment. He longs for a pre-Raphaelite world without the present age's distractions; he would like to turn the clock back – but one cannot understand why he wishes to turn it back for the rest of humanity too. One can, by contrast, wholly understand those who welcome modern dentistry, lap-top computers, television and air travel; who marvel at the beauty and power of science, and what it has revealed about this extraordinary universe of ours; who welcome the fact that more and more people are gaining access to the good things of life, intellectually as well as materially – and who have no wish to send anyone back to life in a hut made of peat, lived under the oppression of priests and warlords, with only the rain and an early death for a horizon.

The long war

To some, writers of O'Hear's persuasion seem to be continuing to fight a battle long lost. Received wisdom has it that, after the bruising conflict between science and religion in nineteenth-century Britain, religion subsided into a period of quiescent decline that, apart from a few twitches and spasms, continues to this day. The conflict was sparked by Darwin's ideas, and fanned by the rapid growth of scientific knowledge and its applications through technology, which to educated people seemed to sweep ancient superstition out of its path with a properly dismissive hand. Only in America, with the Scopes trial of 1925, the continuing determined efforts of Southern fundamentalists to resist evolutionary theory and the secular thrust of the American Constitution, does the conflict still have life.

This picture, however, is not altogether right. It misses one significant and intriguing twist, which is that in the first three decades of the twentieth century a rapprochement between science and religion was mooted by some on both sides, and nearly achieved, but was in the end repudiated not by scientists but by conservative churchmen.

This is a fascinating and instructive lost chapter in the history of ideas, and illustrates an important truth, namely, that the opposing intellectual structures of religion and science are direct and utterly incompatible rivals as claimants to possession of truth about the world. (A cynic might say: 'To get a feel for the rivalry, and incidentally to see which of the rivals to put your money on, try lighting your room by prayer instead of electricity.') Those theologians who recognised that they had better not concede too much to science won the day over their negotiation-minded fellows; and this coincided with a tremor in the churchgoing population as economic and military uncertainties increasingly overshadowed the 1930s, making conservatism in faith once more attractive. It coincided too with a period of increased conversion to Catholicism in England – among the converts, amazingly, some intelligent people – an extraordinary phenomenon of the inter-war years in Britain, a sort of semi-mass hysteria induced no doubt by the shock of the previous war and an inability to cope with the coming of new things in science and thought.

The intriguing central feature of the science–religion story in the early twentieth century is that religiously minded scientists and scientifically minded theologians thought they saw opportunities for a rapprochement (or at least a cohabitation) between their respective outlooks, in two features of contemporary science: the apparent immaterialism of early twentieth-century physics, and the feasibility of giving a Whig interpretation to evolution, construing it as an onward and upward process of improvement, expressive of creative purpose. It was this idea in particular – the idea of progress – that failed in the gloom of the 1930s, and made the susceptible reach, as they always do in such circumstances, for eternal verities in place of unpalatable truths. It is notable that some of those who did not turn to prayer turned instead to Marxism as an alternative nostrum, because it too offered certainty and a form of faith in the future, although it also required belief in progressive inevitability of a quasi-Darwinian kind, and therefore demanded a degree of optimism that many were ceasing to feel. To these latter human nature seemed, as religious thinking postulated, a fixed entity, not innately good (as the doctrine of

Original Sin asserted; and pessimist thinkers like T. E. Hulme gave this doctrine a sociological twist), and anyway limited in its capacities and possibilities. Human beings accordingly required strong government both secularly and spiritually. It is no accident that the Catholic converts and Anglo-Catholics of the period, men like Hilaire Belloc and T. S. Eliot, Hulme and Chesterton, were also political conservatives to a marked and in some cases extreme degree.

So, to disillusioned folk in the 1930s modernism seemed discredited, and traditional pieties accordingly resumed their attractiveness. Some attribute the indifference to science of Karl Barth and other leading theologians to their belief that 'natural theology' is impossible. In their view, humanity's supposed 'alienation from God' seemed a vastly more important matter than study of the physical universe could ever be. So the failure of the enterprise of reconciliation and mutual understanding came down to theologians thinking that science was either an enemy or an irrelevance – and accordingly a spirit of mutual distrust descended, akin to a cold war.

This failed effort at reconciliation offers much incidental food for thought about the future relations of faith and reason in a world in which science has advanced even further, and religion – or some of it – has plunged even further back to its dark primitive roots.

Science and hope

One major hope for the future is science. The other is the study of history, for to know the past is to understand the present. This thought speaks for itself. But the place of science in providing the framework for the good life merits a fuller meditation, as follows.

Imagine a medieval stonemason resting from his labours halfway up a Gothic cathedral spire. He gazes – if he is a man of sensibility, he marvels – at the world spread around him. What does he see? Leaving aside such details as urban sprawl, factory chimneys and passing aircraft, he sees much the same world as we now do. But in another sense of 'see' we now see the world in a way inconceivable for him, because the stories told then and now about the nature and origins of the universe are vastly different. Both stories are strange and in their way beautiful; but the one told by modern science is infinitely stranger and more beautiful than any hitherto dreamed by mankind.

Science is to the contemporary world what art was to the Renaissance: a magnificent creative achievement that transforms humanity's perception of itself and its relationship to the world. By means of the many excellent popularising science books now standardly available, non-scientists can spectate the unfolding sagas of genetics, particle physics, brain research, palaeoanthropology and astronomy – the sciences that most catch public imagination because they lie closest to its philosophical concerns – rather as they stroll through a gallery to look at paintings. This is as it should be, because the more scientific literacy there is, and with it general knowledge about the aims, successes and limitations of science, the better.

In its beauty and transforming power, as in the dangers it can pose, science is mankind's most formidable achievement. Achievements in art, by comparison, for all their supreme importance in themselves, touch minorities only, and even at their most potent are restricted to transfiguring the mental lives of the relatively few rather than the world of the many. But science, particularly through its technological applications, is able to reach everyone, for good or ill.

Moreover, where art seems to flower and decline at the whim of history – not cumulatively but cyclically, each phase existing for itself alone – science since its crucial moment in the seventeenth century has expanded, progressed, risen like a strong upward line on a graph, each phase building on the last and then superseding it, yielding new insights and greater knowledge. The efficacy of science and its cumulative character go together; we seem constantly to be learning more about the world – and knowledge is power.

Yet science's progress has not been without its false starts and wrong turns, just as with any other human endeavour, and it has sometimes been just as susceptible to prejudice and folly. Sometimes, too, its very aberrations contain the makings of powerful scientific advances, only appreciated long after they were first mooted.

Some argue that science's main problem is its inaccessibility. Non-scientists find science difficult to understand and are therefore afraid of it. Until a century ago science was, or at least could be, anyone's business. Now it is as arcane and complicated as the most secret mystery cult, and in consequence has become alienated from much of our culture, which encounters it only through its technological effects. The result is that some think as did Thomas Love Peacock's character Dr Opimian in *Gryll Grange*, who remarked, 'I almost think it is the ultimate destiny of science to exterminate the human race.' This is possibly the first recorded expression of anxiety about the physical threat posed to humankind by science; hitherto it had posed only a theological threat, by impiously claiming to breach the divine monopoly of knowledge about the workings of creation.

The three ugly sisters Ignorance, Superstition and Greed have always been enemies of science. Dr Opimian's fear of science stemmed from the first two. They need no explaining, but the third does; for greed proves itself an enemy of science by perverting it to such ends as the despoliation of the environment for profit, and the invention of ever more destructive weapons of war – thus bringing science into disrepute. An ill-assorted anti-scientific league results, made up of those who know nothing about science, those who understand the horrors that wicked people can conjure from it, and those whose beliefs about the world have remained essentially unchanged since the Stone Age.

Science's defenders say that it need not be a threat either to the environment or – by way of genetic engineering and the like – to the autonomy and uniqueness of human beings. They are especially concerned to show that most of the fears entertained by those hostile to science are unfounded or exaggerated, arguing that the dangers of global warming, environmental pollution, depletion of resources and other kinds of Doomsday threats are all overstated; and that science will anyway help to solve problems and create new benefits as it progresses. They also play down such problems as the risk of radioactive fallout from disasters at nuclear power stations, and environmental damage caused by industry.

Public disquiet and even suspicion about such defences is understandable and sometimes justified. But one can be vigorously pro-science without trying to mask the real dangers that its use can pose. It is better to argue that science is often our best hope for dealing with science's mistakes and misapplications, as our environmental problems and scientific solutions to them demonstrate. The chief point is that the scientific attitude – which as a matter of normal best practice values enquiry, curiosity and observation, rigorous testing of ideas, experiment, open-mindedness, preparedness to think again in the face of new evidence – is what has given us the long list of benefits without which most of us now would not know what we know, do what we do, or even, perhaps, have lived as long as we so far have.

Towards the good life

When science replaces mythology as the framework for understanding the world, it brings with it its enquiring, questioning, open-minded attitudes, and that in turn – as happened when the eighteenth-century Enlightenment applied the inspiration of seventeenth-century science to questions of human nature and society – makes possible a better and finer understanding of what conduces to the human good. The insistence on the adjective 'human' is crucial, for it is insight into human needs and human nature which alone makes possible a grasp of what would promote human flourishing. Many practices of religion and government throughout the ages have depended pivotally on an understanding of how to manipulate human beings, by identifying and inflaming their baser instincts, chiefly those of greed and fear: greed for wealth, position and honours; fear of death, hell and punishment. But a less self-serving enquiry into the human condition, one that had as its aim the identification of what would give humans their best chance of living satisfying, creative, generous lives characterised by pleasure and wisdom, would seek rather to grasp the necessary conditions for this possibility. As humanists of all epochs have seen, these conditions are the things listed in this chapter's opening paragraph: individual liberty, the pursuit of knowledge, the cultivation of pleasures, the satisfactions of art, personal relationships, and a sense of belonging to the human community.

Although there is no ambiguity in any of these notions, most are unspecific – and deliberately so. Take the expression 'personal relationships' for example; obviously, this means love and friendship, but both love and friendship are capacious notions, and the kinds of interpersonal bonds which humans are capable of forming admit many varieties and different degrees. But this is exactly the point of individual liberty: that it leaves to individuals the latitude to work out such details for themselves. The creativity of living resides in the way individual freedom is used in forming relationships, gaining and applying knowledge, and cultivating and enjoying pleasures. And it always goes without saying that these pursuits have to be conducted consistently with the freedom and well-being of others.

In everything that has been said in this book about the humanist conception of the good life, the concepts of freedom and autonomy have been central. From classical antiquity to modern philosophy the fundamental idea has been that people possess reason, and that by using it they can choose lives worth living for themselves and respectful of their fellows. The contrast between a humanist ethics of freedom and a transcendentalist claim that man's good lies in submission to an external authority – the authority of a supposed divine power or transcendent order; which in concrete terms means the teachings of a priesthood or tradition – is therefore a very sharp one. Where humanism premises autonomy as the basis of the good life, religion premises heteronomy. In humanist ethics the individual is responsible for achieving the good as a free member of a community of free agents; in religious ethics he achieves the good by obedience to an authority that tells him what his goals are and how he should live. Given that the metaphysics of religion is man-made, and that human psychology is the source of belief in the power of transcendent authority to reward obedience or punish its opposite ('sin', one must remember, explicitly means disobedience), it follows that the chief motivation for religious ethics is the need felt by potentates of many kinds to exert control over individuals, to limit their freedom, to make them conform, obey, submit, follow where led, accept what is meted out to them, and resign themselves to their lot.

It takes no special insight to see how powerful an instrument of social management this is, and how helpful it is to a ruler to have the aid of an invisible policeman in the form of a deity, who knows even what men think in private. Of course, rulers who cannot tolerate their subjects' freedom have also had to resort to other means besides, ranging from spies and terror to bread and circuses; but gaining a hold on men's minds through the potencies of superstition has long been a crucial instrument. All history, and too much of the contemporary world, is living proof of this unhappy truth. This explains why the ethical and intellectual history of the West can be seen as presented here: as the long struggle for people's minds between the two conceptions of the good, the autonomy of humanism and the heteronomy of religion. By far most of what has been a gain for both individuals and civilisation in the West has come from the endeavours and triumphs of the former.

It is impossible to conceive of a free and creative life in the humanist sense as one lived without alertness, sensitivity and insight. This tells us what Socrates meant when he said that the best life is the considered life. To the question 'What is good?', then, the answer can only be: 'The considered life – free, creative, informed and chosen, a life of achievement and fulfilment, of pleasure and understanding, of love and friendship; in short, the best human life in a human world, humanely lived.'

ACKNOWLEDGEMENTS

Thanks to Catherine Clarke, Ken Gemes, Elizabeth Shenton, Louise Page, Richard Milner, Rebecca Wilson, and especially Katie Hickman, for help of various kinds in connection with the writing of this book. I am grateful also to the librarians of the London Library, Birkbeck College Library, and the British Library. Parts of some of the later chapters, dealing with recent and contemporary ethical concerns, began life as essays in *Prospect*, *Index on Censorship*, *New Statesman* and the *Observer*, and in the review sections of *The Economist*, the *Guardian*, *Financial Times*, *Independent on Sunday* and *Literary Review*, and I am grateful to have had the opportunity to give a first airing to the ideas they contain in those forums. In a couple of places I have reprised short passages from my *The Reason of Things* because, needing to make the same points, I found the way they were expressed there as apt for the task as I could make them. My chief intellectual debt is to the scholars, philosophers and historians past and present whose spadework has made it possible for successors to meditate on the large themes surveyed in this book; for we ride on their shoulders, and see the view courtesy of their high achievements.

SELECT BIBLIOGRAPHY
AND REFERENCES

Chapter 1, Introduction: Shadows and Shapings

Hare, Augustus, *Peculiar People: The Story of My Life* (Chicago, 1995)
Pater, Walter, *The Renaissance* (Oxford, 1998)
Tanizaki, Junichiro, *In Praise of Shadows* (London, 1988)

Chapter 2, The Classical Conception of the Good Life

Ackrill, J. L., *Aristotle the Philosopher* (Oxford, 1981)
Adkins, A. W. H., 'Homeric Values and Homeric Society', *Journal of Hellenic Studies*, 91, 1–14 (1971)
Aeschylus, *Complete Greek Tragedies* (Chicago, 1959)
Allan, D. J., *The Philosophy of Aristotle* (Oxford, 1970)
Annas, J., *An Introduction to Plato's Republic* (Oxford, 1981)
Aristophanes, *Clouds* (Warminster, 1982)
Aristotle, *The Complete Works*, ed. J. Barnes, 2 vols. (Princeton, NJ, 1984)
Barnes, J., *Aristotle* (Oxford, 1982)
Barnes, J., *Early Greek Philosophy* (Harmondsworth, 1987)
Boardman, J., Griffin, J., and Murray, O. (eds.), *Oxford History of the Classical World* (Oxford, 1986)
Bowra, C. M., *Homer* (London, 1972)
Crombie, I. M., *Plato: The Midwife's Apprentice* (London, 1964)
Finley, M. I., *Aspects of Antiquity* (London, 1968)
Finley, M. I. (ed.), *New Legacy of Greece* (Oxford, 1981)

Griffin, J., *Homer on Life and Death* (Oxford, 1980)

Gruber, G. M. A., *Plato's Thought* (London, 1980)

Guthrie, W. K. C., *The Greeks and their Gods* (London, 1950)

Guthrie, W. K. C., *A History of Greek Philosophy*, 6 vols. (Cambridge, 1962–81, 1962)

Hardie, W. F. R., *Aristotle's Ethical Theory*, 2nd edn (Oxford, 1980)

Homer, *Iliad*, trans. R. Lattimore (Chicago, 1951)

Homer, *Odyssey*, trans. R. Lattimore (New York, 1967)

Irwin, T. H., *Aristotle's First Principles* (Oxford, 1988)

Irwin, T. H., *Plato's Moral Theory* (Oxford, 1977)

Jones, A. H. M., *Athenian Democracy* (Oxford, 1957)

Kraut, Richard (ed.), *The Cambridge Companion to Plato* (Cambridge, 1992)

Lear, J., *Aristotle: The Desire to Understand* (Cambridge, 1988)

Lloyd, G. E., *Aristotle: The Growth and Structure of his Thought* (Cambridge, 1968)

Long, A. A., 'Morals and values in Homer', *Journal of Hellenic Studies*, 90, 121–39 (1970)

Moravcsik, J. M. E. (ed.), *Aristotle* (London, 1968)

Plato, *Collected Dialogues*, ed. E. Hamilton and H. Cairns (Princeton, NJ, 1961)

Rorty, A. O. (ed.), *Essays on Aristotle's Ethics* (Berkeley, 1980)

Vlastos, Gregory, *The Philosophy of Socrates* (Garden City, 1971)

Vlastos, Gregory, *Platonic Studies* (Princeton, NJ, 1981)

Vlastos, Gregory, *Socrates: Ironist and Moral Philosopher* (Cambridge, 1991)

Vlastos, Gregory, *Socratic Studies*, ed. M. Burnyeat (Cambridge, 1994)

White, N. P. A., *A Companion to Plato's Republic* (Oxford, 1979)

Chapter 3, The Philosophic Ideal

Arnold, E. V., *Roman Stoicism* (Cambridge, 1911)

Austin, M. M., *The Hellenistic World* (Cambridge, 1981)

Bailey, C. M. A., *Epicurus: The Extant Remains* (Oxford, 1926)

Bevan, E., *Stoics and Sceptics* (Oxford, 1926)

Branham, R. B., and Goulet-Caze, M. O., *The Cynics* (Berkeley, 1996)

Bury, J. B., and Barber, E. A., *The Hellenistic Age: Aspects of Hellenistic Civilisation* (New York, 1970)

Cicero, *On the Good Life* ('On Friendship', the 'Dream of Scipio', and selections from 'Tusculan Discussions', 'On Duties', and 'The Orator'), trans. Michael Grant (London, 1971)

Cicero, *On the Nature of the Gods* (Loeb, 1933)

Cicero, *Stoic Paradoxes* (Warminster, 1991)

Clarke, M. L., *The Roman Mind* (London, 1956)

Diogenes Laertius, *Lives of the Philosophers*, 2 vols. (Loeb, 1925)

Dodds, E. R., *The Ancient Concept of Progress and Other Essays* (Oxford, 1973)

Dodds, E. R., *The Greeks and the Irrational* (Berkeley, 1951)

Dudley, Donald R., *A History of Cynicism* (London, 1937)

Epictetus, *Discourses and Encheiridion*, 2 vols. (Loeb, 1925)

Erskine, A., *The Hellenistic Stoa* (London, 1990)

Ferguson, J., *The Heritage of Hellenism* (New York, 1971)

Ferguson, W. S., *Hellenistic Athens* (London, 1911)

Green, Peter, *Alexander to Actium: The Historical Evolution of the Hellenistic Age* (1990)

Inwood, B., *Ethics and Human Action in Early Stoicism* (Oxford, 1985)

Jones, H., *The Epicurean Tradition* (London, 1989)

Long, A. A., *Hellenistic Philosophy* (London, 1974)

Long, A. A., and Sedley, D. N., *The Hellenistic Philosophers* (Cambridge, 1987)

Lucretius, *On the Nature of Things* (Loeb, 1975)

Marcus Aurelius, *Meditations* (London, 1970)

Mitsis, P., *Epicurus' Ethical Theory* (New York, 1988)

Navia, Luis E., *Classical Cynicism* (Westport, 1996)

Pliny the Younger, *Letters* (Cambridge, Mass., 1969)

Plutarch, *Moralia* (Loeb, 1949)

Sandbach, F. H., *The Stoics* (London, 1975)

Seneca, *Letters* (Cambridge, Mass., 1925)

Seneca, *Moral Essays* (Loeb, 1920)

Walbank, F. W., *The Hellenistic World* (London, 1981)

Chapter 4, The Ordinances of God

Augustine, *City of God* (Loeb, 1968)

Augustine, *Confessions* (Loeb, 1912)

Bernstein, A. E., *The Formation of Hell* (London, 1993)

Bible, King James Version (1611); New Revised Standard Version (1989)

Brooke, R., and Brooke, C., *Popular Religion in the Middle Ages* (London, 1971)

Brown, P., *The Body and Society: Men, Women and Sexual Renunciation* (New York, 1988)

Chadwick, O., *Western Asceticism* (London, 1958)

Childress, J. F., and MacQuarrie, J. (eds.), *Westminster Dictionary of Christian Ethics* (London, 1986)

Cochrane, C. N., *Christianity and Classical Culture* (Oxford, 1944)

Gill, R. (ed.), *The Cambridge Companion to Christian Ethics* (Cambridge, 2000)

Gill, R., and Porter, J., *Moral Action and Christian Ethics* (Cambridge, 1999)

Gilson, E., *Christian Philosophy in the Middle Ages* (London, 1955)

Gorun, J. R., *Living the Christian Scriptures: Walking in the Footsteps of Jesus* (Dubuque, 1997)

Gula, R. M., *Reason Informed by Faith: Foundations of Catholic Morality*, Paulist Press (1989)

Hamilton, B., *The Medieval Inquisition* (London, 1981)

Kaye, B., and Wenham, G. (eds.), *Law, Morality and the Bible* (Downers Grove, 1978)

Lane-Fox, R., *Pagans and Christians* (London, 1960)

Lietzmann, H., *The Founding of the Church Universal*, 2nd edn (London, 1950)

Longnecker, R. N., *New Testament Social Ethics for Today* (Grand Rapids, 1984)

McCarty, M., *Living the Catholic Sacraments* (Dubuque, 1994)

Marrou, H. I., *Augustine and his Influence Through the Ages* (New York, 1957)

Mitchell, B. G., *Morality: Religious and Secular* (Oxford, 1980)

Moynahan, B., *The Faith: A History of Christianity* (London, 2002)

Outka, G., and Reeder, J., *Religion and Morality* (Garden City, 1973)

Pennock, M., *Living the Message of the New Testament* (Notre Dame, 1992)

Prochaska, L. M., *Living a Moral Life: Gifted and Growing*, 2nd edn (Mission Hills, 1992)

Stoutzenberger, J. M., *Morality: Christian Vision in Practice* (Dubuque, 1993)

Stump, E., and Murray, M. J., *Philosophy of Religion* (Oxford, 1999)

Chapter 5, The Second Enlightenment

Allen, P. S., *The Age of Erasmus* (Oxford, 1914)

Aretino, *Ragionamenti* [1534]

Armstrong, A. H. (ed.), *Cambridge History of Later Greek and Early Medieval Philosophy* (Cambridge, 1970)

Baker, H., *The Dignity of Man* (Cambridge, Mass., 1947)

Bamborough, J. B., *The Little World of Man* (London, 1952)

Baron, H., *From Petrarch to Leonardo Bruni* (Chicago, 1968)

Bentley, J. H., *Humanists and Holy Writ* (Princeton, 1983)

Boccaccio, *Decameron* [1350] (Oxford, 1998)

Bolgar, R. R. (ed.), *Classical Influences on European Culture* (2 vols., 500–1500, 1500–1700) (Cambridge, 1971 and 1976)

Bouwsma, W. J., *The Culture of Renaissance Humanism* (Washington, 1973)

Breen, Q., *Christianity and Humanism* (Grand Rapids, 1968)

Burckhardt, J., *The Civilisation of the Renaissance in Italy* (New York, 2002)

Burke, P., *Culture and Society in Renaissance Italy* (New York, 1972)

Bury, J. B., *History of the Freedom of Thought* (New York, 1975)

Bush, D., *The Renaissance and English Humanism* (Toronto, 1939)

Gilmore, M. P., *The World of Humanism* (New York, 1952)

Grafton, A., and Jardine, L., *From Humanism to the Humanities* (London, 1986)

Heller, A., *Renaissance Man* (London, 1978)

Knowles, D., *The Evolution of Medieval Thought* (London, 1962)

Kretzmann, N., et al., *Cambridge History of Later Medieval Philosophy* (Cambridge, 1982)

Kristeller, P. O., *Eight Philosophers of the Italian Renaissance* (Stanford, 1964)

Kristeller, P. O., *Renaissance Thought* (New York, 1961)

Kristeller, P. O., *Renaissance Thought II* (New York, 1965)

Kristeller, P. O., *Renaissance Thought and its Sources* (New York, 1979)

L'Engle, M., *The Glorious Impossible (Life of Giotto)* (New York, 1990)

Levi, A., *Renaissance and Reformation: The Intellectual Genesis* (London, 2002)

Mackail, J. W., *Studies in Humanism* (London, 1938)

Mann, N., *Petrarch* (Oxford, 1984)

Pfeiffer, R., *History of Classical Scholarship from 1300 to 1850* (Oxford, 1976)

Pico della Mirandola, *Oration on the Dignity of Man* [1486], trans. Russell Kirk (New York, 1996)

Randall, J. H., *The Making of the Modern Mind* (Cambridge, Mass., 1940)

Rashdall, H., *The Universities of Europe in the Middle Ages* (Oxford, 1936)

Saunders, J. L., *Justus Lipsius: The History of Renaissance Stoicism* (New York, 1955)

Schmitt, C. B., *Aristotle and the Renaissance* (Cambridge, Mass., 1983)

Schmitt, C. B., and Skinner, Q., *Cambridge History of Renaissance Philosophy* (Cambridge, 1988)

Siegel, J. E., *Rhetoric and Philosophy in Renaissance Humanism* (Princeton, 1968)

Taylor, H. O., *Thought and Expression in the Sixteenth Century* (New York, 1920)

Tracy, J., *Erasmus: The Growth of a Mind* (Geneva, 1972)

Ullmann, W., *The Medieval Foundations of Renaissance Humanism* (London, 1977)

Weiss, R., *The Renaissance Discovery of Classical Antiquity* (Oxford, 1969)

Wilkins, E. H., *Life of Petrarch* (Chicago, 1961)

Yates, F. A., *Collected Essays* (London, 1982–4)

Chapter 6, The Third Enlightenment

D'Alembert, J., *Preliminary Discourse to the Encyclopaedia of Diderot* (1751)

Anchor, R., *The Enlightenment Tradition* (New York, 1967)

Becker, C. L., *The Heavenly City of the Eighteenth Century Philosophers* (New Haven, 1932)

Bredvold, L., *The Brave New World of the Enlightenment* (Ann Arbor, 1961)

Brown, S. C. (ed.), *Philosophers of the Enlightenment* (Brighton, 1979)

Cassirer, E., *The Philosophy of the Enlightenment* (Princeton, 1951)

Condorcet, Marquis de, *The Future Progress of the Human Mind* (Paris, 1970)

Diderot, D., *The Encyclopaedia* (Selections), trans. S. Gendzier (New York, 1967)

Furbank, P. N., *Diderot* (London, 1992)

Fussell, P., *The Rhetorical World of Augustan Humanism* (Oxford, 1965)

Gaskin, J., *Hume's Philosophy of Religion* (Oxford, 1988)

Gay, P., *The Enlightenment: An Interpretation*, 2 vols. (New York, 1966, 1969)

Hankins, T., *Science and the Enlightenment* (Cambridge, 1985)

Harris, R. W., *Reason and Nature in the Eighteenth Century* (London, 1968)

Hazard, P., *European Thought in the Eighteenth Century* (London, 1954)

Hulme, P., and Jordanova, L. (eds.), *Enlightenment and its Shadows* (London, 1990)

Hume, D., *Enquiries Concerning Human Understanding and Concerning the Principles of Morals* (Oxford, 1975)

Hume, D., *Principal Writings on Religion, including Dialogues Concerning Natural Religion and the Natural History of Religion* (Oxford, 1998)

Hume, D., *A Treatise of Human Nature* (Oxford, 1978)

Hutcheson, F., *A System of Moral Philosophy* (London, 1755)

Kant, I., *Critique of Practical Reason*, trans. Lewis White Beck (Indianapolis, 1956)

Kant, I., *The Grounding for the Metaphysics of Morals*, trans. James Ellington (Indianapolis, 1981)

Locke, J., *An Essay Concerning Human Understanding* (Oxford, 1975)

Locke, J., *Two Treatises on Government* (Cambridge, 1960)

Lough, J. (ed.), *Essays on the Encyclopédie of Diderot and D'Alembert* (Oxford, 1968)

Lovejoy, A. O., *Essays in the History of Ideas* (Baltimore, 1948)

McKay, J. P., and Hill, B. D., *A History of Western Society*, vol. 1: *From Antiquity to the Enlightenment*, 5th edn (Princeton, 1995)

Mackie, J. L., *Hume's Moral Theory* (Oxford, 1980)

Mandeville, B., *The Fable of the Bees* (Oxford, 1924)

Manuel, F., *The Eighteenth Century Confronts the Gods* (Cambridge, Mass., 1959)

Martin, K., *French Liberal Thought in the Eighteenth Century* (London, 1929)

Outram, D., *The Enlightenment* (Cambridge, 1995)

Paine, T., *Essays on Religion* (New York, 1908)

Paine, T., *The Rights of Man* (1791–2)

Passmore, J. A., *The Perfectibility of Man* (London, 1970)

Payne, H. C., *The Philosophes and the People* (New Haven, 1976)

Raphael, D. D., *The Moral Sense* (Oxford, 1947)

Rockwood, R. (ed.), *Carl Becker's Heavenly City Revisited* (Ithaca, 1958)

Rousseau, J. J., *Confessions*, trans. J. Cohen (Cambridge, 1987)

Rousseau, J. J., *Profession of Faith of a Savoyard Vicar* [1782]

Sambrook, J., *The Eighteenth Century*, 2nd edn (London, 1993)

Schouls, P., *Reasoned Freedom: John Locke and Enlightenment* (Ithaca, 1992)

Shaftesbury, Third Earl of, *Characteristics of Men, Manners, Opinions, Times* [1711], ed. P. Ayres, 2 vols. (Oxford, 1999)

Smith, A., *Theory of the Moral Sentiments* (Edinburgh, 1759)

Smith, A., *The Wealth of Nations* [1776]

Smith, P., *A History of Modern Culture*, vol. 2, *The Enlightenment* (New York, 1934)

Venturi, F., *Utopia and Reform in the Enlightenment* (Cambridge, 1971)

Voltaire, *Candide* (1759)

Voltaire, *Philosophical Dictionary* [1764], trans. P. Besterman (New York, 1924)

Voltaire, *A Treatise on Toleration* (1763)

Wickwar, W. H., *Baron D'Holbach* (London, 1935)

Willey, B., *The Eighteenth Century Background* (London, 1953)

Willey, B., *The English Moralists* (London, 1964)

Yolton, J. (ed.), *Philosophy, Religion and Science in the Seventeenth and Eighteenth Centuries* (New York, 1990)

Yolton, J., et al., *The Blackwell Companion to the Enlightenment* (Oxford, 1991)

Chapter 7, The Crisis of Outlooks

Bentham, J., *Collected Works* (London and Oxford, 1968)

Darwin, C., *The Descent of Man* (London, 1871)

Darwin, C., *The Origin of Species* (London, 1859)

Feuerbach, L., *Essence of Christianity*, trans. George Eliot (London, 1841)

Gribbin, J., and White, M., *Darwin: A Life in Science* (London, 1995)

Hennell, C., *Inquiry Concerning the Origin of Christianity* (London, 1838)

Huxley, T. H., *Collected Essays* (Bristol, 2001)

Jones, G., *Social Darwinism and English Thought* (Brighton, 1980)

Jowett, B., et al., *Essays and Reviews* (London, 1860)

McLellan, D., *The Thought of Karl Marx* (London, 1971)

Marx, K., *Theses on Feuerbach* (1845)

Marx, K., and Engels, F., *Collected Works* (London, 1975)

Mill, J. S., *Autobiography* (London, 1873)

Mill, J. S., *On Liberty* and *Utilitarianism* (London, 1864)

Mill, J. S., *A System of Logic* (London, 1841)

Mill, J. S., *Three Essays on Religion* (London, 1874)

Nehamas, A., *Nietzsche: Life as Literature* (Cambridge, Mass., 1985)

Newman, J. H., *Apologia Pro Vita Sua* (Oxford, 1913)

Nietzsche, F., *Beyond Good and Evil: Prelude to a Philosophy of the Future*, trans. and ed. Walter Kaufmann (New York, 1966)

Nietzsche, F., *On the Genealogy of Morals* and *Ecce Homo*, trans. and ed. Walter Kaufmann (New York, 1969)

Nietzsche, F., *Thus Spake Zarathustra*, trans. R. J. Hollingdale (New York, 1999)

Nietzsche, F., *The Twilight of the Idols* and *The Anti-Christ*, trans. R. J. Hollingdale (Oxford, 1998)

Safranski, R., *Nietzsche: A Philosophical Biography* (London, 2002)

Sidgwick, H., *Miscellaneous Essays and Addresses* (London, 1904)

Spencer, H., *First Principles*, rev. edn (London, 1902)

Spencer, H., *The Principles of Ethics*, 2 vols. (London, 1892)

Strauss, D. F., *Life of Jesus*, trans. George Eliot (London, 1835)

Ward, W., *W. G. Ward and the Oxford Movement*, 2nd edn (Oxford, 1890)

Willey, B., *The Nineteenth Century Studies* (London, 1955)

Willey, B., *More Nineteenth Century Studies* (London, 1956)

Chapter 8, The Rediscovery of Ethics

Ayer, A. J., *Language, Truth and Logic* (London, 1935)

Baier, K., *The Moral Point of View* (London, 1957)

Camus, A., *The Myth of Sisyphus* (London, 1955)

Crisp, R. (ed.), *How Should One Live? Essays on the Virtues* (Oxford, 1996)

Dunayevskaya, R., *Philosophy and Revolution* (New York, 1973)

Foot, P. (ed.), *Theories of Ethics* (Oxford, 1967)

Freud, S., *The Basic Writings of Sigmund Freud*, ed. A. Brill (New York, 1938)

Freud, S., *The Essentials of Psycho-Analysis* (London, 1986)

Glover, J., *Humanity: A Moral History of the Twentieth Century* (London, 2000)

Hare, R. M., *The Language of Morals* (London, 1952)

Hursthouse, R., *On Virtue Ethics* (Oxford, 1999)

Levi, P., *The Drowned and the Saved* (New York, 1989)

Levi, P., *Survival in Auschwitz* (New York, 1995)

Mackie, J. L., *Ethics: Inventing Right and Wrong* (London, 1991)

Moore, G. E., *Principia Ethica* (London, 1903)

Nowell-Smith, P. H., *Ethics* (London, 1954)

Rawls, J., *A Theory of Justice* (Cambridge, Mass., 1971)

Ross, D., *The Right and the Good* (London, 1930)

Sartre, J. P., *Essays in Existentialism* (New York, 1993)

Sartre, J. P., *Existentialism and Humanism* (London, 2002)

Singer, P., *Writings on an Ethical Life* (London, 2000)

Solomon, R. C., *Existentialism* (New York, 1974)

Stevenson, C. L., *Ethics and Language* (London, 1944)

Todorov, T., *Facing the Extreme* (London, 2002)

Toulmin, S., *Reason in Ethics* (London, 1948)

Wallace, G., and Walker, A. D. M. (eds.), *The Definition of Morality* (London, 1970)

Williams, B., *Ethics and the Limits of Philosophy* (London, 1985)

Chapter 9, Laying the Ghosts

Holloway, R., *Godless Morality* (Edinburgh, 1999)

McKay, J. P., and Hill, B. D., *A History of Western Society*, vol. 1: *From Antiquity to the Enlightenment*, 5th edn (Princeton, 1995)

Masterson, P., *Atheism and Alienation* (London, 1971)

O'Hear, A., *After Progress* (London, 1999)

Todorov, T., *The Imperfect Garden* (London, 2002)

INDEX